MAKING MOVIES ON YOUR OWN

Practical Talk from Independent Filmmakers

by

Kevin J. Lindenmuth

WITH A FOREWORD BY
Ted V. Mikels

McFarland & Company, Inc., Publishers
Jefferson, North Carolina and London

British Library Cataloguing-in-Publication data are available

Library of Congress Cataloguing-in-Publication Data

Lindenmuth, Kevin J., 1965–
    Making movies on your own : practical talk from independent
filmmakers / by Kevin J. Lindenmuth.
        p.   cm.
    Includes index.
    ISBN 0-7864-0517-1 (softcover : 50# alkaline paper) ∞
    1. Motion pictures—Production and direction—United States.
2. Low budget motion pictures.   3. Independent filmmakers—United
States—Interviews.   I. Title.
PN1995.9.P7L477   1998
791.43'0232—dc21   98-16263
                                                                                        CIP

Manufactured in the United States of America

McFarland & Company, Inc., Publishers
  Box 611, Jefferson, North Carolina 28640

 University of
Hertfordshire

College Lane, Hatfield, Herts. AL10 9AB

Learning and Information Services

For renewal of Standard and One Week Loans,
please visit the web site **http://www.voyager.herts.ac.uk**

This item must be returned or the loan renewed by the due date.
The University reserves the right to recall items from loan at any time.
A fine will be charged for the late return of items.

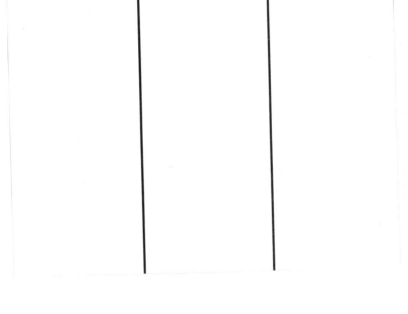

Special thanks to:
Audrey Geyer
Tom Piccirilli
Ron Ford
John & Nancy Lindenmuth
Marie Urban
Sid the Mutant Cat

Contents

Foreword

by Ted V. Mikels

If there was anything to read or study prior to making a film or video it would be Kevin Lindenmuth's book, a compilation of the works of a number of filmmakers in addition to the down-to-earth and matter-of-fact approach expounded by Kevin himself. Nowhere in my nearly fifty years of independent filmmaking have I seen or read anything so correctly spelled out in agonizing detail of what is experienced by those creative and dedicated souls who make the attempt to put their genius onto film or videotape.

I am asked constantly, when lecturing at colleges or film schools, how does one get started in making a film? There is no one answer that covers all, but in the reading of Kevin's book, you will experience an eye-opening adventure into the process. There is required, above all, a determination that knows no bounds, and you will be taxed beyond what you could imagine. Finding a way to put your story or script into a cohesive film or video is merely the first step in a long walk to completion and a measure of success.

The words of those who contributed to Kevin's book are so rare that you may have never heard them before. That is due to the fact that unless you make a film or video yourself, you cannot possibly imagine what you may be called upon to do. You may be the director, or the producer, possibly also the writer, but be prepared to perform every single thing you cannot afford to pay someone else to do.

Independent filmmakers *never* have enough money to do all the things they want to in their film. Some talented people who commit to you to stay with you throughout the production may suddenly face conditions beyond their control, and have to leave the show. That is to say, "Leave you holding the bag." You must learn all you can about every phase of the filmmaking process, as you may in fact be called upon to perform the necessary service at any time. It may be in lighting, sound recording, makeup, cinematography, special effects, cooking (yes, cooking to feed your crew), truck driving, or any other of 300 jobs utilized in the filmmaking process.

In Kevin's book, I read almost every word that has ever come out of my own mouth, relating to the difficulties encountered in making a film. I have always stated, "*There are three things that are important in the making of a film,*" and I will relate them here in the order of their difficulty.

The first and most difficult is raising the money. The second most difficult thing is getting the money back. The third thing, and the easiest, is the actual making of the film. (The first two prerequisites are so difficult, it makes the making of the film amazingly simple.)

1

Ted V. Mikels, director-producer.

In fact, you may have to make do without raising the money, making the film on a total shoestring or without money, as I have had to do many times. Then you encounter the criticisms when your film is then compared with those costing millions of dollars. Unfair, but who says anything in the world is fair? Then, you may never experience getting back any dollars at all from your production, even though many other entities and businesses may make a lot of money from selling and marketing it. However, take hope. You can always entertain yourselves and close friends by showing your film in your own home late at night. "Put salt and pepper on it and eat it," they used to say in Hollywood, where I spent nearly thirty years. The celluloid (film) tastes better that way.

I will say that if you are determined to the point where nothing can deter you in your obsession to make film, "let no power on earth stop you."

Do yourself a big favor, and read then reread Kevin's book. There is a wealth of factual and valuable information in it. I would suggest that it is an absolute "must read" for anyone attempting to make a film or video production. Those who have already done so will identify with every word and savor the memories.

TED V. MIKELS

Mr. Mikels is a director, producer, writer, cinematographer, editor and distributor. He is the director of such films as *Astro Zombies* (1969), *The Corpse Grinders* (1971), *Doll Squad, Dimension in Fear* (1998) and upcoming *The Corpse Grinders II.*

Introduction

As a kid I always knew what I wanted to do when I "grew up": make movies. I think this was primarily because I was subjected to so many films, particularly horror movies, when I was very young. In fact, the first movies I remember seeing were a double feature of *The Corpse Grinders* and *The Undertaker and His Pals*. Then there was the *Planet of the Apes* and *Dr. Phibes* movies at the drive-in with my father, and all the horror TV hosts on Saturday nights. For years I thought that Captain Kangaroo was really Dr. Phibes (they do look alike!) and it always puzzled me why he didn't talk through that hole in his throat to Mr. Green Jeans. That was simply television, I thought. And if not for my grandmother, a big horror fan herself, I probably wouldn't have been able to get into the theaters to see the early *Friday the 13th* movies.

I began making short "epics" with my family's Super 8mm camera in elementary school and continued shooting films in high school and as a Film/Video Studies major at the University of Michigan in Ann Arbor. I also worked at a public access television station during college, where the public was at my mercy subjected to the films I would make for classes and subsequently air on the channel. I think my films received the most viewer complaints that year because they were often aired after religious shows, catching all those particular viewers off guard.

After I graduated from college I moved to New York City as I couldn't afford to move to California at the time. I landed jobs as production assistant on a few independent films I can't even remember the names of, then started in the video production industry because work was readily available, though I had always wanted to shoot narrative films. Then, one day I decided I had to make that first feature, *Vampires & Other Stereotypes*. This was to be followed by the anthology *Twisted Tales*; another feature, *Addicted to Murder*; and *The Alien Agenda* series.

In talking to the 25 other filmmakers whose ideas, attitudes, and experiences you will also read about in the following pages, I discovered that they make films for the same simple reason I do: they have to. Movies enable them to express themselves in a way no other medium quite satisfies. Through film and video they can literally create something from their imagination and then show it to people, whether it be to enlighten, entertain, or disturb. Although some may maintain that they're simply making films they want to see and that no one else is creating—and that it's incidental if other people view them—these filmmakers *do* want audiences to see their work, not only because it will give them incentive to move on to the next project but because they want to share whatever is was that drove them to make the movie in the first place. I know, because I'm

Kevin Lindenmuth, 1992.

one of those filmmakers. I want to disturb and entertain you all.

In the following chapters I'll give you my two cents on moviemaking, mostly by comparing and contrasting my projects. Following my remarks, the other independent filmmakers will give their invaluable advice on making a feature-length movie, whether it be a horror film, comedy, or drama, sharing their successes and mistakes.

I want to thank these filmmakers who have contributed their insights to this book: Jeffrey Arsenault, Steve Ballot, Howard Berger, Ron Bonk, J.R. Bookwalter, Gabriel Campisi, Ronnie Cramer, Ron Ford, Hugh Gallagher, Mike Gingold, Matt Howe, Evan Jacobs, Michael Legge, Mick McCleery, Scooter McCrae, Blair Murphy, Mark & John Polonia, Tim Ritter, Eric Stanze, Nathan Thompson, Tim Thomson, Doug Ulrich, Tom Vollmann, Gary Whitson & W.A.V.E. Productions.

KEVIN LINDENMUTH

About the Interviewees

Jeffrey Arsenault (*Night Owl, Domestic Strangers*) began making films in New York's lower east side in the early 1980s. His films were shown at bars, cafés, clubs, galleries, and underground screening rooms. In 1988, a short film was shown at the New York Film Festival Downtown, and later toured Europe with a program of films by Alyce Wittenstein. His first feature, *Night Owl* (starring John Leguizamo), premiered at the American Film Institute's Los Angeles International Film Festival in 1993. This was followed by the Festival of Fantastic Films in Manchester, England; Equinox Valley of the Sun Film Festival in Phoenix; the Rome Florence Film Festival in Rome, Italy; the New York Underground Film Festival; the Northwest Film Festival in Southport, England (where it won Special Jury Award); and Fantasy FilmFest, which toured six cities in Germany. He edited the feature film *Heaven's a Drag* (UK title: *To Die For*) in London for director Peter Litten, which was released by First Run Features. He also just completed *Domestic Strangers*, his second feature as director. New York University recently listed Jeffrey Arsenault as one of the most accomplished alumni to have graduated from Tisch School of the Arts. Arsenault lives in Manhattan with his two cats, Spider Baby and Dementia 13.

Steve Ballot (*The Bride of Frank*): Like many others, Steve Ballot wanted to do something creative with his life, but was stuck at a job where he needed to stay to pay the bills. His creative pursuits were relegated to part time. In 1986 he composed a song parody for Howard Stern's radio show that won him a trip to London. In 1991, Ballot created a video invitation for his upcoming wedding that won grand prize in *Video* magazine's Home Video Contest (a two week trip to Germany). Before bailing out of the warehouse and trucking company where he worked for ten years, Ballot managed to capture the real life characters he worked with, in what's "gotta be one of the sickest movies ever made," *The Bride of Frank*.

Inspired by John Waters, Russ Meyer and George Romero, Ballot reasoned that if he was going to produce a feature on video, the only way to transcend the limitations of the medium was to come up with something bizarre, twisted and totally over the top. *The Bride of Frank* achieves those questionable goals in a big way. Ballot now runs his own video production company and most recently produced a video that won him a part in Howard Stern's *Private Parts* movie. He plays the sleazeball husband who tries to talk his wife into taking her clothes off for Howard's producer, Gary DellAbate (Baba Booey), in front of the Metropolitan Museum of Art next to a donkey.

Howard Berger (*Original Sins, The Blood Between Us*) always says the wrong thing to

Steve Ballot.

Ron Bonk.

the wrong people, is always at the wrong place at the wrong time and stylistically emulates the directors that nobody else seems to like. Lately, he feels that cinematic language is a lost art and that there is no excuse not to say more in a film than what is spoken. He has attended the film department at SUNY Purchase, written comedy for the Nickelodeon channel and appeared as "Mr. Large Pants," a recurring character on Nickelodeon's game show *Sudden Panic*. He has worked on *Basket Case 2*, sharing Belial-breathing chores with Scooter McCrae and has contributed interviews and articles to *Fangoria* magazine and *European Trash Cinema*. Berger is currently working on four new feature scripts, two to be shot on 35mm and two for digital video.

Ron Bonk (*City of the Vampires, The Vicious Sweet, Strawberry Estates*) began working in film and video back in 1992 with the

release of the antique instructional video *What a Deal! Secrets to Buying and Selling at an Antique Flea Market*. The success of that video inspired him to move on to bigger and better things. In 1993 he shot his first movie, *City of the Vampires*, and released it through his own successful distribution company, Salt City Home Video, which has gone on to distribute *Savage Harvest, The Scare Game, Darkest Soul, Creep, Wicked Games* and *Ravage*, as well as several instructional videos on the B-movie biz, with more titles lined up for the coming year. Since *City*, he has served as director of photography and second unit director on *The Sandman*, plus producing the anthology *Dark Descent*, which includes the two shorts *Permanent Waves* and *I've Killed Before* (the short that inspired *Bloodletting*). He wrote, produced and directed *The Vicious Sweet* and *Strawberry Estates* recently, and produced, edited, photographed and acted in *Gut-Pile*. He also cowrote Tim Ritter's *Screaming for Sanity* with Tim and Kevin Lindenmuth. His short film *Less of 2 Evils* was one of five finalists for the *Looking for Richard* contest. He spends what little of his time left maintaining his web site (B-Movie Theater, http://www.b-movie.com—over 100,000 hits a month strong!), and writing for publications like *Cool Stuff*, *Alternative Cinema* (managing editor at one time as well), and *Manic Shopper*. Briefly, he published and edited *TV Scene* magazine, currently edits and publishes an online-only magazine called *Dark Gallery* (http://www.b-movie.com/dghome.html). In the next year, he will be involved in *Sonny and Gino Vs. the World* (cowriter, codirector, coproducer), and an untitled alien abduction movie (producer, director of photography), as well as a couple of undisclosed projects. He also hopes to find the time to direct a segment of Lindenmuth's *Alien Agenda* series, as well as to return to horror directing with the ambitious vampire action epic *Little Sister* by early '98.

J.R. Bookwalter (*Dead Next Door, Ozone, Sandman*) began his filmmaking career at the tender age of 11 in suburban Akron, Ohio. After making over 40 short films from 1978–1985, Bookwalter landed financing for his first full-length feature, *The Dead Next Door*, from Detroit, Michigan, horror icon Sam Raimi (*The Evil Dead, Darkman*). In 1989 he landed a multipicture deal with producer David DeCoteau (*Creepazoids*) which included the 16mm *Robot Ninja* and *Skinned Alive*. Bookwalter is also the producer of *Night of the Living Dead* cocreator John A. Russo's *Midnight 2: Sex, Death and Videotape*. In 1992 he broke out on his own with *Ozone*, a high-energy thriller that has been likened to *El Mariachi* and voted Best Outlaw Video of the Year. Most recently he was the cowriter and director of *The Sandman*, an old-fashioned monster movie with '90s-style effects. Recent projects include *Polymorph* and producing *Bloodletting*.

Gabriel Campisi: At age 8 he grabbed his father's Super 8mm camera and shot a series of random narratives that, although amateur, were a sign of things to come. At age 15 he was beating out the competition in film festivals and contests across the country with his intricate, low-budget film productions. *The Lost Creature* and *Monster Busters*, two 15-minute shorts, took top hon-

ors at national tournaments. Just two years later he received several breaks and took his first steps toward professional filmmaking: working in movies and television shows as a technician, script supervisor/rewriter and assistant director.

Besides writing, producing and directing his own work, he provides production services to a variety of projects through his company, Starlight Pictures. This includes music videos, national commercials, corporate videos and other producers' films. He recently completed writing and producing the pilot episode to *Lost Birds*, a television documentary series that recounts historic aviation disasters. He currently finished his feature *Shadowdance*, an alien movie.

Ronnie Cramer (*Back Street Jane, Even Hitler Had a Girlfriend, The Hitler Tapes*) started making 8mm films at age 13 (1970), mostly for fun. He studied painting and other fine arts in school and spent most of the 1980s playing guitar in various rock bands (*Alarming Trends* the longest) at venues such as San Francisco's Mabuhay Gardens and New York's CBGB. He worked in the audio field for a while until he was hired to record the sound for a 35mm horror film around 1981-82. During the shoot he observed all aspects of the production and took a lot of notes. Afterward he bought a used camera and began making music videos (16mm films, actually) for the bands he played in and for others. During this time he produced a self-financed 30-minute musical film ("Alarming Trends") for about $2,000, which led him to believe he could make a feature for not much more. In 1989 he wrote and directed a crime feature called *Back Street Jane*, which ultimately cost $15,000. The film eventually grossed about five times its cost to date. He was hired to direct *Even Hitler Had a Girlfriend*—which Joe Bob Briggs called "The Best Drive-In Movie of 1992" and "one of the greatest independent comedies ever made." This film was financed by a trio of investors from Nebraska who have made quite a tidy sum from it. In 1994 he made the sequel, *The Hitler Tapes*.

Gabriel Campisi.

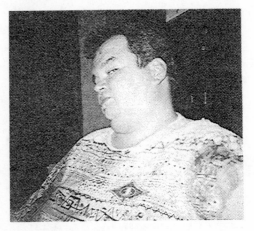

Ron Ford.

Ron Ford (*Alien Force*): Born in Bremerton, Washington, in 1958, Ford received his drama degree from Olympic College in 1980. While in college he was nominated for the Irene Ryan Acting Award for his performance as Dodge in Sam Shepard's *Buried Child*. He wrote a play, *Outlaws*, which was produced for the American College Theater Festival and nominated for the David Library Literary Award. That same year (1983), Ford married the woman who played his wife in *Buried Child* in the same theater in which the play was produced. In 1985 they moved to Tucson, Arizona, where Ford worked on the production crew of many motion pictures (including *Can't Buy Me Love* and *World Gone Wild*) in many capacities, from driver to makeup artist. There he got his first professional acting roles in the TV series *Hey, Dude* and *The Young Riders*. He made a public access video of Forrest J Ackerman's Lon Chaney story *Letter to an Angel*. Ackerman

appeared as narrator in the short, which won an award in American Film Institute's 1985 "Visions of U.S." competition. In 1990 the Fords moved to Los Angeles. Ron has since appeared in *Killer Tomatoes Eat France, Addicted to Murder, The Fear, Alien Force, Blazing Force, The Alien Agenda: Endangered Species*, and the upcoming *Extraterrestrial Highway*. He played Bottom in a film of *A Midsummer Night's Dream*, and will play the titular character in the upcoming *American Terrorist*.

After winning the 1992 Christopher Columbus Screenplay Discovery Award, Ford wrote the 1995 release *The Fear*. He cowrote *Blazing Force* and several upcoming pictures for Wildcat Entertainment. He has sold two horror scripts to David DeCoteau, and also did uncredited dialogue work on *Germans*. As a director Ford helmed the first segment of Kevin Lindenmuth's *Alien Agenda: Endangered Species* and the current science fiction feature *Alien Force*, both of which he also scripted. Recently, he directed and wrote *Mark of Dracula* and *Riddled with Bullets* for Wildcat Entertainment.

Hugh Gallagher (*Gorgasm, Gorotica, Gore Whore*) says "I think maybe all the tragedies in my life may be responsible for a lot of the dialogue in my movies. If you can get past all the sex and gore, there are some things being said. They say everyone needs an outlet, and my movies are definitely

Hugh Gallagher.

Michael Gingold shooting *Mindstalker.*

mine. Most people are shocked when they first meet me; they expect some sadistic monster and instead they get me. I read once that the more violent a movie is, the moviemaker is that much more quiet—if you've seen any of my movies, then that phrase should give you a better understanding of me.

"At this point in my life I continue to publish *Draculina* on a much bigger scale than ever before. Draculina Publishing is now a full time occupation, and my movies are second in line. I'm pretty happy with the way things are going for me now.

"When you're young all you want to do in life is become rich. And although money is a strong incentive for some of the things I do, most of what I do is just because I want to." (Taken from *Playgore: An In-depth Look At The Making of Gorgasm, Gorotica, and Gore Whore* Draculina Publishing).

Mike Gingold (*Mindstalker*): began his filmmaking career in the manner of most independents: shooting short Super 8mm movies, most of them in the horror genre. These projects ranged from his own version of *Day of the Dead* (a few years in advance of George Romero's real thing) to his magnum opus, a 40-minute slasher flick about a killer stalking foreign exchange students, *Deadly Exchange.* At one point during high

school he entertained ideas about shooting a feature on Super 8 and trying to get it distributed somehow, but soon dismissed this as unlikely and impractical. From 1985 to 1989 he attended New York University's film school, where he completed a 19-minute horror short called *Hands Off,* "inspired" by Clive Barker's short story "The Body Politic," which played a few conventions and festivals and may be released as part of a video compilation.

During his junior year at NYU, he began writing for *Fangoria* magazine, which led to his joining the staff full-time in 1990 as associate editor and then managing editor, the position he holds now. It was here that he discovered the films of Mark Pirro and realized that shooting and releasing a Super 8 feature was not an impossible dream after all; thus was born *Mindstalker* (originally titled *Tracker*), based on an idea he'd had in college. For reasons of financing, lack of facilities and plain old creative stagnation, the movie has taken several years to complete, but it is now complete. He is currently planning his next project (to be shot on professional video), which will most likely be a suspense thriller called *Angel of Mercy.*

Matt Howe (*Original Sins*) grew up in the rural town of Thomaston, Connecticut, where he started making movies at the early age of 8 and continued to make them through high school. After graduating from the State University of New York at Purchase, where he learned some rudiments of the craft, he began a career as a cinematographer. He shot hundreds of educationals, industrials, commercials, shorts and five features, including *Original Sins*. Two of the features were made on Betacam SP, one on 16mm, and two on 35mm. The most recent one, *Virtual Hell*, was a $500,000 sci-fi action epic starring Robert Davi. His features and shorts have been featured in festivals around the world, including Sundance, Telluride, Toronto, Rotterdam and Johannesburg, South Africa. *Desolation Angels*, shot on 16mm for $30,000, won the Best First Feature awards at both the 1995 Telluride and 1995 Toronto film festivals. Both *Desolation Angels* and *Parallel Sons*, which were done in 35mm for under $100,000, are scheduled for theatrical release. Currently he wants to shoot more feature work and continue to develop independent feature projects.

Evan Jacobs (*Walking Between the Raindrops*) was born in Queens, New York. The youngest of two children, his family moved to Southern California when he was 4. He attended the local schools, and through his four years in high school he studied drama. He went to Orange Coast Junior College, and it was there that he declared he wanted to be a screenwriter. He lived in San Francisco for a semester, but came back to Southern California to make his first video movie, *Walking Between the Raindrops*. He is currently 23 years old, attends Cal State Long Beach and is majoring in film. He has also completed *Safety in Numbers* and *The Toll Collector*.

Michael Legge (*Working Stiffs, Loons, Cut-Throats*): went from regular 8mm film to Super 8mm during high school, making dozens of shorts. He went to a "broadcasting" school in Boston, where he learned video production and made his first 16mm film. After college he made a 16mm feature, entirely self-funded, which taught him more about production than school ever did. He made dozens of Super 8 films during the years 1979–1986, getting awards, trophies, and even money from various film festivals around the country, particularly the Ann Arbor Film Festival. He also had films screened at festivals in Venezuela, Canada and Australia. One of his shorts, *The Lemon Man*, was licensed to the USA Network program *Night Flight*. After this he went back to making features. *Working Stiffs, Loons, Cut-throats*, and *Sick Time* have all been made during the past ten years. He finally made the plunge into video with his new feature, *Potential Sins*, and the new anthology *Creaturealm*.

Mick McCleery (*The Killing of Bobby Greene, Don't Watch This Show*) started shooting films when he was 12 years old. He admits that these were *Halloween* rip-offs, *Road Warrior* rip-offs, and *Star Wars* rip-offs. When he was eighteen he did a series called *Twisted Tales*, which at first sounds like a *Twilight Zone* rip-off. But as he made more episodes (12 in all) he clearly began establishing his own style. It wasn't until he went to college that he started to think more about filmmaking. When he turned 21 he decided to make the jump to a full length feature movie to be shot in Betacam SP, which would become *The Killing of Bobby Greene*. It took some four years to finish and during that time he learned a lot about how to (and how not to) go about making a film. As of late his directorial efforts have been concentrated towards a half hour sketch comedy series called *Don't Watch This Show*. It's a wild, irreverent comedy in the same vein as Monty Python. In addition to establishing One by One Film & Video in New Jersey he has also established somewhat of a cult following as an actor.

Scooter McCrae (*Shatter Dead*) studied film at the State University of New York at Purchase, graduating in 1988. He is legendary there for being the only film student to be on probation for every single semester.

Scooter McCrae.

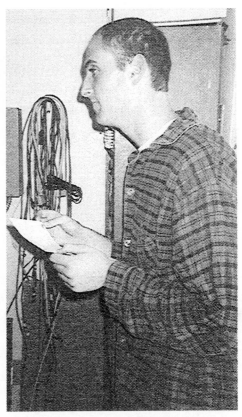

Evan Jacobs.

Other fine achievements include setting the soundstage on fire and having masterminded the theft of a hydraulic lift from the dance department (both for his senior thesis project). It should also be noted that, although he was passionately interested in experimental films, he has since gone on to fashion projects of a much more narrative nature. He has just finished *Sixteen Tongues.*

Blair Murphy (*Jugular Wine: A Vampire Odyssey, Steps, Black Pearls*) was raised in a funeral home in New Jersey and has a bachelor of fine arts in cinema from the University of Bridgeport, Connecticut. His 40-minute student film, *Steps*, was winner of the New England Outstanding Student Film Award (Boston Film and Video Foundation) and the Festival Special Edison Award (New Jersey Young Film and Videomakers Festival). After graduation he worked as a PA on the *Robocop* movies (and too many other movies), worked two years as assistant for Stan Lee at Marvel Films, and two years as a cameraman for Prince as well. *Jugular Wine*

was his first feature film, which was picked up by Blockbuster, Tower, and other stores and released in a dozen countries so far. He currently lives in Venice Beach, California. He runs Empyre Films, a small independent production and distribution company. His second feature film, *Black Pearls*, is about to be released.

Mark and John Polonia (*Splatter Farm, Saurians, How to Slay a Vampire, Feeders, Terror House*): A brother/team company (Polonia Bros. Entertainment) with several feature film productions under their belt, including the infamous *Splatter Farm, Saurians, How to Slay a Vampire, Feeders* (currently available for rental at Blockbuster Video) and *Hellspawn*, the Polonia brothers supervised the direction and postproduction of two independent producers' films, *3000 Bullets* and *Savage Vows.* They currently have a complete editing and production outfit utilizing

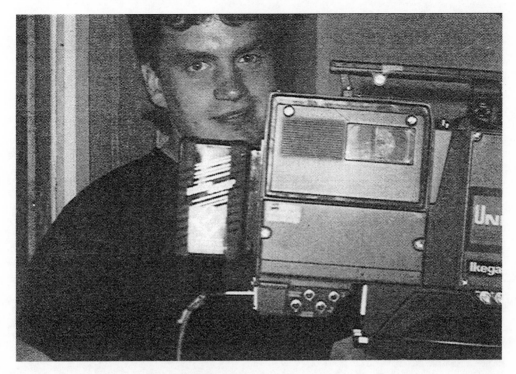

Mick McCleery on the set of *Twisted Tales*.

Blair Murphy and actress Rachelle Packer in 1993.

high-end video equipment and most recently, professional 16mm gear. They began pursuing filmmaking at an early age and graduated to higher levels of production over the years. Their first shot-on-video feature was made as seniors in high school and found release through the now defunct Phoenix Home Video, the company that released *Abomination* and others. The brothers work as a team from concept to final edit and are anxious to move from shooting on video to 16mm film.

Tim Ritter (*Truth or Dare, Wicked Games, Creep*) was born, appropriately, on Friday, October 13th, 1967. Since a youngster he has always been obsessed with making films. He started out with an old S&H Green Stamp Super 8mm camera in 1978. While still in high school he worked at a company which specialized in making industrial videos and commercials and during that time completed two feature-length movies before graduating, *Day of the Reaper* (1984) and *Twisted Illusions* (1985). Immediately after graduation he was able to successfully sell his writing and directing talents to a Chicago-based distributor which financed his next film, the $250,000 *Truth or Dare—A Critical Madness* (1986), which became one of the first feature films shot directly for the home video market. *Truth or Dare* was a worldwide phenomenon, selling over 30,000 copies in the United States alone and hitting number 16 on the national rental charts. Ritter followed this, as writer-producer-director, with *Killing Spree* (1990), *Blinded by the Blood* (1993), *Wicked Games* (1994), and *Creep* (1995). He was also the music coordinator for Donald Farmer's *Scream Dream* (1990), associate producer on *Vampire Cop* (1991), and creative consultant on Joel D. Wynkoop's *Lost Faith* (1992). *Screaming for Sanity*, his last *Truth or Dare* movie, was completed in 1998. Currently, Ritter resides in Palm Beach County, Florida, where he is the president of his own feature film production and distribution company, Twisted Illusions, Inc. The company is in its 12th year of business.

Eric Stanze directs, writes, and pro-

Tim Ritter.

duces low-budget movies in St. Louis, Missouri. He was 18 years old when he made his first movie, to gain domestic and foreign home video distribution. The project, titled *The Scare Game*, shot in 1990, which according to Eric is "a now-embarrassing bit of bad dialogue cheese cinema that was, however, a priceless learning experience." After *The Scare Game* he went through college video production classes and, at age 19, landed employment in the corporate/industrial/broadcast video industry, mostly shooting and editing. His next movie was *The Fine Art* (shot in 1992)—a character driven, Hitchcockian drama, featuring stylish visuals shot with more professional equipment. *The Scare Game* and *The Fine Art* were discovered by a home video distributor and released (in greatly superior edited-down versions) *The Scare Game Double Feature*.

His next project, shot in 1993, was a

Eric Stanze (photo by Larry Kemmerling).

Nathan Thompson.

more ambitious shot-on-video movie called *Savage Harvest*, an all-out horror movie which is currently being distributed to the home video market. After this movie he stayed busy writing more screenplays, co-producing experimental short subjects and directing music videos for several local bands.

At this time he is completing work on *Ice from the Sun*, an extremely intense and very experimental dark fantasy which is being shot in Super 8mm film with a budget of $11,000, which the director states is "the most original movie I have ever written. The finished product will be hard to categorize into a specific genre; it will be too progressive for some markets and is sure to offend conservative viewers (if I do my job right)."

Nathan Thompson began his career at the age of 9 with a standard 8mm film camera. He has been shooting film and video for over 20 years. After graduating from Ben-

nington College he began his own video company and did work for everyone from the March of Dimes to the Defense Department. In 1986 a recruitment piece was named "Most Effective Video" by the National Association of College Counselors. In that same year he finished his first full-length feature, *Blood Harvest*. For the next two years he shot and cut almost 400 cable TV spots that he hopes you never see. He now edits national TV spots for McCann-Erickson, the largest advertising agency in the world. In recent years, his work has been awarded both ADDY and EFFY awards. Reviews of his most recent feature, *Contact Blow* (available for rental at Blockbuster) suggest his is a name to watch in the future.

Tim Thomson (*No Resistance*) was born in Chicago in 1966 and spent his formative years making stop-motion dinosaur movies in the basement with his Super 8mm camera. That and spending too much time in front of the TV or at the movies was his first and real education. This continued through high school, where he was always involved in drama and performance–type activities. When it came time to pick a career in college in the mid–80s he focused on radio, TV, and film because it was fun—and because he knew that's what he wanted to do for a living. During that time he worked at a local PBS station and gained valuable hands-on experience and access to some equipment. By the time he graduated college he and his friends had four or five "movies" to their names. After college he moved to Houston to work in industrial-commercial production and gained access to more equipment and money, never losing the drive to make movies. *No Resistance* is his first feature intended for an audience. He is currently attempting to raise funds to produce a continuation of that movie in 16mm. Tim Thomson is also responsible for digital special effects in *Alien Agenda* series, *Alien Force*, and *Creaturealm*.

Doug Ulrich (*Darkest Soul*) started making movies at the age of 13 when he bought an old 8mm camera at a flea market for a measly $5. His first film was a horror movie called *Horror at Midnight*, which he says "sucked," but as time went on he learned from his mistakes and improved, using a Super 8 sound camera. When he turned 18 he retired from moviemaking because he just didn't have time with working a full time job and the friends he used just weren't available anymore. During this time he started getting into makeup effects—full head rubber masks and eventually foam latex masks—and won quite a few costume contests. In 1991 he ran into an old high school friend, Al Darago, and the moviemaking resumed. At first Doug was to do a music video for Darago's band but the band broke up. "Al then talked me into making a short slasher movie," Ulrich says, "since Al always wanted to get into acting and loves slasher films." They came up with the production company name Nobudget Productions and the first film was *Sliced in Cold Blood*, which was made a part of the anthology *Scary Tales*, their first full-length movie. The next project was *Grave*

Tim Thomson.

Diggers, which is being released as *Darkest Soul* because the original title gives the false impression that it is a horror movie. The film has been reviewed by a few magazines and has garnered positive reviews. Their new project, *Screen Kill* is a horror-gore movie about two guys who make low-budget horror movies and eventually kill the actors for real.

Tom Vollmann (*Dead Meat*) first caught the filmmaking bug at the early age of 5, which he attributes to his mother buying him an issue of *Famous Monsters of Filmland* and taking him to matinee showings of *Tarantula, Monolith Monsters, Flesh Eaters* and the like. In grammar school, armed with his trusty J.C. Penney's Super 8mm camera, he began filming such things as a spy yarn, a sci-fi extravaganza, and a *Night of the Living Dead* rip-off entitled *Day of the Dead*. After high school, working as everything from an electrician to caretaker to carpenter to set

Tom Vollmann shooting *The Clinic*.

builder and coowner of a video production facility that specialized in film-to-tape transfers and wedding videos, he never lost sight of making his own movies. *Dead Meat* (1993)

was his first feature. Currently he has just completed an installment for *The Alien Agenda: Under the Skin*, a mafia-inspired alien movie, and a segment for *Creaturealm*.

Gary Whitson (W.A.V.E. Productions) is the owner and founder of W.A.V.E. Productions. His first film, *If a God Should Fail*, was shot on Super 8mm (1976) and dealt with the return of Hercules as he tried to stop a crazed scientist and his cyborg from taking over the earth. In the 1970s and '80s he was an amateur artist and did custom work for various people. This led to the idea of making custom videos for people. In 1987 he ran an ad asking for people interested in doing horror movies and since has gained the able assistance of Sal Longo, Aven Warren, Clancey McCauley, Mike Brady, and Dave Castiglione, who help in varying capacities. Since '87 over 30 video features have been completed, ranging from super heroines to lovesick vampires to jungle women to crazed killers. These movies are produced from someone else's script or story idea for a fee. They then turn around and sell the movie through their outlets and the writer receives a royalty for each sale. Recent releases include *Rana, Queen Of The Amazon, Sorority Slaughter, Hung Jury*, and *Bloody Creek*. Whitson has directed every W.A.V.E. movie produced.

1. Getting Started

Both of my features, *Vampires & Other Stereotypes* and *Addicted to Murder* started the way most any independent features start—with a bunch of people who wanted to make a film because that was the only way it was going to materialize. That is what independent filmmaking is all about.

Ironically, my low-budget moviemaking career began at the 1991 Fangoria Weekend of Horrors convention. The previous month I was contacted by a guy out in California who was interested in banding together East Coast filmmakers to make films that he, in turn, would distribute. He got my name off the end credits of a cable public access show I was still producing and syndicating throughout the United States. He explained that we would direct and produce the movies and he would distribute them. There were a few problems, though. He had no money to advance for the productions, and I got the distinct feeling he was simply a disembodied voice on the phone. Although I appreciated the list of local filmmakers he provided me with, I wondered why I should go through him to make a movie. If I was going to endure all the hard work to make a movie, I might as well do it on my own without an outside producer.

So, the following month, I met a special effects outfit called Imageffects during my annual visit to the Fangoria convention. They liked my ideas and were gung-ho on doing another feature after having completed

work on Rolfe Kanefsky's *There's Nothing Out There* the previous summer. They, in turn, recommended a friend who had studio space to shoot in. This was Mick McCleery and One by One Film and Video in Vorhees, New Jersey—an integral part of my first two features as well as my most recent endeavor, *The Alien Agenda*. Everyone got along, agreements and contracts were made up, and then I began writing the script, really having no idea what went into making a feature-length movie.

After waiting and working on other people's projects since I first came to New York, I couldn't wait any longer. I had to make *my own film*. I had to do what I always wanted to do.

Why a horror movie as opposed to a comedy or drama? Well, having watched thousands of them during my childhood they were the most familiar form of entertainment for me. I enjoyed them and wanted to make one myself. And why a vampire movie? Because watching *Dark Shadows* when I was four years old, as well as drive-in movies like *The Return of Count Yorga* and *Scream, Blacula, Scream*, definitely left an impression on me. I was *going* to make a *vampire movie* and it was going to be a little bit *different*. The result was *Vampires & Other Stereotypes*.

Twisted Tales was shot after *Vampires* but actually completed before that feature

17

Kevin Lindenmuth and crew on the set of *Vampires & Other Stereotypes* (1992).

was edited. I utilized some of the leftover sets from *Vampires & Other Stereotypes* and cast some of the very same actors. It was an anthology in three parts directed by Rita Klus (who was my continuity person on *Vamps*), Mick McCleery, and myself. With three different directors, who each edited their own segments, the production was completed much faster. We all came up with the stories fairly quickly, arranged schedules, and shot it during the next few months. I would say that our biggest influences were *Tales from the Darkside* and *The Twilight Zone*, with a good deal of ourselves thrown in. The feature had a very limited distribution some years ago, but is currently being rereleased with a behind-the-scenes supplemental.

The influences on *Addicted to Murder*, done some five years after *Vampires & Other*

Stereotypes, were pretty much the same and I had not quite gotten over the vampire thing. But rather than rehash certain elements from the first film, which had comedic overtones, I decided to go in the other direction and make it very dark and serious. In preparation for writing a script that dealt with serial killers I read dozens of books on the subject and watched quite a few "serial killer movies," making sure I would not do anything that had been done before. My biggest problem with serial killer movies is that they were becoming predictable, so I decided having a serial killer created by a vampire would add something new to the genre. Also, the serial killer aspect would ground the film a bit more in reality. So, I took one of my favorite genres and combined it with one I thought could use some new blood.

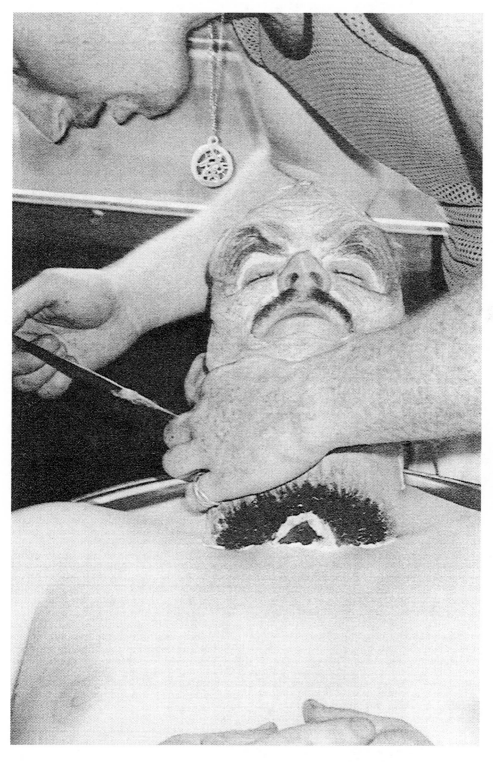

Special effects technician Scott Sliger applies makeup to the face of an actor on the set of *Vampires & Other Stereotypes*.

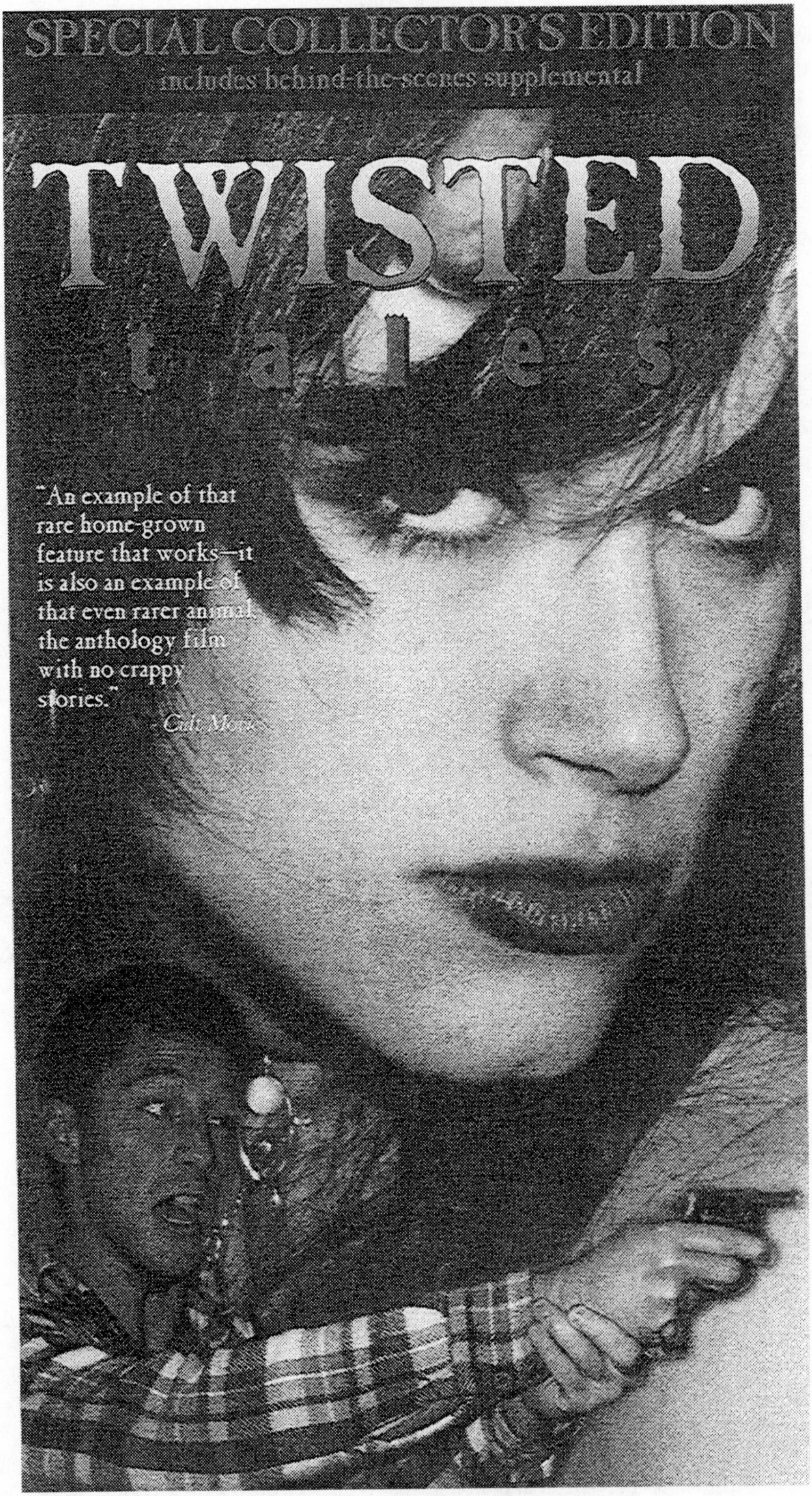

TWISTED
tales

"An example of that
rare home-grown
feature that works—it
is also an example of
that even rarer animal,
the anthology film
with no crappy
stories."
— *Cult Movies*

Home video artwork for *Twisted Tales*.

"A very serious, disturbing horror feature. The film is filled with horrific and gruesome happenings."
- *SHOCKING IMAGES MAGAZINE*

Addicted to Murder

MICK McCLEERY • LAURA McLAUCHLIN • SASHA GRAHAM
ADDICTED TO MURDER
Starring GORDON LINZNER • CANDICE MEADE • SEWELL WHITNEY
JOLEE BECKER and BERNADETTE PAULEY
Original Soundtrack by STEVE MARUZZELLI and HECTOR MILIA
Special Make-up Effects by RON CHAMBERLAIN and DEREK BECKER
Written by KEVIN LINDENMUTH and TOM PICCIRILLI
Produced and Directed by KEVIN LINDENMUTH

Home video artwork for *Addicted to Murder*.

THE INTERVIEWEES WERE ASKED,
What are your influences and aspirations and what got you into wanting to make movies?

ARSENAULT: I think in some way I'm influenced by almost everything I see that I respond to in some way. Basically, my first influence would have to be *Dark Shadows*, the daytime serial which was broadcast from 1966–71. I remember watching it as a very small child, only five years old, and here was an afternoon soap opera that dealt with vampires, witches, ghosts, werewolves, dementia, and all kinds of fun stuff. I think that moody, gothic atmospheric horror had a big influence on what I responded to in films. To this day I prefer straight horror to anything with a comedic edge. What influences me most is other filmmakers. The first three that come to mind are Hitchcock, Argento and DePalma. These are by far the top three in my book. I would like, some day, to make something as suspenseful as Hitchcock. I love the choreographed violence of Argento's films, and I love the visual style of DePalma. *Notorious*, *Suspiria* and *Dressed to Kill* are my favorite films from each director, respectively. On the independent scene I think Gregg Araki [*The Living End*, *The Doom Generation*] is the freshest and most original filmmaker working today. His wit and style are unmatched. I don't agree with his heavy politics but his films are an exhilarating experience, no matter how many times I see them.

BALLOT: My influences are all the movies I've ever seen. Every movie has had some kind of effect on me, even if it was just boredom or nausea. For me, movies are the most potent art form. When a film is really powerful it burns images into your brain. The images of the Wicked Witch and the flying monkeys from *The Wizard of Oz* have been in my head since I was a child. Movies have the power to scare you, change the way you think, move you to tears, excite you, delight you, or just bore the shit out of you. No

other art form can fuck with your emotions so effectively.

Reading a great book can affect your mind and emotions, but a few hundred people can't sit in a dark theater reading the same book and collectively react to the same thing at the same time. When consumer video technology reached the public it became possible for any schmuck to pick up a video camera and make a movie. Before that, the average consumer could shoot 8mm or Super 8mm film with sound, but it was costly, more difficult than video, and because of film processing, the results were not immediate. With video: point, shoot, play back on your television set—instant moviemaker! Now, people who loved movies could not only rent them at a store and watch them at home on their TVs, they could get a camera and make their own. So my biggest influences have not only been the movies themselves but the new video technology that enabled me to make my own.

BERGER: To be honest, I want to make films that can seriously screw up children. This doesn't mean that my films have to be NC-17 to do that. I could screw a child up with a G rating! That's my goal. Every film that screwed me up when I was little—*Night of the Living Dead*, *End of the Road*, *Night Must Fall*, *Blood and Black Lace*, *The Tingler*, *Eyes Without a Face*, *Scream and Scream Again* and *Ring of Bright Water*, to name a few—have since become favorites of mine and have helped to shape the direction of my own psychology towards cinema. Influences aside from these are far and wide. I'm influenced by screenwriting that is tightly constructed and subversively plotted—love *The Innocents* and *Hi, Mom!*—and directors who can interpret such writing with imagination and vision. Directors who matter to me:

Robert Aldrich, Claude Chabrol, Alfred Hitchcock, John Huston, Mario Bava, Jesus Franco (was on to him twenty years before the bandwagon, proud to say), John Frankenheimer, Jean Rollin, Frank Perry, Joe Dante, Sam Fuller, Curtis Harrington, Sam Peckinpah, Joseph Losey, Terence Fisher, Brian DePalma and of course, Ken Russell. Too many others to mention. I've wanted to make films since I read my first issue of *Famous Monsters* back in '71. That screwed me up, too. So, I'll consider myself successful the moment I hear my first prepubescent casualty—that joyous sound of a child screwed up—not necessarily scared, just screwed up—bawling his eyes out—hyperventilating—because of one of my movies—to the accompaniment of an agitated parent desperately trying to console.

BONK: George Romero and Steven Spielberg stand as my two biggest influences. It was Romero's *Dawn of the Dead* that I saw, and decided that I wanted to be a moviemaker. I think I knew it all along, but seeing that movie on that grand scale, with so many levels and so many meanings, yet so simply entertaining, I was just absolutely "wowed." I knew that I wanted to tell a story like that! And I saw it on a video on a small television for the first time—not in a theater, where the experience can be so magnified!

Spielberg's body of work has always been so wholly entertaining. Every time he is associated with a project, I come away from it with some satisfaction. But it's his early work—*Duel, Jaws, Close Encounters, E.T.*—that is really inspiring. He is such a great director. For it to take so long for him to win the Academy Award makes me think that we still really don't appreciate him like we should.

But my favorite single movie, the movie that created my love of watching movies, that stunned me and affected me more than any other movie, and more than most any other experience in my life, was *Star Wars*. Right from the beginning, with that Star Destroyer coming over the top of the screen to the great dog fight battle at the end ... it just took me to another world like nothing

before or since! There can never be another movie like it!

I also find a lot of inspiration in the works of Orson Welles. Hell, his life history itself is an incredible story. The work he was still able to produce with all that interference ... if only Hollywood had left him alone! John Carpenter is also a huge influence—he could scare like no one else. His early work was like old E.C. Comics brought to life. His music as well is quite inspiring—I have written many a script and story listening to it. And, of course, Alfred Hitchcock. I would have to write a small book just to touch on how important his work is to me. Maybe in the next book...

BOOKWALTER: George Romero was the biggest influence on me. I remember having the very strong vision of a zombie eating a bug off a tree and not really knowing what movie it was from or where I saw it. Home video wasn't around as much when I was growing up, and even if it were, my parents would never have gotten it! Finally in high school we orchestrated this screening of *Night of the Living Dead* as a fundraiser and I finally figured out that was Marilyn Eastman eating that bug. Of course, by this point I had been a Romero junkie after seeing that exploding head from *Dawn of the Dead* in *Fangoria #1* years before. I just really dig his stuff; Romero has a real gift for making a lurid subject or title play very mainstream. My other influence is Steven Spielberg, and specifically *Raiders of the Lost Ark*. I grew up at the right time to be properly affected by *Star Wars*, so I guess that any sort of "escapism" movie is my bag. Sci-fi used to be my big thing when I started making Super 8mm home movies in 1978. Gradually I discovered gore and went a little nuts for that, and it's really been in the last few years that I've completely tired of making and or seeing gore movies. But horror will always be in my blood! I have my mother to thank for that; she used to watch *Dark Shadows* religiously, and she claims I'd be sitting right there as a baby, my eyes glued to the TV.

CAMPISI: Like so many people across the world I was literally blown away by George Lucas's galactic tale of a young boy who conquers the universe. I was about 9 years old when I saw *Star Wars*, and my life has never been the same since the experience. I wanted to remain in that world, be a part of it, or at the very least try to mimic it. Hence began my foray into the world of make-believe. With a Super 8mm camera I began shooting "Star Wars" in my backyard, writing dialogue for the characters and putting lighter fluid and matches to my toy Frisbees and model airplanes.

Steven Spielberg influenced me greatly as well. *Jaws, Raiders of the Lost Ark, Close Encounters* and *E.T.* all had an immense impact on my motivation and desires in the early years. Spielberg's current projects continue to motivate me. James Cameron, Robert Zemeckis, Ridley Scott and John Carpenter all have told tales and accomplished feats I hope to accomplish some day.

The films I enjoy watching are *good* films. If they're good, I'll watch them. There are too many duds out there, and one has to wonder where the hell some people get the financing to back their films. Besides good films, my choice of genre varies. I am positively biased toward enjoying science fiction, fantasy and horror. For the most part, I like for stories to be set in contemporary present day—an easier way for the audience to identify with the experience. If it has a twist ending, a pinch of the supernatural or the unknown, count me in. I'm there. I'm watching and enjoying it.

CRAMER: I kind of went about this in reverse as I had made a few films before I really started watching films critically. These days I love artists like Luis Buñuel and Vittorio De Sica, but I can't say my no-budget exploitation pictures are influenced by them.

FORD: The first movie I can remember seeing is *Little Shop of Horrors*, which I found highly disturbing, but also fascinating. Its tongue-in-cheek attitude was completely lost on one so young. And, well, I guess it warped my psyche, because I have been completely obsessed with genre movies ever since. It's a real sickness. My greatest childhood memories are of watching *King Kong* and *The Incredible Shrinking Man*, not of, God forbid, actually *doing* something.

For many years I would watch nothing but horror, sci-fi or fantasy movies. If a picture didn't fit squarely in those genres, then I wasn't interested. Fortunately, later on, I did relax the genre restriction and found that I could also enjoy Westerns and dramas and comedies and *noir* and arty foreign pictures and noisy musicals and all the other marvelous variety offered in the cinema. Nowadays, when I just feel like watching a favorite old movie, I often find myself reaching for an Orson Welles movie rather than a Roger Corman, and sometimes that scares something deep down inside of me that doesn't want to be lost. It never is lost, though, as the highbrow and camp somehow continue to coexist in my bizarre universe. If I were to compile a list of favorite films, it would include *It's a Wonderful Life, Horrors of the Black Museum, City Lights, Touch of Evil, Terms of Endearment, Invasion of the Body Snatchers* (the original, of course) and *Stagecoach*. So I guess the point is I just love movies and have been influenced by all kinds, but my first love is genre movies, especially horror movies. The love of those movies is what drives me to make movies. I want to express myself in that language I love so much.

My aspiration is to just keep making movies that I like to watch and to make a living at it; hopefully making bigger and better and more ambitious pictures each time. I want to do it all, writing, acting and directing, getting better and more confident with each project. Someday maybe even do a movie that says something special in a new way. I don't know if I have that in me or not. Time and others will tell.

GALLAGHER: I was a big horror fan as a kid, loved Hammer movies and just cheap exploitation films. I always wanted to make my own movie but never had the equipment or enough people to share my interest. Plus, I always had the delusion that movies were made in Hollywood—not rural Illinois. It wasn't until video became popular that I saw *The Rats Are Coming the Werewolves Are Here*, I then realized anyone could make a movie.

GINGOLD: I've been into movies, particularly genre films, ever since I was very young; my early favorites were the Japanese monster movies, which I continue to enjoy to this day. At the age of 12, just as the late '70s horror boom was getting underway, I started checking out the heavier-duty genre films, and in late fall 1979 I had the young film fan's equivalent of a religious experience: I saw John Carpenter's *Halloween*, which left me terrified yet loving every minute of it and transformed me into a horror fan for life. Thus, most of my Super 8 projects were slasher films (it also helps that this is the cheapest subgenre to work in—no monster makeup or extensive F/X required); I even shot a spoof of this type of movie at summer camp titled *Halloween the 13th Part 4*.

In my student film and *Mindstalker*, I can't say I had any conscious influences; I was just trying to tell the stories as best I could, and keep a focus on the characters as much as the horrific events. One of my favorite filmmakers in any genre is Stanley Kubrick, and at the risk of sounding pretentious, I think there's a bit of his influence in *Mindstalker*, in the use of long takes and wide-angle shots to set a mood. But it certainly wasn't something I was thinking about while shooting the movie; I was too concerned about getting the filming done to worry about what inspirations I should bring to bear on it!

JACOBS: I spent my youth in movie theaters and video stores. I was always watching something, writing something, or filming something with the video camera. With movies I went in stages. I watched films like *The Last American Virgin*, *Bachelor Party*, *Mr. Mom*, and *Caddyshack*. Then, my parents

would tell me about people like Robert De Niro and Al Pacino. I started watching films like *The Pope of Greenwich Village*, *Raging Bull*, and *First Blood*. I think I found my genre in Woody Allen films. I remember being enthralled with *Broadway Danny Rose*, and when I watched *Annie Hall* I felt like crying at the end. I related so much to the situations and the dialogue and identified with the "little man" character. I also liked how he portrayed women, how he dealt with his problems, et cetera. Then there's the new crop of directors like Tarantino, Rodriguez, and Kevin Smith. I'd like to take a little bit from all of these directors. Tarantino's directing style [pacing] and dialogue. Kevin Smith for his dialogue and Robert Rodriguez's energy and efficiency. Three movies that inspired me to make *Walking Between the Raindrops* are *Annie Hall* [Allen], *Clerks* [Smith], and *Who's That Knocking on My Door* [Scorsese]. I hope to continue to be inspired by a wide range of directors while at the same time coming more into my own as a visual artist.

HOWE: I've always loved horror movies. I used to beg my parents to let me stay up Saturday nights when I was a kid and watch *Creature Feature*. I hit high school just as the big *Halloween*-inspired horror craze was getting up to speed. I tried to see as many of those pictures as possible; most sucked, but the films of Carpenter, Romero, and Cronenberg made a huge impression on me. *Scanners* was the first Cronenberg movie I saw and it excited me more about movies than anything I've seen before or since. The films that sucked were as big an influence on me as the good ones. Watching the lousy horror flicks made me think "gee, it can't be that hard to make a movie better than this piece of shit." While somewhat naive, it was a healthy attitude for a burgeoning filmmaker. Film school introduced me to a number of directors I might otherwise never have gotten interested in, such as Kurosawa, Welles, and Sam Fuller, three filmmakers who remain inspirations to this day. As for what got me interested in making movies, I believe I've always wanted to make movies since I saw my first, *Lady and the Tramp*, at a local drive-in. Something about looking at those giant, moving, talking images that have the power to suck you into their world that made me, even at a very tender age, think "Yep, this is for me."

McCLEERY: My influences are wide and varied. As a kid I liked horror films and action-adventure. John Carpenter was one of my favorite directors. Today I like all types of films as long as they are good. But to be honest I don't get to see too many films. It's a struggle to sit down for two hours and watch one. The films I saw and loved as a kid were: *Conan the Barbarian*—saw it on TV again recently and still like it—*Cat People*—haven't seen it since '85 so I don't know if it's still good—*The Outlaw Josey Wales*—seen it recently, still great—*Escape From New York*—still good—and *O.C. and Stiggs*. You haven't heard of it? It's funny but it should be cut differently. All of these films aside, the thing that got me wanting to make films was the whole package of creativity. I enjoy the writing, directing, acting, editing, shooting, the works. The only thing that I don't really like is dealing with the other actors. That's always a headache when you have to rely on other people. What does it boil down to? I got into filmmaking because I needed to create, and I can't draw for shit.

LEGGE: Since all I do is comedies you would think that would be my biggest influence. But I had two equal loves growing up: comedies and horror films. I admit straight out I'm a fuddy duddy about horror films—I prefer the old classics that relied more on mood and suggestion, but I can take a good gore fest, too, if there's some thought behind it, which there usually isn't. I love comedy in all its forms, low to high. I am a fan of the Marx Brothers for their verbal wit and surreal aspects, and Laurel and Hardy for their slapstick genius coupled with two very human characters. Yes, I like the Three Stooges,

Abbot and Costello, W.C. Fields, et cetera. I was a fan of Monty Python and Peter Sellers. Growing up watching all this is what I guess made me want to do more than watch. I know it sounds corny but, being a misfit in my youth, movies were one of the few pleasures I had, and I wanted to bring that pleasure to other misfits.

McCRAE: *Star Wars* is the film that made me want to make movies. Until I saw it, although I grew up watching an endless stream of flicks on television—before VCRs—I had never really thought about having anything to do with the film industry. I must have purchased every single magazine ever to publish a story on the damn thing; I read anything I could get my hands on about the special effects—thank you, *Starlog*—and design work. But *Dawn of the Dead* is the film that made me want to make horror movies. Having said that, I'm sure it's obvious to anyone who has seen *Shatter Dead* that the George Romero and Lucio Fulci zombie movies were a major inspiration for my first feature-length project. I especially love the earlier Romero works like *The Crazies* and *Martin*; they are marvels of editing that are worthy of study by anyone who is interested in seeing that you don't have to move the camera around very much to impart a feeling of momentum to the proceedings. The Fulci films are especially fascinating as studies in the lack of a linear narrative in a work to provoke irrational fears, i.e., "What the fuck is going on?!" or, "Why are the dead returning to life?!" et cetera. *The Beyond*, which is a masterpiece, has a narrative structure so disjointed that it appears to be almost completely senseless on a first viewing. But that confusion only exists if you pursue its story in a traditional narrative strand; this work should be examined as a majestic tapestry, not a single taut story-string. This kind of oblique storytelling really appeals to the experimental narrator that still dwells within my fevered subconscious. Gads, what a pretentious thing to say…. Finally, a few other films and filmmakers who have cracked me open and poured their inspirations into my sponge: *Solaris* and *Stalker*, both by Andrei Tarkovski, are two of the best science fiction films ever made and possibly two of the most beautiful films ever. *Solaris* especially is such a nakedly open wound of a love story that it has convinced me that every film I write must have such an incredible passion at its base for viewers to connect with. Nobody is sure what a monster might look like or do, or what it feels like to get stabbed with a knife in a shower after sex, but everybody knows what it feels like to be in love—the good way or the bad way. *Last Year at Marienbad* by Alain Resnais and Alain Robbe-Grillet is yet another work of genius from which I learned that how you choose to tell the story, and not the story itself, is the single most important thing about establishing yourself as an expressive and individual storyteller; it is a film that, like no other film, concerns itself with being a product of the collective narrative memory that is unique to the language of cinema. So I really like it a lot, okay? I think part of making a career out of this filmmaking disease is learning to mix ambition with practicality in such a way that does not undermine the strength of an artistic vision, nor does it so distill the initial inspiration as to make it flavorless.

MURPHY: I was raised in a funeral home so I had a predisposition toward dead bodies and death and all that which was accompanied by Saturday Creature Double Features. Plus my father, the funeral director, was big into home movies. So, somehow, that soup of things made my path cinema. My favorite films are the Bob Fosse movies—*Lenny*, *All That Jazz*, and *Star 80*—and then a bunch of others from there—*Apocalypse Now*, *Ciao! Manhattan*, *Taxi Driver*, et cetera, et cetera, et cetera. There was a lot of *Apocalypse Now* and *Thx-1138* influencing me when I made *Jugular Wine*. Also Godard. And *2001*. I like all the stories of psychosis that go on behind the scenes in movies. And I like mythic depth. I don't care much for films that only aspire to be ironic or a course of ac-

tion without relevance. I've always aspired toward building a huge empire. I like Disney. And the opening of *The Hunger* was pretty cool, too.

Black Pearls was influenced by the movie *Sherman's March* as well as Jack Kerouac's novel *The Subterraneans*.

POLONIA BROS.: Some of our major influences would have to be early '70s sleaze movies and sci-fi on the late night TV and the horror films of the early '80s. Not so much influenced by a particular director, but by the whole scope of the genre. After falling in love with these movies we just decided we had to make our own. It was that simple—we were five.

RITTER: My influences for horror filmmaking include pretty much all the slasher movies I grew up on in the late '70s and early '80s. The movie that actually had me wanting to film horror flicks was probably *The Incredible Melting Man*, when I saw the trailer as a kid. I was too young to see the movie but the trailer really got into my imagination. Of course, *Halloween* was probably the movie I began carbon-copying in my early Super 8mm films. And all of the *Friday the 13th* movies—I'm one of the few people who freely admits to enjoying all of those! Every sequel was cool in my book—I guess I just grew up with them, but I always loved the Jason character. And Michael Myers, too! I've always been a horror and science fiction fan as long as I can remember. Stephen King was and still is a big inspiration; I've read all his works. Romero, Carpenter, Craven, Cronenberg, and John Russo ... I was always a big fan of their works. I think I was and still am just your basic *Famous Monsters/Fangoria* fanboy! Kind of a horror junkie. The type of movies I watch now include lots of independent low-budget works from other filmmakers, just to see what's happening. Some of them are quite good and inspiring. *Darkness* and *America's Deadliest Home Video* come immediately to mind. I also enjoy big flicks like *Speed* and *Jurassic Park*: they're just great entertainment. Personal favorite films include *Henry: Portrait of a Serial Killer* and *Jaws*. And any of those great Cannon movies from the eighties that starred Bronson or Norris are great. I guess I aspire just to make movies that I would like to see personally and have other people enjoy them on the same level that I would.

STANZE: My greatest influences emerged from the horror boom of the '80s and late '70s. As with many other filmmakers my age, Sam Raimi and George Romero were huge influences. In the past, my movies have not disguised their sources of inspiration. *Savage Harvest* especially sports a heavy Raimi style—without the goofy Three Stooges humor. When, in my youth, I first realized the thrills of 8mm film and consumer camcorders, I started making movies specifically to do bloody special effects. That's when I realized how fascinated I was with all the *other* aspects of making movies. As I progressed, I concentrated more on the stories, the camera work, and directing the actors, leaving the special effects in more capable hands.

Now, I am still a horror fan, though few good horror movies are being made these days. I enjoy a very wide variety of movies, from some Hollywood blockbuster mainstream films like *Jurassic Park* to artsy independent films like *Man Bites Dog*, to the micro-budget stuff like *Shatter Dead*. My all-time favorite movies include *Apocalypse Now*, *The Evil Dead*, *Star Wars*, *Pulp Fiction*, *Full Metal Jacket*, *Dawn of the Dead*, *Night of the Living Dead*, *Alien*, *Cinema Paradiso*, *True Romance*, *Citizen Kane*, Carpenter's *The Thing*, and, of course, many others.

THOMPSON: I have always been fascinated by the power of the visual experience (be it in a theater or looking at a painting) to send a message. All of the key emotions from laughter to fear are things that one can relate to and share sitting side by side with someone she or he doesn't even know personally. Or in some cases, sitting next to someone you don't even like. I was empowered by the potential for political understanding that came from works like *Missing* or *Salvador*. You might not agree with the perspective from which they came but they certainly left you with an understanding of the issues. The visual moving image can bring otherwise abstract issues to life. There is much evidence to suggest that the effect of seeing war at home on America's televisions has had an effect on the country's willingness to go to war. In the case of Vietnam, it appears that the camera helped America lose its stomach for war. In the case of the Persian Gulf, it may have actually had the opposite effect. Without taking sides on any of those issues, one can still appreciate the power of the moving camera to change our futures. The political example is only an obvious concrete one. I believe these truths apply to all emotions.

The first horror movie I ever saw when I was a kid was *Blacula*. I'm from Oakland, California, and this was the thing to see at the time. I just thought it was way past cool. The horror genre also seemed to offer one of the few routes for a young, broke filmmaker to break in. My early inspirations came from magazines about low budget sci-fi and horror work. Cunningham, Carpenter, Romero. But even they had each at least done one or two pieces by the time I was reading about them. The real inspirations for me were the Don Dohlers, the Dan Beuhls, who were putting out low budget magazines that invited everyone to send in their work. I never did send mine in because my projects would just keep getting bigger and bigger. I was crushed when *Amazing Cinema* stopped coming out. I honestly don't know if these guys have any idea how many people they inspired with their down and dirty encouragement. I'd like to take this opportunity to thank them since you asked. While my full length pieces to date lean in the action-horror direction, there are messages jammed in them about everything from race, to politics, to whatever is pissing me off. If you care about what you are making, then you will do it no matter the obstacles. My next piece is a '90s corporate vampire piece reflecting my perception of the huge corporate world in which I am currently working. I'll probably get fired for it. My understanding of what is important to create may never coincide with those of the people who give Academy Awards. But my mother is an artist in California and she helped me make peace with that a long time ago.

THOMSON: Nothing can make you want to make movies like the simple love of watching movies. I was raised on TV shows, cartoons and monster movies. My first love was and is science fiction, fueled by movies, comics, Saturday morning TV and books. My first heroes were James Bond, Bugs Bunny and Godzilla. As I got older, I discovered how many different kinds of films there are out there, and I really gained an appreciation for all of them. In my high school and college years the cable–VCR revolution was born, where for the first time we gained access to almost everything there was on film and video. Now we have unlimited choices of what we can watch, and although my first loves remain there buried deep, my influences now come from everywhere: Orson Welles and Roman Polanski, David Cronenberg and Dario Argento, Peter Greenaway, Soviet sci-fi, surrealists, black comedies, *film noirs*, silent horrors, New Wave stuff, seamlessly styled action, spaghetti westerns, music videos, computer games, anything Japanese, Buster Keaton, all the Hong Kong stuff, industrial films, Mexican films ... the list is endless. Basically, I'm drawn to highly visual things with a great depth of character; I enjoy films with silences filled with subtle nuances, well-told stories, different styles and expressions. I enjoy finding new things. I think you benefit more by expanding the realms of what you watch. Having American Movie Classics has taught me more than weeks of college classes, just by being able to sit down and study what people have done in the past, and bringing little bits into my own work.

ULRICH: I basically watch all kinds of movies but the one type I love the most is horror. When I was young I loved the feeling of being scared; it gave me a rush. The movie that influenced me the most was *The Exorcist*. In my opinion it's the best horror movie ever made. It had everything—a great story, great acting, great special effects and great direction. And to top it off it had a big budget for the time. When I was about 10 years old, me and my friends would make up little action stories and play them out. We'd choreograph fight scenes and act them out and I always wished that I had a movie camera to film them. When I did get that first 8mm movie camera the first movie I made was a two-minute horror movie. But the second movie was an action film.

VOLLMANN: It was those nuclear monstrosities from the 1950s-60s that tugged at my ever growing imagination. As I entered grammar school my love for horror-sci-fi films grew to a fever pitch. I bought every monster magazine I could get my hands on. Armed with my trusted J.C. Penney's Super 8 camera, I began filming anything and everything. *Night of the Living Dead* inspired this zombie ripoff I made called *Day of the Dead*. What vision, huh? I also had a keen interest in stop-motion animation. Ray Harryhausen's films were a great inspiration to me. Most of my summer vacations during high school were occupied by shooting short films using stop-motion techniques I'd read about in *Cinemagic* magazine. The best part of these films was blowing up the miniature sets using fireworks and chemicals, camera always rolling, of course. In 1979 I saw the much anticipated sequel to *Night of the Living Dead*, George Romero's *Dawn of the Dead*. I couldn't believe how great the film was. The writing, acting, special effects, cinematography, editing and music were outstanding. This is a near perfect film. To see how Romero brought all these ingredients together on such a small budget and still maintained such a massive scope is simply amazing. Reading in *Fangoria* about how this film was made made me realize that film-making would be in my blood for the rest of my life.

GARY WHITSON: My main influences were the old monster movies from the '50s. And *King Kong* was my favorite monster movie. And I always loved the cliffhangers. That's why I came up with the character of Fanny Starr, who is always finding herself in some deadly trap or another. And I loved the old Hammer horror movies as well as just about anything that was shown at a drive-in. And comic books were a big influence, too. Ever since I was in high school I've wanted to make movies and with the advent of video, it became a reality.

2. Thoughts on Film Schools

I went to college at the University of Michigan, in Ann Arbor, as a "Film/Video Studies Major" and have a bachelor's degree that proclaims as much. Although a part of me thinks college was a way to keep from finding a real job for four years, I think my filmmaking would have suffered if I had not gone to school. This is because it made me watch movies I normally would not have watched, provided me access to equipment I could readily create with, and threw me into a group of students who I had to try and out do with my films and projects. Most importantly, it gave me time to develop my own style and filmmaking skills.

During my college years, I watched about six or seven movies a week, from Altman to Bergman to Welles and Ken Russell and Bakshi, analyzed them, wrote papers on them, and learned about what went into creating a narrative or experimental film—and I absolutely loved it.

Yet, classes had certain requirements and the teachers were, more often than not, conformists. They taught you to study Hollywood movies 90 percent of the time and set that type of filmmaking as a goal. They didn't stress independent filmmaking beyond the college experience. It was always alluded to that jobs were next to impossible to find, and if you actually landed one, it would be as a production assistant and you'd be "paying your dues" for the next several years.

Graduation with a film degree was not made to seem like a great goal.

Well, I completed the class requirements, but I also took the option of making short films instead of writing term papers and took independent studies classes where I was given more freedom to do what I loved and still receive credit. What they taught in classes was theory—such as the use of a point-of-view shot to show what a character sees and how he or she sees the world or how a low angle can seem to empower a character. All useful information for creating your own films. *But they weren't teaching us how to make films.* A huge difference! There was little hands-on or practical training so I figured I had to do this myself.

I wanted to transform my ideas, those nightmares I had, into a tangible thing others could also experience. I have to acknowledge that some of my early college films were disturbing, such as *Die Pumpkin Head* and *Roadkill*, but they went over pretty big in class. In fact, when I told my teacher what *Roadkill* was about—a man whose job it was to go out and hit as many people as he could during his eight hour work shift—and that it was supposed to be a comedy, she didn't understand how I could pull this off. It wasn't until I showed it in class—and all the students laughed in the right places—that I felt vindicated.

As for fellow students, there was support,

such as in getting actors and crew, but the actual circle of active filmmakers was small.

The most annoying classmates were those who would go on and on about this director or that director and dismiss anything that was low-budget as exploitive schlock. These were also the same people who didn't like horror or fantasy films. They talked and talked and talked. They're probably *still* talking about doing a film, and I graduated a decade ago. *That's* the difference between someone with a film degree and a filmmaker.

A person with the film degree knows about theory—the filmmaker takes those theories and utilizes them and makes their very own film.

The important thing during my college education was to never relinquish those dreams, to always keep in mind that I was going to make movies, even if it took years to do so. So yes, I'm glad I went to film school—I was able to watch a lot of great movies.

THE INTERVIEWEES WERE ASKED,
What's your take on film school?

ARSENAULT: Film school is not necessary, but it can be extremely helpful. For me, it was learning all the technical background. I always knew I wanted to direct, but I learned how to operate a camera, operate a Nagra, thread a projector. I can still do all those things today. That's very helpful in learning how to run a film set, understanding delays, and knowing how to remedy them. On-the-job experience is great, but most people start as a P.A. [production assistant]. Chances are you'll be so worked to death as a P.A. that you won't have time—or won't be allowed—to learn the equipment. Film school gives you the opportunity to do everything and it's wise to take advantage of that opportunity.

BALLOT: Because I never attended film school, my opinion is somewhat unqualified. Do you need to go to film school to make a film or a video movie? John Waters got thrown out of NYU. Kevin Smith withdrew after one semester and used the $25,000 he had set aside for future tuition to make *Clerks*. Quentin Tarantino never went. Then again, Spielberg, Coppola, Scorsese and countless others all graduated.

If you have the time and the money I'm sure that going to film school couldn't hurt.

If you're a rich kid in your late teens or early twenties and your mommy and daddy can pay for you—go ahead, go. And when you get out make the 900th film about slacker, generation-X angst. When I see it I'll puke.

You have to live before you're capable of doing anything significant. Does a 22-year-old, whose life experience consists of living at home for eighteen years and going to school for four, have enough knowledge about the human condition to make a great film?

In some cases, yes. Todd Solondz's *Welcome to the Dollhouse* was brilliant and it was about junior high school. In most other cases, however, the answer is "no." If your frame of reference is limited then the scope of what you can accomplish artistically will also be limited. Maybe it would be better to skip film school and go out to experience the world. Roam the globe, go to Bosnia, live with homeless people, get thrown in jail.

Am I serious? Well, half serious. I'm not telling anybody what to do. All I'm saying is that you can become technically proficient by attending film school, but if you have nothing to say, then what's the point? Film school can teach you the craft of moviemaking but it's not the only way to learn. Read books, talk to people, and learn by doing. Work as a production assistant for a film crew or intern for an established director. Also, connections are probably the most important thing. If you can schmooze, network, and figure out how to acquire important contacts, then film school or not, you're ahead of the game.

BERGER: If you have good teachers, then you could learn a lot. If you're taught by a bunch of tired old jerks, you're doomed. Working with other students is a valuable experience. It prepares you well, I feel, for the "real" or "reel" world. In other words, it will allow you to work closely with a bunch of selfish, arrogantly deluded cut-throats who will pretend to appreciate you just as long as you slave for them diligently for free and with no prospect of help in return. That's the way it is. Don't believe anyone who tells you otherwise; they probably just want you to trust them so that they can use you. Key warnings about film schools and the profession in general: (A) Trust no one—depending on false friends sinks ships—and (B) watch and learn all that you can. "God helps those who help themselves" as they say. Wise words.

BONK: I just think you have to do what works for you. You only know yourself best. Film schools are great for providing info, getting updated on all the technical jargon. But I honestly believe that if you are really going to learn anything that you have to get out into the field. The hands-on approach! That's the only way you can really learn. And I also believe that you can become a quality filmmaker having never gone to film school. I mean, everything you need to learn from is right there in front of you! Your own vision—how you see the world, how you remember events. Shelf after shelf of movies at your local video store. Numerous, quality books on film aesthetics. Watch these movies and study them. Go back to the classics! Note how you feel while watching any movie, as well as immediately after. Even hours after. And then go back and look at the movie and

figure out why. Is it the story? The acting? The music? The shot selection? How the shots are cut? What's in the background? How the set is lit? What is it? Is it the reaction on the actor's face? What? What does it? And then gradually you can learn how to become a quality storyteller, which is what a filmmaker really is. It can be tough and frustrating at this level, because of the lack of budget, equipment, et cetera. Being a filmmaker at this level is like having a great visual imagination and not being able to draw. But you learn your boundaries and make them work for you, and you can still tell a most affecting story.

BOOKWALTER: I don't have a high opinion of film school. Personally I never really considered it as an option. I was so dumb that after I graduated high school I found the Art Institute of Pittsburgh, which I attended for a year to take photography classes ... just in hopes that I could get a production assistant job for Romero! Of course, that never came to pass, but I did get to be an extra in *Day of the Dead* during that time. My method of learning has always been to read about it and then go do it. If it doesn't work, I alter what I'm doing until it does ... or until I fail enough to warrant stopping the insanity! I think film school is probably great if you want to be a technical guy—a grip, a gaffer, a cinematographer—but for aspiring writers, producers and directors, the best way to learn is to do.

CAMPISI: Like all colleges, and all choices of education, film schools work for some people and fail for others. It depends largely on which film school you go to, and how strong your desire to learn is.

I believe, however, that the days are gone where film school was the premiere entry into Hollywood. Today, you must prove yourself with a good project, whether you're a student or independent filmmaker, or borrowing money from your friends and family and put something together. In a film festival you compete with *everyone*.

I also believe that today there are a lot more movies being produced, with the independents and with the introduction of inexpensive home video equipment, thus allowing more entry level positions for people who want to learn from hands-on experience.

I personally learned production and filmmaking skills from hands-on experience. By 15, I was working on my first *real* movie, as a production assistant. Hardly an inspiring title, but an actual movie position nonetheless.

I get phone calls every week from film students at the local university who call to ask for advice. "How do you do this? What about that? Can I do this? Which camera filter do I use? What film stock? How 'bout video?" Sometimes I wonder what they're learning in college, since obviously many of them are clueless.

Does this mean hands-on experience surpasses film school? Absolutely not. It means there are no engraved rules on how to learn filmmaking. Again, what works for one person won't work for another.

CRAMER: I don't know anything about them but I can't imagine enough film jobs out there for all those graduates.

FORD: I didn't go to film school, so I don't know how much my opinion is worth. While in college I interviewed director Martin Brest when he previewed his new (at the time) film *Beverly Hills Cop*. He came out of the American Film Institute. He told me that the only thing the AFI did for him was to give him the resources to make his first film. But I think Brest was a bit unfair. I think film school is probably an excellent idea. You learn the mechanics of filmmaking, get to try everything, as well as having the resources to make your first film. I wish I could have done it. The danger of it, of course, is in getting too academic about it and losing the passion that makes your films your own. The people from film schools sometimes tend to make movies by the book,

and those people are doomed to episodic television. But if you want more, you have to be true to yourself and not let them package you. Film school is the one time when you can make a movie without worrying about its commercial potential. Take advantage of it. Make your movie the best way you can, even it's a splatter monster movie.

GALLAGHER: If you are just someone who wants to make a movie I don't see the need. I've always gone by that "live and learn" school of training. But, if you are looking to make it in the industry, with technology the way it is today, it seems you'd have to go to school because you'd never be able to afford to get that close to that type of equipment without going. Things have changed dramatically in video in just the last couple years.

GINGOLD: Film school is a different experience for everyone who attends one, and personally I found that there are both pros and cons to the experience. The first thing I can say is that graduating from film school, even with a great short movie to show for it, does not guarantee that you'll jump right into directing a professional feature. For every NYU or USC hotshot who begins shooting a $50 million studio production the week after graduation, there are dozens of his or her classmates who go on to work in much lower-level positions or in a field outside the business entirely. And winning awards at the school festival doesn't mean anything, either. Many people who took home major prizes at the NYU fests while I was there have gone on to do nothing significant that I'm aware of; on the other hand, two of my old classmates, Dean Lorey and Vince Gilligan, never won any awards but are currently working quite successfully, as a feature scriptwriter and a coproducer on *The X-Files*, respectively.

One of the pros of film school is that it's a place to make mistakes, to learn by doing and in my case to get various adolescent indulgences out of your system and streamline your craft. On the other hand, this can be an expensive proposition—I was fortunate enough to have parents willing to put me through it—and you can certainly learn by doing just as much on your own. Film school allows you access to better and more sophisticated equipment than you might be able to get your hands on otherwise; depending on which one you attend, however, there are only a certain number of students who actually get to direct higher-end projects. And one of the biggest advantages of film school is the ability to make contacts, both in the industry and among friends and fellow students whom you can go on to work with after graduation. However, all of the people who worked on *Mindstalker* were friends from around where I lived, not former classmates.

Some people who work in the horror field have reported encountering a bias at film school against people interested in working on genre projects. I never really had that problem; what ticked me off were the people who already considered themselves "professionals" and carried this attitude with them on student film sets, looking down on people who weren't entirely sure what they were doing, wanted to experiment or even have some fun, dammit, while shooting. To these people, my attitude always was, "This is film school, for God's sake. If you're so professional, go off and work on a studio movie and leave those of us who want to learn alone."

I guess there's really no right or wrong answer to whether film school is a benefit or not, or whether it can teach you how to be a moviemaker. What it can do is help you hone your craft, and provide you with opportunities in other areas—without my writing for college papers and a trip to the *Fangoria* offices to apply for an internship, I might not have eventually would up with a full-time job there. To go or not to go is ultimately a decision each potential student has to make based on their own individual experiences and ambitions.

HOWE: Film school can serve an important purpose in the development of a young filmmaker, but you have to go through a lot of bullshit, too. With that in mind, here's some of the good and bad you can expect from a film school education:

(1) Contacts. Upperclassmen and friends can form a lifelong network of people who can help you get jobs, crew on your movies, help you evaluate your own work and offer moral support. Nearly all the people I'm close to and work with are friends I met in film school; the torments of school has forged a lifelong bond between us. Competing against other students may seem the proper course of action when immersed in a program but cooperation will yield more positive results in the long run.

(2) A basic education in the fundamentals of filmmaking. And I do mean basic. Film schools want you to think they're teaching you everything there is to know about moviemaking but at best you're just scratching the surface. Graduate from USC and walk onto any feature set as gaffer or even key grip and you'll quickly realize how little you know. Learn what you can while at film school, but face up to the fact that there's still more to learn after graduation.

(3) Exposure to filmmakers you'd never seek out on your own. For me this included three of my now favorite directors: Kurosawa, Welles and Fuller, as well as a number of others.

(4) The grand prize. Those truly talented and lucky will walk out of film school with real industry contacts, for example, agents and producers. This is rare, even at big schools. And many of those who do land these contacts often never get anywhere with them. Don't expect a film school diploma to get you a job directing a feature. It won't.

Then, there are the negatives. Here's some things to watch out for.

(1) Bergman is not better than Cronenberg. Many film school professors look down

at genre movies. Most likely your teachers in film school will do their best to
keep you from following your heart and
making horror movies. This happened
to me and the result was me dropping
15 grand on a "serious" senior thesis film
that was one of the biggest pieces of shit
ever put on celluloid. In fact, as soon as
Original Sins was finished I threw the
whole thing, negative and all, into the
garbage. Never let anyone, respected
professor or not, tell you what kind of
movies you should be making.

(2) The arrogance trap: you are not the center of the universe. Film schools, in order to justify themselves, like to instill
in students a sense that they're important. As a result, many students graduate with an attitude that they know
everything there is to know about filmmaking. Let me stress again, at best
you'll know a very little. This arrogant
attitude has gotten more P.A.'s fired on
shoots I've been on than any other factor. People in the business don't give
two shits that you went to film school.
They don't want to hear how cool your
senior thesis film was, and they aren't
particularly impressed with your analy-
sis of *Fanny and Alexander*.

If you are lucky enough to actually land a job working in production after
you graduate, keep your film school career a secret. People not only don't care,
they tend to resent little know-it-alls.
Work hard, be enthusiastic, and keep
your mouth shut. Don't think that just
because you went to film school and the
gaffer didn't, that you know more than
he does.

(3) Woe is me. Film students get so focused
on making it to senior year, then ex-
pend so much time and energy struggling through their always nightmarish
senior thesis project, that graduation
becomes a horrific rather than joyous
event. What now, is the major question.
Suddenly, you left the womb with no
career, virtually no contacts, and cer-

tainly without anyone beating a path to
your door to beg you to make another
movie. This period is extremely depressing and can last several years. Trouble
is, at most film schools you won't have
any on campus agency setting up job
interviews and you won't have any internship programs offered. Basically,
you've been thrown in the pool and left
to sink or swim.

Had I been a tad smarter, I would have
taken some of my energy I was directing at
my oh-so-important student films and put it
towards making some job contacts while I
was still in school. Thus, I might have avert-
ed a few years of tortured soul searching
after graduation.

Something else that happened to me,
as well as to a number of my associates, is
that we felt like our creative spark got beat-
en out of us by film school. You enter as a
freshman all bright-eyed and bushy tailed,
and you leave a senior depressed and con-
fused by a world that doesn't care. It took me
a few years to rediscover that spark I had
going into school. I did it by getting back to
the type of movies I really wanted to make,
Original Sins. Others get through it in other
ways. Some never do at all and go back to
school to become accountants.

JACOBS: To make films you do not need
to attend film school. You can watch movies
and learn that way, mess around with cameras, et cetera. I just think that film school
gives you that much more of an option. All
a degree is is a certificate of accomplishment.
It's valid, but a degree doesn't insure you
anything. There is no security in any job or
vocation. I am a film major because I'd like
to earn a degree. I don't want to study English or law. I love film, so why not major in
it? Some production companies take into account that someone has a degree; some don't
care. If you can get one, why not get it? I'm
going to learn things that I'm sure I'll eventually learn anyway, but it's just another avenue for the films that I make. I'm going to

be in the filmmaking community, which if anything, will be beneficial. Everything I'm doing now, making my video movies, looking for distributors, and writing, is all being done irrespective of my film courses. It has nothing to do with my "film major." I think that's the key. I'm going to do the classwork, as well as my own work. If anything, I'll just keep getting more experience.

LEGGE: I don't really have an opinion on film schools since I never really attended one. I'm hesitant about any place that teaches you "the rules," although I realize some are needed.

McCLEERY: As far as film schools go, I think they are a great place to learn that filmmaking isn't just pointing your camera at some cool shit and pushing the button. Film is a powerful medium and it should be regarded and respected as such. Plus—if you go when you are young—it gives you time to grow up, see other people's work and network with people with similar interests. I went to Temple University in Philadelphia for four years and graduated with a film degree. Did I need all the classes I took? Probably not. Did I learn something from all of them? Absolutely. And sometimes you learn things you don't expect. I still believe the class that taught me the most about writing was my acting class. We would spend hours improvising scenes and that was real helpful for coming up with stuff, plus it helps you to write realistic sounding dialogue. Always remember that people don't speak in proper English nor do they use complete sentences. Being an actor has helped me keep this fact in mind. My film theory classes taught me to look at the way you select shots and angles so you can affect the audience the way you want.

There is no doubt that school is a positive experience, the only question is ... do you want to go to a technical school that is just going to teach you about production or do you want to go to a university and take 63 credits in your major and 63 credits in all

the other crap? If your main goal is to just become technically competent enough so your film looks and sounds good then the technical school is probably enough. If you want a cool looking degree from a big time university that your mom can hang on her fridge, then college is it. Nonetheless, take a look around your area for technical schools that don't cost much money. I teach at a public school (as a result of having a fancy college degree) where adults can pay a measly hundred bucks and have access to some pretty decent S-VHS equipment for ten months. Maybe your area has something similar.

McCRAE: Film school is great if: A) You're going to one where the tuition is not so prohibitively expensive that you can no longer afford to buy film stock and experiment like crazy both within and without of the established curriculum. Most of the reason you want to go to one of these institutions is to get your hands on the equipment and shoot enough stuff so you begin to discover an inner voice and how to express it— i.e., establish a personal style. How can this happen if you don't have the financial room to make mistakes or have as much access to the equipment as possible?; and B) You're going to have to find time to study other subjects as well so you won't have wasted four years learning to use equipment that will be obsolete before graduation day. I can't imagine anything more horrifying than discovering that upon entering the "real world" you know how to load an Arriflex magazine but can't compose a grammatically correct sentence.

The school I went to was great because it was dirt-cheap and access to the equipment was better than average—from what I've heard from other people. I feel sorry for anyone who's only experience with film school is a dumping ground like New York University. I'm sure it had its glory days, but it's ridiculously expensive to attend now; also, it's more of a trade school then an arts school. You come out of that place as "a director" or "a gaffer" or "a dolly grip"; the smaller and cheaper programs seem to turn out more well-rounded "artists"—God, I hate that word. And you have no fucking right to make a film about politics if you don't understand how this kind of stuff actually works; Spike Lee and Oliver Stone, you know who I'm talking about.

MURPHY: I think it was George Lucas who said that if you're going to make it, you're going to make it, film school or no film school. I went to the University of Bridgeport in Connecticut. My feeling at the time was that all schools were simply bullshit. But now that I'm a little older I can see in retrospect how stupid I was being. I really believe that you can cheat yourself out of a lot of education by holding on to too much rebellion.

First off, on campus nobody knows anything about what life is really like (unless you're working your way through school).

But what we did manage to study and create in film was invaluable. Everyone from my school has since moved to Los Angeles. And we're all doing okay. School wove us into a network that has been very helpful. Also, it was a great training ground to get your hands on equipment whenever you wanted to shoot something. Some of the bigger schools only allow you a camera a few times a year. But we had stuff nonstop. Anyway, just to have guidance was cool.

Ultimately, it's all up to you. School or no school, parents in the industry, whatever … it all comes down to your own perseverance. Luck helps, too. But it's really you. Make films. Make films. Just keep making films. That's the way to do it. I know a lot of people that went to film school who are waiting for something to happen and that's not the way it works. I know a few people that have amazing self-drive but they don't really know beans about filmmaking. But if they want it badly enough they'll learn what they need to learn. Film school can give you that initial foundation in a neat, pampered package. And filmmaking on campus can be really fun. But the rest is up to you.

My teacher used to tell us to do the work or get out! That he didn't ever want to hear any complaints because nobody's parents ever forced them to go to film school!

POLONIA BROS.: We believe film schools have some advantages, but we learned our craft at the school of hard knocks, by trial and error, and by just doing. That is as valuable, in my opinion, as a school would be. The bottom line is, *just do it*! A person out of film school has no greater chance of getting their foot in the door as you or I because once they leave the front door of the school where are they? On the street, scrounging for work like the next guy. Do what you think is best for you.

RITTER: Well, I never went. I don't think they are bad, though. There are no direct routes to getting "into the business." Each success story, each project that a person manages to get off the ground is always very different in circumstances. I think film schools are probably a great place to learn about equipment, get your hands-on experience, and meet other people with your interests. But the way I learned about equipment and such was actually working at a video company and being taught how to use stuff as I went along to earn money. So, that is another way … get an entry level job at a video/film production company and work your way up, learning as much as you can.

The only thing film school cannot teach you is creative stuff—you either have it or you don't. The passion to do what you have to do … you have to have that to begin with! Also, I've heard that film schools really don't get too much into *how* to raise funds for projects and such.

My final thought on film schools would be, on a personal opinion, why would you invest all that money to go to school for four years and end up with a "thesis film" that is creatively limited by the rules and specifications of the school when you could have taken your money, made a feature film on your own terms, and have it in the marketplace. Again,

I'm talking about people who aspire to write and direct, not technical buffs. But that's a much better way these days to get noticed—just do it.

The best reason to go to film school would be if you didn't have a core group of filmmaking partners to help with your projects. In film school you will meet people with similar interests.

STANZE: I think film school is an expensive and not-as-effective alternative to hoppin' off your butt and making some movies. Even if the movies are technically rough and no one ever sees them outside of their cast 'n' crew, the experience will, in many ways, be more educational than film classes. Finding someone who is making a movie and volunteering for their crew is also more educational than film school, and a hell of a lot less expensive. There is no substitute for hands-on, in-the-trenches experience.

While film school *can* provide valuable technical knowledge, creatively it tends to limit the students to making uninspired, ultra-conservative, paint-by-the-number films. At least that is the case here in the Midwest. If you do spend the dough to gain cinema education in a classroom, you should supplement this education by going out and trying things your professor told you to never do.

THOMPSON: I didn't go to a college for film training. I'm sure it's great for many things. Today as a production person, I know that you get someone who can do it for you if you can't do it yourself. For me that has been the real trick. I have friends who went and some who opted not to go for graduate school because it seemed to them that the real world was better than graduate school. One friend explained how while she was auditing a class of students who were about to graduate they asked questions that suggested to her that they hadn't been versed in reality at all. She opted for a job instead. My company is full of film school graduates who are trying to make their first real film. I thought that was what they went to school to do. I

know one person who went to graduate school for film with the clear expectation that the best function it could serve was to make contacts. I am only recounting what people tell me though, as I didn't go to film school myself.

The issue of getting trained, however, is very different for me. It's hard to get experience on equipment and you have to do it. I work on an Avid and a VideoCube. The nature of this technology is constantly changing and there are times when it seems the only way to get the training is to already be working (kind of like the union acting situation). In high school there was a cable station nearby that would train you and then use you as cheap labor on the cameras. I wrote a script and made enough noise that they eventually let me make a piece of my own. A lot of people will go to film school, but having something you wrote, shot and cut, puts you in a whole different category. This is part of a bigger economic picture in the world today. When my boss interviewed me for the editing position, he couldn't care less where I went to school. He wanted to see what I had done recently. When I talked to people who might give me money for a project, they don't ask where I went to school. They want to see what I can do for them. So to loosely quote Eddie Murphy, it's not where you've been but "What have you done for me lately?"

THOMSON: Here's what I think: The very first and best thing that teaches you about how to make movies is to see them. A lot of them. Because then you instinctively know what works, what's been done, et cetera. The second best thing that teaches you is that you go out and do it. There's absolutely no substitute for getting at it, making something, learning by mistakes, not being afraid to get goofy and do whatever the hell you feel like doing. That's why working in TV is better than school: TV makes you do a bunch of stuff, right away. And you learn how to do things in an up-to-date everyday practical environment, which, I think, schools tend to be removed from. Nothing beats the doing.

School was good for me first because it taught me disciplines and a few basic rules, and it gave me access to equipment for free. But after landing a job, school couldn't teach me as much ... real life does it better. I think the tendency is with some schools to teach things that are a little bit out of date and teach what the teacher believes, as opposed to what people want out of their TV channel, for example. So there comes a time when you just have to move on and do the real thing.

You can't beat schools for equipment access, though. At the end of my college days I was getting course credits for just grabbing the film stuff and going out to make my own projects: learning by my own mistakes, and they picked up the tab, offered a lot of encouragement, et cetera. You definitely lose that when you get out into the real world.

There's a benefit from saying you went to a prestigious school, I guess, but in the end your work speaks for itself. And believe it or not, most film departments don't even require you to finish your own completed film to graduate!

ULRICH: I think film schools are great for learning the basics and learning technical things but I feel the best school is on the job experience. I can't say much on film schools because I never went to one, but I do know a handful of people who have and they all lack the knowledge that non–film school filmmakers have—*experience*. That's where us non–film school filmmakers learn everything, on the job training. You're forced to learn little tricks of the trade that they just don't teach in schools. This is just one man's opinion.

VOLLMANN: Having never attended a film school my opinion may be slightly prejudiced. I believe anyone can learn filmmaking techniques by reading books, watching other people's films, or by just going out and shooting films by trial and error, as I have done. On the other hand, if someone chooses to enter a film school, he will need to network with other filmmakers. Take advantage of the school's resources and manpower to make films. If someone attends a film school just to acquire a sheepskin, then I believe your time and money would be better served making your own film. I also have a theory: If a film school offers someone a scholarship based on short films they have done, skip school. You're already talented enough to be successful in this industry.

WHITSON: As far as film schools, I'm sure you'd learn a lot. But I'm really not into making the "American classic." I just want to have fun and do what I like. If I had the time, I'd take some classes. But there's not much time to go around.

3. The Script

The script must be the strongest aspect of your low-budget movie, as you cannot rely on name stars or state of the art special effects. The characters and story have to propel the movie. The script also has to accommodate what resources you have available. After all, you can't make *Terminator 2* on a few thousand dollars.

If you have not written a script before, there are numerous books at your local bookstore and at the library on the basics of format and structure. Also, read other people's scripts—again available at bookstores and libraries. And, of course, view the movies you watch more closely. Analyze what works in terms of character development and story. Take notes if you have to. Learn. And if you spend four months to a year writing that first script you will learn all this. You'll be confronted with it every day.

With *Vampires & Other Stereotypes*, I wanted to make a film that would appeal to genre fans. I also wanted to make a movie I wanted to watch.

After I met with some of the people who would be involved in the movie, I wrote the script, keeping in mind what resources I had available—decent special effects and a studio.

Two months later, plugging away every day at my electric typewriter, I held 94 pages of the script in my hands, estimating one page of script to one minute of screen time.

It was a semi-comic, apocalyptic, F/X-filled horror film about a group of irresponsible kids who open a gateway to hell, which is guarded by vampires. A genre movie along the lines of *Evil Dead II*. My intention was to have all the stereotypical characters of a horror movie—the blond in distress, the reluctant hero, the annoying supporting characters, put them all in a familiar setting, such as the "trapped in hell" scenario—and create a movie that had a sense of humor about itself, not a spoof, but an homage to all those films that had such an influence on me.

Originally titled *Hellions*, the script was then given to the special effects house and they assured me they could do all the effects/props before we started shooting in the summer. During the next month or so some of the dialogue would be changed, in part thru improvisation on the set. Further changes occurred in postproduction. All in all, the script formed over a four month period.

In contrast, the script to *Addicted to Murder* took nearly a year and a half to write. With my second feature I wanted to keep away from the comedy slant, primarily because I had done it before. This time I wanted to create a very serious, disturbing horror feature. I expanded upon the premise of a short film I had shot in college, *If You Love Me*. It was about a man who seems to repeatedly kill his wife over and over again and it's questionable whether or not she's a ghost or if he's insane and has been killing different people all along and simply sees her in their place. It was a fairly disturbing short film (shot in Super 8mm) and I always wanted to expand upon it. Because I didn't have access to a studio or the time to deal with many special effects I decided the entire thing would be shot in New York City and the effects kept to a minimum. But after months of writing, reading every possible book on serial killers, I still wasn't happy with the first version of the script. I couldn't do anything more with it. I was at a standstill. So I approached my friend, horror novelist Tom Piccirilli, to take a stab at it, as I'm a big fan of his writing. I first met him at a writing group I belonged to some years ago. Piccirilli is the author of such novels as *Dark Father*, *Pentacle*, and *Shards*, as well as a prolific short story writer whose writing can be seen in numerous magazines and anthologies such as *Hot Blood* and *365 Horrors a Year*. He's also coeditor of the magazine *Pirate Writings*. During the next few months we'd each work on the script, passing it back and forth, finally coming to the version which was ultimately shot.

Addicted to Murder tells the gory tale of Joel Winter, a serial killer who becomes involved with a beautiful female vampire whom he must "kill" each night, partly for her sexual gratification. As Joel slips into the vampiric life himself, he paradoxically finds the humanity he lacked when he was alive. He no longer has the desire to kill humans, so he uses his natural talents to track down and destroy the creatures who made him. There's no gore in the first half-hour of the movie but when it happens it goes overboard, chainsaws and all, to appeal to that part of the horror market. Hopefully, the picture is upsetting because of its psychological and surreal terror.

I like the *Addicted* script much better

because the story and characters are much stronger—there's a *reason* why everything happens in it, rather than in *Vampires* where everyone was trapped in this warehouse and shit just started happening to them for the sole reason of having cool special effects. I think it's also a much stronger script because four years passed between the movies, which gave me more experience as a writer and filmmaker and a person, and the actors involved, Mick McCleery and Laura McLauchlin (both minor characters in the first movie), greatly improved their acting skills. They were very capable in handling the challenges of the new script.

If you're writing the script and don't know script format go to the library and check out some books or go to the local bookstore and check out the movie section. It's relatively easy, like writing a detailed comic book, with one page of script usually equaling one minute of movie. What's also helpful is getting your hands on some actual scripts—find them at the various film conventions—become familiar with how they're written, what makes them readable and interesting.

Once you've written a draft that's ready to show, give it to several people to read—and I don't mean just your mother or your girlfriend. Give it to people whose opinion you respect, who know the genre as well as you. Then, when you get all three or four scripts back and they all complain about the same thing, that probably means you should change it.

Remember, before you ever make a movie you should have a very clear idea what you want, even if it takes years to come up with a story you really want to do. It is the absolute one thing on a low-budget production that shouldn't be rushed, because the script is usually the low-budget film's strength.

THE INTERVIEWEES WERE ASKED,
How important is your script? Does your budget determine your ideas or vice-versa?

ARSENAULT: I think it is crucial to have the script in the best and most polished form possible before filming starts. This, I feel, is the shortcoming of my first two features. I never felt the scripts were 100 percent there, but I went ahead and started shooting anyway because I figured it would never be 100 percent there in my opinion. The lesson I learned is that I should now work with a collaborator.

Also, *shoot everything in the script.* Don't make the mistake of "editing" your film on the set by saying "Oh, we're running out of time, this scene isn't really necessary." This is a big mistake. *Shoot everything in the script.* In both my features I made the mistake of tossing scenes during production. The result? I found myself in the editing room, on both pictures, without enough material for a solid feature-length film. That's why both my features only run 77 minutes, and why they're somewhat slowly paced. Lesson learned: hire a good producer who will keep your ass on track. Sometimes it's not always best for a director to be in total control because you can lose your objectivity on the set.

The budget doesn't necessarily determine my ideas, nor do my ideas determine the budget. I basically write what I want and raise what I can raise. The only correlation between budget and script in my work was on *Domestic Strangers.* I deliberately wrote a script that would take place almost entirely on one location. That way, I could shoot it in a shorter period of time and save some money.

BALLOT: The importance of the script depends upon the movie and the moviemaker. For Alfred Hitchcock, the script was of paramount importance. Once his films were storyboarded Hitchcock considered them basically finished. Shooting, for him, involved following the storyboards to the letter. Charlie Chaplin placed much less importance on the script. He would change it as he went along, reinvent it, improvise, and sometimes not use it at all. For *The Bride of Frank* the script was simply a blueprint. Because most of the characters were nonactors I wanted the dialogue to be delivered in their own words. I gave them a basic idea of what I wanted them to say and I let them phrase it.

BERGER: The script is the thing. Get yourself a good grasp of character, location and incident and don't rely on stealing from other movies to do it for you. Nothing more depressing than to witness a scene repeated verbatim from another movie. Usually the messages are different and transpose awkwardly into the new environment. Try to push character, dialogue and behavior in a direction that is opposite to the familiar, but at the same time don't be quirky for quirky's sake. See how boring all the Tarantino clones are getting? Do everybody a favor and create new fiction.

Story and gimmick should always be secondary to character and incident. However, like a good author needs to understand the many possibilities of sentence structure with words, a good director needs to understand the many possibilities of filmic structure with images and sounds. Plain and simple. The rules bend this way and that depending upon the degree of our imagination—but they were designed to do so. Not enough writers or directors today, especially in the no-budget videofilm arena, have taken the chances they have at their disposal. I can't stress enough the importance of pushing as far away from formula as possible and having faith in developing character, set-piece and subtext—this makes up for any lack of budget you could possibly suffer from.

Budget definitely guides the course of the scriptwriting. You can always try to bite off more than you can chew—that should be a goal, in fact. Just try to remain practical. Keep in mind how much money your project stands a chance in recouping while you write.

But beyond budget, I think that format determines market and market determines depiction of subject matter. I feel video demands a different guideline of perception than does a theatrical film. I am from the school of "balls nailed securely to the wall," especially if I am making a horror film. On video, the screen is small and I like to have copious helpings of blood and nudity mixed evenly with a fairly intelligent script to keep my interest. On a larger format, 16mm or 35mm, you can get away with more subtle and less obviously exploitive material. I enjoy and intend to make both types of feature. Some people might and have disagreed with me on this and argue the value of blood and nudity. I say to them: "Have fast forward button will travel!"

BONK: Easily, it is the most important thing. It's the basis of the whole movie. It's the foundation on which all stands. You can be the greatest director, with cool shots and strong acting and neat special effects, but if the story sucks the critics will notice. Just witness Hollywood—lots of glossy, slick stuff, but much of it lacking soul. The script is the soul of the movie.

Writing at this level can be a bit of a conflict. I would love to write my own *Star Wars*, but I stay away because I know it is beyond anything I can do at this level right now. I try not to restrict myself when I write, though—I don't worry about the budget and how we might pull off what until after the script is done. Then it is either compromised in the best possible way or we come up with some new, unique way to pull it off. Or we just don't do it at all. But if I go into a script worried about budget, I just hit a brick wall. I give myself major writer's block. If it proves too big for me and my current status then I figure I can just option it out to an agent and maybe get it into someone else's hands or buy it until a future date when the resources are there. Eventually I do hope to do all of it.

BOOKWALTER: Hey, the script's the thing, isn't it? "If it's not on the page, it's not on the screen," as they say. When I wrote *The Dead Next Door*, there were very few

things that I changed due to budget constraints. It was too bad I didn't have $125,000 up front to make that movie—I would have put even *more* in there! As I made movies for David DeCoteau [*Creepazoids*], I had to downscale, which frustrates me. I remember showing DeCoteau the final cut of *DND* and as we started closing the deal for *Robot Ninja* him telling me "I don't want thousands of extras or aerial shots, just get it done on time." But, that's my thing! I want spectacle! A movie on an epic scale! I always used to wonder why my mother called me Cecil B. DeMille, Jr., back in my short film days.

For me the challenge is to make the story as solid as possible and then dazzle them with the production itself. That's not to say that I'm an advocate of "all sizzle and no steak." I think if your concept is strong and your execution is good, the rest will hopefully follow. Everyone seems to agree that the script for *Ozone* is weak but that doesn't stop anyone from saying it's a good flick and that it works for them. My movies are usually made in postproduction; I wind up spicing things up after all of the writing and shooting is done.

CAMPISI: The script is the most important element in any film production. It is the blueprint of the entire project. Imagine building a house without a blueprint. How well do you think that house will turn out?

Although making movies is a collaborative effort, it all begins with a good script. Take the time necessary to make sure the entire project works on paper before committing time and money and energy into something that doesn't work.

When you've got financial backing, you can pretty much write anything that comes to mind when it comes to production value and effects. The money is there. You can get away with it.

When, however, you are limited in funds, special care must be taken to write a script that you *know* you can shoot. This means gathering all available materials—actors, locations, props, vehicles, effects—*before* writing

Marcus (Andren Scott) is caught peeping and chased by an irate Mark Webster in Ronnie Cramer's *Even Hitler Had a Girlfriend*.

your script. Once you have all that at your fingertips—on index cards—you should try to dictate a screenplay that contains all these elements—*and nothing else.*

Essentially, if you don't have the money, your lack of it should dictate what kind of script you write, and if you *do* have money, you should let your imagination run wild.

CRAMER: Script verses budget. It would be nice to be able to shoot a script as written, but there are always corners that must be cut. One thing I liked about *Even Hitler Had a Girlfriend* script was that it was about a guy moping around his apartment most of the time. I thought, "Now *there's* something that won't cost much." One of the few things I changed was the scene where the guy visits the Statue of Liberty. I made it Mt. Rushmore since it's much closer to Denver.

FORD: Let me answer the second part of the question first. All of the scripts I have sold were written with budgetary considerations very much in mind right from the start. Very definitely it influences and shapes my ideas to a great degree. *The Fear* was written with four specific locations which the producer had secured. *Masque of the Red Death*, which I wrote for David DeCoteau, had to be set entirely within a Romanian castle he has access to. Another script I wrote for Dave was *Mad Crush*, which also had to be set in one location for budgetary reasons. We chose a Victorian mansion, revamped into an elite medical school. *Blazing Force* was a job in which I had to write scenes to expand a threadbare 40-minute featurette into a full-length feature, using the same actors and locations, of course. *Alien Force* was written with specific actors, locations and resources which I had available in mind. In many cases, however, we wound up abandoning the locations which the scenes were written for in lieu of others which provided more production value. So I guess it's all relative, but budget is always a big consideration for me.

You have to be realistic if you want to get movies made. You can't go ape shit and write the most amazing things you can imagine, figuring you'll let the technicians figure out

Trace (Tyrone Wade) fights Gorek in the body of Diane (Jane Mun), a woman he has just saved from street thugs, in Ron Ford's *Alien Force*.

how to do it later. Because if your script isn't possible to do on a realistic budget, it will remain merely a script, a piece of literature. And bad literature, at that, because a script is merely a blueprint for a film. Except for honing your writing craft, writing a script serves no function if the script never becomes a movie.

How important is the script? It's extremely important, of course. I am a very fast writer, and sometimes I think in retrospect that I should slow down and polish my work more. But one thing I do spend a lot of time on is the structure of the plot. I spend most of my time in the prescripting stages figuring plot points and getting the plot to conform to the common, accepted three-act structure which I believe is necessary to make a genre movie commercial in today's market. The structure is the most important thing. Then pacing. Then dialogue. If those things are working for you, then your script is doing all right.

I am a bit of a radical, however, in that I do not think the script is the most impor-

tant factor in determining a movie's success or failure. To me, film works on emotions and on subliminal levels. Its most poignant effects are achieved through visuals and through subliminal sound bites; not through dialogue or plot. Film is a visual medium first. So few directors remember that any more. It's not first about telling stories. If it were, we'd all be novelists, where we'd have more control and more freedom. No, movies are about images first, words second. There are many movies I can think of where a good director made a terrible script watchable because of his solid imagery. *I Was a Teenage Werewolf* springs to mind as a minor example. It is a horrible script, it has absolutely no direction whatsoever. But through his imagery and cutting, director Gene Fowler made a visual sketch of teen angst that is fun and interesting. I can also think of movies which had good scripts which were fouled up by poor directors. I don't need to name those. The point is, the script is very important to a good movie, but not as important as the direction.

GALLAGHER: I never really think in a high budget manner. All my scripts are tailored to be able to pull off with the amount of money available to me, and the locations. But you can tell a pretty good story with no money. *Gorotica* was shot very inexpensively in about four to five days. It looks like shit and sounds like shit but the story is so bizarre and interesting that people still love it. I think it's considered a classic in the horror genre. And that seems to prove that the story is the main ingredient. I would probably be better off just writing scripts, since I have so many ideas that I feel are original. I feel I'm a better writer than I am a moviemaker … but I still enjoy making them when the elements and people are right.

GINGOLD: A script is one of the most important components—if not the most important one—of any production, and I learned this the hard way, because I began *Mindstalker* without a finished screenplay. By the time I knew I was going to make the movie and had established my actors and locations, I realized I was going to be losing some of them in a very short time: an amusement park where I wanted to film would be closing for the season; one of my actors was about to move out of a house where I wanted to shoot; another was about to go into the Navy, et cetera. So I started with a completed outline and a script that hadn't been refined, and I finessed the individual scenes as I needed to film them. Needless to say, this is not the best procedure to use, and I think the movie suffers a bit for it, particularly in terms of the exposition. Working around scenes that I didn't have time to thoroughly think through is one of the things that resulted in the editing taking so long, and I'm still not entirely happy with some of them; the sequences that are "pure film," involving little or no dialogue, are the stronger ones in the movie. I'll never go into another production without a script that I've taken the time to develop to my complete satisfaction.

On the other hand, working independently, without scheduling or creative restrictions hanging over your head, can free you to improvise, and come up with new scenes after the fact to flesh out your story or clarify narrative points. At one point during shooting, for example, I realized that the first act didn't establish the malevolence of my alien villain, the "Tracker," strongly enough; he just appeared on the fringes of the action for a while, not taking an active part in it. So I wrote and shot an opening scene in which he terrorizes and kills a girl working in a library, which not only starts the movie off with more of a bang but—through a shot in which he looks at a book of maps after the murder—explains how he knows his way around the area during his subsequent pursuit of the heroine.

Another impromptu scene came about because of a lucky opportunity to indulge in a bit of guerrilla filmmaking. Some time after we started work on the movie, Greg Gonzalez, my coproducer-cocinematographer, found out that a scene involving a burning house was going to be filmed for a major movie near where he lived. I won't mention which major movie, just in case anyone connected with it might get upset, but a clue to it will be found in my end credits. After ascertaining the location beforehand, we drove there the night of the shoot, where the house was merrily blazing away as a group of local residents looked on. It was too crowded on the street to take any shots from there, so we asked some people standing on the deck of a house across the street if we could join them. They were happy to oblige; in fact, they even thought our little Super 8 camera was part of the actual production! I shot about ten minutes' worth of footage, and then was faced with a dilemma: How do I integrate it into the movie? Eventually, I came up with a scene that not only made use of these shots, but helped clarify that fact that there are two alien beings in the movie's first act—the Tracker and an enemy that he has already wounded as the story begins. Originally, the other alien simply expired off-screen after appearing in a couple of scenes, in which (I realized) he could be easily mistaken

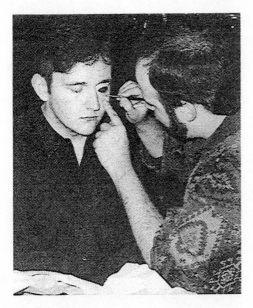

Makeup F/X artist Vincent Guastini applies alien eye appliances to actor Walter O'Reilly on the set of director Mike Gingold's *Mindstalker*.

for the Tracker, so I added a new sequence in which the Tracker follows his dying opponent to a house's basement. He sets the other alien on fire and departs; cut to the guerrilla footage of the house in flames. Presto! Instant production value, plus an extra bit of action before the main story kicks in.

This also addresses the question of how the budget influenced the script. My approach was, since the bulk of the story involves the Tracker chasing my heroine all over creation, I would use any free and interesting location I could think of. Therefore, *Mindstalker* has scenes set in a few different suburban houses and apartments, two train stations (and on a train), a concrete ledge overlooking a roaring dam, two different restaurants and the aforementioned library and amusement park, not to mention that the climactic action takes place in a mansion where one of my actors lived. Originally, the finale was set in an isolated cabin, but when that became unavailable, I decided to rewrite a bit and use the mansion as my locale. It's not entirely believable, I suppose, but it's damn cinematic.

To me, using a lot of interesting locations is one way to belie the cost of your movie.

There are enough low-budget films—both indie and "professional"—set in basements and cabins. It also gives your audience something interesting to look at instead of the same four walls for ninety minutes, and allows you to get creative with your camerawork; at the amusement park, for example, I took shots from the Ferris wheel and haunted house rides, among others. And when you're working on the true independent level, you don't have to worry as much about permits; as long as you don't have a ton of crew and actors or excess equipment, people will just assume you're taking home movies with your Super 8 or video camera. And should you get seriously busted, it's a lot easier to pack up and come back another day for another try when you're working with small-scale equipment.

JACOBS: The budget has almost no bearing on my ideas. Since the films I make are generally slice of life, dialogue driven pieces, and I'm working with almost no money anyway, I just write with a general idea of my resources. I have friends who have apartments, some who own warehouses, a lot of them are musicians, some work in markets and convenience stores, et cetera. I write the story with an idea of what I have at my disposal. Like I said, I'm usually not making science fiction, horror, or special effects work. The story is told through the words of the actors and actresses. Surely, I'd love to film scenes on a much grander scale, but I'm also a realist about all of this stuff. I don't have the money to rent out a hall or a soundstage. The warehouse that I have access to functions as a business for a record label. There are only certain times that I can use it. I just try to write the best script, with the most real or believable dialogue that I can. I try to tell stories that I would like to see. I also try to answer questions through my scripts. I just sit down and write, and a lot of times I'm surprised by what the characters say. I think of situations that maybe I've been in, or situations that I'd like to be in, or just situations that I have a curiosity about.

That is the aspect that I enjoy the most. I consider myself more of a writer than a director.

HOWE: A solid script is the key to making a good film, at any level. A hundred million dollars will not make a bad script into a good movie, it will just make a bad, expensive movie. Any number of recent Hollywood outings will confirm this.

Your budget should, to some degree, influence your script. You obviously have to limit yourself to what you can afford. Sure, if you really wanted to you could do *Goldeneye II* on VHS for two thousand bucks, but let's face it, it's probably not going to measure up to the original.

Don't get overambitious. Biting off more than you can chew only hurts your chances of making a solid picture. The one advantage micro-budget filmmakers have over Hollywood is that we have total control. There's no committee telling us what to do. Take advantage of that freedom to make the most interesting, original film you can.

And remember, because you don't have a lot of money, you have to give the audience something they can't get anywhere else, otherwise why bother with your crudely produced film? Be audacious. Be inventive. Unleash that geek imagination that's hiding somewhere down in the depths of your twisted mind. Go for it and give the audience that thrill they can't get anywhere else, otherwise you'll end up making crummy retreads of boring Hollywood pictures.

And finally, never go into production with a script that's not as perfect as you can make it. Never assume that you'll figure things out while shooting, or fix it in the edit room. You'll be too harried on the shoot and fixing things in post is often harder than it seems. A good rule of thumb to go by is this: If it's not on the page, no way is it going to be on the screen.

LEGGE: To me and to anyone making a fiction film, script is all important. How anyone wings it is beyond me. I'm too neurotic to hope that I'll come up with something as I go along. I script and plan everything I can to the last detail. I don't pay actors or crew, so I don't want to waste their time or mine. Everyone who works with me knows that I will get them in and out as efficiently as possible, which makes it more likely they'll want to work with me again. I've also learned never to write a story I couldn't pull off realistically because of the costs involved. I'm not going to do a period piece where I'll need elaborate costumes, or come up with great-sounding ideas that I can't pull off. Fortunately for me, I can get away with murder. With comedy, I found you can use your liabilities to humorous use. Since I don't deal with ordinary reality in my movies I can play around with locations and such. If I needed to represent the president of the United States, for example, since I don't have access to the White House interiors, I'd come up with some stupid idea to put his office in some weird place instead. Maybe they're painting the oval office so they move him outside to the street ... something like that. It's comedy; I can do whatever suits my purposes. So anyway, I keep things contemporary, and I don't plan elaborate effects. I work with people, and I concentrate on human foibles, pomposity, and the ridiculousness of everyday life.

McCLEERY: Of course the script is the most important thing in your production. It is the one place where you don't have to spend any money—provided you are writing it yourself—so you can spend all the time and effort you can afford into making it right. Without the script your production will go nowhere. As far as letting your budget dictate your script, I'm sort of split on it, but I'm changing fast. When I was younger I thought it hurt your writing when you write around a location or a prop or a car or anything, it hurts you by forcing you in one particular direction—in a sense boxing you in—but now I realize that making low-budget movies is about putting dollars on the screen; the more expensive you can make your production look the better off you will be when you go to sell it. So in the end I would say that it is necessary to write to what you have. So if you have a really cool-looking abandoned building near you … use it. If you have a cool prop and you can use it in a scene and it's going to help your production value, then go for it. It can also improve your writing skills in the long run by forcing you to write for given situations. Speaking of good writing skills, as far as becoming a good writer goes you have to do two things. The first is to write, and write a lot. Keep a notebook to jot down ideas and then make sure to follow through with the ideas and write them out as scripts. The more you write the better off you'll be. Secondly, you have to be able to be critical of your own work. This is the hard part because you really have got to read your own stuff and decide if it's crap or not. If you can't do it for yourself then get into a writers' group or find a person whose opinion you respect and let them read your stuff. But remember, use your writing time wisely and get the script right, because if the script isn't there and you go into production anyway, thinking you can fix it as you go along, you'll be sadly disappointed.

MCCRAE: In case I haven't already made it clear enough, *the script is everything*! The way the second part of the question is phrased is interesting; yes, the budget does affect the scope of the ideas I have, but not the basic idea itself. With *Shatter Dead*, I have an apocalyptic zombie movie that takes place—more or less—in six rooms with people doing a whole lot of talking about the things that I could not afford to shoot. The scope of the film is limited by its almost nonexistent budget; the few attempts I made to establish a sense of scale in the first fifteen minutes—i.e. the deserted city streets, a "crowd" of zombies attacking a car—are, frankly, embarrassing in the cheapness of their presentation. But on an intellectual level it was necessary to present these sequences for other scenes later in the film to have some power behind them.

Sometimes these limitations are helpful in establishing the point of view that a screenplay can take. For example, writing a film about a serial killer takes on a very different flavor if you have the money and resources to shoot it as a police procedural—complete with uniforms, police cars and station facilities—as opposed to only having the money to shoot it in the grimy confines of the killer's apartment and his stalking grounds. Personally, I couldn't care less about the details of a police investigation, but I am interested in what the serial killer is going to have for breakfast—this should be obvious from his nomenclature, right? Well, I guess it's a good thing I like working with low budgets. I guess what it boils down to is the same old argument: which came first, the budget or the idea? For me, the two are currently inseparable.

MURPHY: The script is very important. And don't just study other scripts. Because then you'll just end up rehashing the body of other screenwriters' works. Study life and take note of the lessons you learn. Your life will make what makes your scripts juicy and relevant and cool and worthy.

And learn about screenwriting and story structure. It's such a nightmare to try and create your structure in the edit with a lot of half-thought footage. Even a spontaneous movie like Henry Jaglom's *Venice, Venice* is still working its way through a preconceived process.

If you don't want to think about a script it may be that you just don't understand the relevance of its blueprints. Or you may be just lazy.

I think if you want to become a filmmaker you should want to learn everything from screenwriting to production to post-production to how they put the glue under your damn postage stamps for when you mail your work out to festivals later. It's all just empowerment. Why wouldn't you want to learn screenwriting as well?

POLONIA BROS.: The script is very important. It is the foundation of your film.

Home video artwork for *Shatter Dead*.

Without one you're probably going to have an incohesive movie with lots of ideas with nowhere to go. There are some people who don't script, like those self-proclaimed art filmmakers who throw jumbled ideas together and turn out crappy movies and then use the excuse that it doesn't matter because it is an "art film." You need a script! You need to storyboard! You need to plan! The more prepared you are the more polished your production will be. It doesn't matter if you have a budget of $500 or $5,000, there is absolutely no excuse for lack of planning, plain and simple.

RITTER: The script is the most important thing about any project. You have to believe in it and want to see that movie made. It's important to have the most satisfying screenplay that you can possible have before heading into preproduction. Changes will always occur, but that initial script is the spine of your project—make sure it's what you want.

The budget of any given project does indeed determine the final shooting script. If you only have $12,000 to make a finished movie, obviously big explosions and car chases are out the window. When I sit down to write a movie I plan to produce and direct, I consciously avoid writing anything I know I won't be able to afford or get away with on a shoestring. You never want to exceed your budget and try to get away with things that will never work.

Truth or Dare was a case where I originally wrote everything on a smaller scale, but when we got bigger money I added lots of effects and explosions. That was fun, knowing I could smash up cars and stuff. With *Wicked Games*—the sequel to *Truth or Dare*—I ended up cutting lots of things I wanted to do because of their expense or possible danger. Special effects can get expensive and time-consuming, so some of my more elaborate gore scenes became simple strangulations and aftermath shots as opposed to big murder sequences. Also, a car chase was changed to a foot chase because of the po-

tential danger of staging such an event in public with no insurance. No matter what, no movie is worth putting someone deliberately at risk for a shot. In my book, safety is first and if there is an obvious danger I'll avoid doing that scene. I'll change it to something else. It sometimes works out better this way; it forces you to be very creative on your project. For *Creep*, I wrote the whole script around props that we had laying around from other movies and things I knew I could get very inexpensively or for free. Surprisingly, the script, to me, was very unlimited in terms of story and twists and turns. The process of writing around actors I knew, locations I knew, and props I knew I had access to did not stifle the creativity of my story. I actually think it's the best script I've written and I had a blast writing it. I wrote it quick, like in ten days or something. Some of the bigger things in *Creep*, like the exploding building, were added in as we filmed when the opportunities arrived. I'd never try to plan something like that for a small movie. Sometimes you just get lucky with things happening around you. You simply seize the opportunity.

If you have access to minimal funds, concentrate on your story and characters. Bring twists and turns into your plot. Think of all the *Twilight Zone* shows that were so great with minimal effects and maximum storytelling techniques!

STANZE: I feel the script is very important. However, if you work hard on a screenplay and revise it to the point where you think it's perfect, you shouldn't assume you can simply show up, shoot the script, and get perfect results. Equal attention and preparation should be devoted to camera shots, camera movements, locations, visual effects, et cetera. The script may be a main ingredient, but many other things go into the soup.

When writing the script, one should try to incorporate what you have available to you already. Writing in a lot of elements that you have to go out to find can be time-consuming,

Explosive stunt scene from Tim Ritter's flawed but very successful slasher hit *Truth or Dare—A Critical Madness* **(1986).**

more expensive, and in many cases, impossible. If you know you have access to a specific element, write it in!

THOMPSON: The script rules. If you can't do the script, do something else. Having said that, I admit to having done something else a lot. My first completed piece was about a gang initiation. I was extremely faithful to the script and it ended up being a piece with two guys in a bathroom for most of the show. In written form, the reader went wherever the subject of conversation went. On screen, the whole thing was in a bathroom. I now

take a different approach with my low budget work. For both *Blood Harvest* [now rereleased as *Fraternity Massacre*] and *Contact Blow*, I literally sat down and made a list of all the places to which I had access. Then I made a list of all the crazy stuff I wanted to do. Next, I took my story idea and tried to build in as many locations and events—translate to production value—as I could. In between these projects I have written other scripts. But they each required things I don't have. A courtroom drama, for instance, I believe will require some "name" actors. Maybe next year. Another piece needs to be in a small town that I can take over for awhile. I am shopping these scripts but in the meantime I will make a piece that I can make. So while I don't let the production cost stop me from writing what I want, I also understand that I will have to wait on making some of them.

When you are making an acknowledged low budget film it sort of frees you up. You can take suggestions and run with them. This excites the crew. If an actor has a particular skill or comical way to play something, you are free to say "Let's shoot a take that way and it works, I'll go with it." Of course, you make the ultimate decision alone in the editing room much later. That's the freedom you have when you are doing a project that you begin knowing is low budget. It's all yours.

THOMSON: To me the script is *the* most important thing. It defines everything you can do on a project. It's also the cheapest thing you can do to get a project rolling: writing words on paper. Finish that, and half the work is done ... plus, you can communicate what you want from other people, get their attention and enthusiasm. Also, it's vitally important to take your script and break it down well, organize it well, learn how to make shot-sheets and storyboards and know as much as you can about what you are going to do *before* you go out and do it. I like to edit a film on paper before it's shot, then change it later at my discretion. It's free to do, so why not? People tell me, "Well, that diminishes spontaneity and creativity on the set." That's bullshit. The more planning you do in advance, the more you *have* the ability to create on the set because you know exactly what you need to pull it off, and can move on from there. The more stuff we had planned out, the more we made up new and better stuff ... and we got everything done, and left almost nothing out.

If you have no money, you have to write a script to what you have. On *No Resistance*, we made a list of all the cool-looking places we knew we could shoot ... and we wrote our script to those places. We only wrote special effects we knew we could make. It sounds overly simple, but it's easy to forget sometimes. It's easy to think up stuff like huge gunfights and car crashes because we see them all the time in films ... but then you are faced with the reality of actually buying a car to crash, or physically blowing a squib on someone. And it's tougher and infinitely more expensive than you thought. Better to put your money to better use, and just figure out a way to write around it ... and the cool thing is, usually it turns out better anyway.

Always register your script with the Writer's Guild in Los Angeles or New York City and then get a copyright registration from the Library of Congress. Each costs about $20. These steps are simple ways to protect yourself from infringement, but more important, they make you look good to a distributor ... then they know you can prove you own the project, and everyone is happy.

ULRICH: The script is the heart of the movie. I try to make sure my scripts have all the right elements, like three acts, strong characters and a decent plot. I notice a lot of low or no-budget movies out there lack a good script. Hell, they usually lack even a decent script. When I write I make sure it's makable on the tiny budget I usually have to work with. As someone once told me—don't try to make *Star Wars* on a dollar and a dream. Always write your script to what you have available or to what you can get access to. Good scenery can make up for lack of money.

VOLLMANN: When *Dead Meat* was written we knew how much money we had to spend. Locations, special effects, and even how much film we would need to shoot to adequately finish a scene were taken into consideration. Since *Dead Meat* was our first script, we used a book on how to write screenplays as our guide; this helped us in shaping our script properly. For instance, we only picked locations we knew we could get for nothing, or that we already had. Our special effects were written so as to not cost too much money. We

(From left) Tim Thomson, Dave Ward, Irving Cutter, Pamela Parker, Jay Harvey, David Rains and Jed Wollison on the set of Thomson's *No Resistance*.

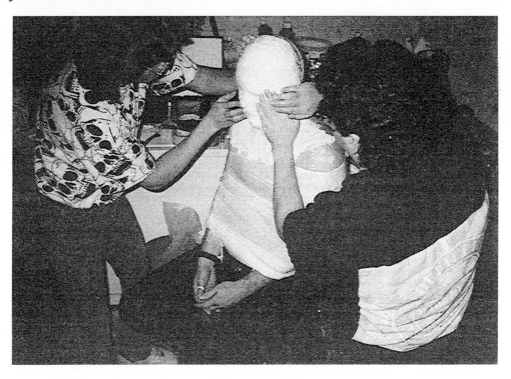

Headcasting Simon (Nick Kostopoulos) on the set of Tom Vollmann's *Dead Meat*.

figured creative lighting and editing could help us there. I would recommend anyone writing their first screenplay to acquire a book on writing scripts. It will help you to lay out your ideas into a format that will make a better movie. Trust me on this one.

GARY WHITSON & W.A.V.E.: The script normally comes from the customer, although there are exceptions where all we're given is a basic outline and we fill it in from there. *Sleepover Massacre* is a good example. The customer wanted six women returning for a class reunion. He wanted them to be attacked by a demon vampiress. He went into great detail about how they should be bitten. The rest was left up to us to flesh out. In our case, we always try to give the customer more than he asked for, so hopefully those sequels will keep coming.

4. Equipment and Format

Both *Vampires & Other Stereotypes* and *Addicted to Murder* were shot on Betacam SP (broadcast quality), then put through a "film-look" process to make them look more professional. I shot in video because I had access to broadcast television equipment and I couldn't afford to rent and shoot in film. I didn't want lack of access to film equipment to stop me from making a movie. But Betacam SP, the broadcast standard, is very different than regular VHS, which degrades horribly every time you make a copy of it, or "go down a generation."

If you're going to shoot in video make sure it's Super VHS, which holds up fairly well, ¾" (the industrial format), or even Hi-8. But if you shoot in Hi-8 make sure you transfer it immediately to one of the other formats (Super VHS, ¾", Betacam) since it tends to crinkle on playback because the tape is so small and thin. You can shoot an entire day and ruin all the footage by replaying it *once* in your camera. *Do not shoot* in regular VHS or regular 8mm—the format does not hold up when you make one copy of it. I recently shot the sequel to *Addicted to Murder* with the new mini-digital camera and the image is incredible.

Also, when you are editing, on whatever format you have available to you, try to edit on the highest format available. If you shoot on Hi-8mm bump your footage to S-VHS, ¾", or Betacam to edit on, or download it into a nonlinear system and bypass the tape

formats entirely. If you shoot on S-VHS edit to S-VHS or ¾" or Betacam. You never want to go down formats when editing, such as recording on Betacam and editing on S-VHS—it defeats the purpose of shooting on Betacam to begin with.

I'm also a believer that if you shoot on video you should put the feature through a "filmlook" process to make it look like film because it's what people expect in a narrative. It also adds to the production value because if people immediately see that it's video they assume the project cost no money to make and that it's unprofessional. There are a dozen sources out there that provide a "filmlook" service. A bigger reason to do that is that distributors and subdistributors are less likely to take anything that looks like video. It's a bias they all seem to have and you're going to have to deal with this prejudice.

I've shot many short films on Super 8mm (you can see them listed on the "Production Board" in old issues of *Cinemagic*) but there's always the chance the camera isn't working correctly or that the film will be ruined in development. Yet, there are segments of *Addicted* that were shot in Super 8mm, for old time's sake. The most important thing with Super 8 film is getting a good transfer to video (for editing), which can cost anywhere from $500 to $2,000, depending on how you do it. The same goes for 16mm film.

But with video you can see right away

what you shot and be secure that it's there. It also expedites the shoot by alleviating that worry. It's far cheaper than film and it's a more secure medium to work on for a first project.

THE INTERVIEWEES WERE ASKED,
What equipment/format do you use and why?

ARSENAULT: Film, film, film. I do everything on film. I shoot on film. I edit on film. I like the feel of film in my hands, I like to touch it, hold it and caress it. Film is my friend. The advantage of film is that you can project it on a big screen just like a real movie. If you have a lot of money, you can even blow up your 16mm negative to 35mm. Film, I believe, is taken more seriously by critics. Also, a good film festival screening can launch a career. Distributors like film better. And it's fairly cheap to edit.

The downside is that it's so expensive to shoot, process and print. As for rentals, what I try to do is hire a cameraperson who owns his own equipment. If he doesn't, a good cameraperson will know where to get the best deals. Otherwise, you can try low-end rental houses like Film Video Arts, or check the trades—*Filmmaker, Independent Film & Video*—for ads from renters.

BALLOT: I shot *The Bride of Frank* on S-VHS because I find those 35mm film cameras just too bulky and cumbersome. No—obviously, that's all that I had at my disposal and all that I could afford. I didn't seek funding from outside sources. The budget came out of my pocket so I was quite limited as far as choosing equipment.

As technology advances and prices come down the little guy benefits. The bane of every videomaker's existence has been generation loss. Shoot some footage, looks O.K. Make an edit master—second generation—doesn't look so good. Make a distribution copy—third generation—looks like shit.

The new DV [Digital Video] format promises to change all that. Right now a few manufacturers already have consumer DV cameras out on the market. Panasonic and Sony offer three-chip models, both of which retail for less than $3,500. These cameras shoot video that looks far better than either Hi-8 video or S-VHS with image quality that comes close to Betacam SP [broadcast standard]. In fact, this DV technology seems so promising that the industrial divisions of JVC, Sony, and Panasonic have all developed their own professional, proprietary versions of the consumer DV format. JVC calls their new format Digital S, Sony's is called DVCAM and Panasonic uses the name DVC Pro. The Sony and Panasonic formats are downward compatible with the consumer versions but none of these new formats are compatible with each other.

The generation loss problem will be addressed by the cameras and decks that sport the new DV in/out ports. Through the newly developed Firewire you can output digital video onto the hard drive of your computer. Because the signal is digital all the way the claims are that there will be no picture degradation, no generation loss. You edit with your PC, then go back through the Firewire with your finished product into the DV in/out port of your camera or deck.

If you're a little guy you can't afford to work with film. You can't even afford to work with Betacam SP and pay off the bills from the editing studio. But now, for an investment of $10,000, you can build your own production facility. Working within the DV format you can produce images that look broadcast quality to the naked eye. If, however, you do have the resources to work in film, good luck. Just remember, the more you have to spend the more you have to lose.

in BUTTERSOUND™

Too Disturbing
to Watch . . .

Too Compelling
to Turn Away

Trade ad for *The Bride of Frank.*

BERGER: *Original Sins* was shot on many formats, including Betacam SP, ¾", Hi-8mm, 16mm film all edited to a Beta SP master. *The Blood Between Us* is being shot on digital video. Our SP camera broke under mysterious circumstances early on in the *Sins* shoot so we couldn't light certain key scenes as dark as we'd have liked. With the impressive light latitude of the new Sony digital camera, I intend to make the look of

Blood much more radical than most shot-on-video features. Lots of flame source light. Most videomakers tend to ignore the sensitivity of video to Lowell-kit lights. I feel a lot of believability is blown when a scene is overlit or when the "Argento" color gels are dusted off. I haven't seen this extreme sort of stylization work yet on video, so I've vowed to veer away from it in my own projects. One problem with digital video is that, if you ever plan to press your work onto DVD or laser, you are going to want the best master you can get and that will have to be on the order of Digital Beta or D2. Something like that. As strong a source as possible. Post production will definitely get costly, but it's worth it in the commercial long-run.

BONK: So far, outside of a few small projects during my one year of film and video school, I have always shot and worked on pictures that utilized S-VHS technology. And all have been shot and edited on equipment I own. My first projects (*What a Deal!* and *City*) were edited linear between a full-size Panasonic AG-455 S-VHS camera and an AG-1960 S-VHS Panasonic VCR, all running through the Video Toaster 2000. I didn't even have a controller! I would time the shots out in my head, usually counting down 3-2-1, and hoped I had just gotten it as close as possible. Titles and effects were done on the Video Toaster as well. The entire movie would be cut first, with all the sound recorded on the hi-fi tracks. Then, with the use of the Carlson-Strand CS250 attached right to the AG-1960, I would lay down any extra sound effects and music to the linear track. The CS250 basically allowed you to utilize both the hi-fi and linear tracks on the AG-1960 separately, giving you as many as three audio tracks to work with.

City was filmlooked for $150 by Eric Stanze [*Savage Harvest*]. *Permanent Waves*, *I've Killed Before*, and the rest have been or will be edited on an IBM computer using Adobe Premiere. Having edited this way, in the much easier nonlinear format, I'll never go back to the old ways. Premiere allows me to cut in shots exactly where I want without having to recut the entire movie after, as well as to trim and output the edited shots to exact frame accuracy. No more slipping, no more missed edits! Also, you can get a pretty decent "filmlook" by capturing the footage at half screen. It also saves space on the computer, since video on the computer takes a lot of memory. Premiere also allows a decent amount of tweaking to the audio itself, as well as 99 audio tracks to put as much sound into your project that you could possibly want.

All of my movies have been shot on a JVC 707U camera, except for *Permanent Waves*, which was shot on the Panasonic AG-455. I'm currently exploring the digital camera options.

Though there are still many film purists out there, with the consistently increasing technology coming to video, I don't see any reason that a person can't make a quality film on this format. The "filmlooking" can be duplicated with varying degrees of success on a variety of different pieces of equipment. By utilizing video you can also keep down the usual film costs, such as stock and developing. You can also edit at home and won't have to own or edit on one of those huge flatbed film editors! All this money you save can be put towards actors, locations, or just plain increasing production values. Sure, if you want to see your movie play on the big screen, you'll have to get a transfer done to film, which is quite costly [about $8,000 from video to 16mm film for a ninety-minute feature]. But it's not impossible, and there are also a variety of video projectors out there which can do a respectable job for movie-theater viewing.

And think about it: What happens if you screw up? It's a mistake that could be extremely costly with film. Video allows you to test your wings and cover your ass at a minimal cost. If a movie is good or bad, it's not good or bad because it was shot on film or video. If it's a dung heap on video, then wouldn't it still be on film? And if it's some sort of breakthrough project on video, don't you think that the powers that be—i.e. Hollywood, distributors—will take notice.

BOOKWALTER: I've shot on Super 8mm, 16mm, S-VHS and Digital Video. Under no circumstances would I recommend that anyone ever shoot on Super 8mm film again. And if you do, you had better pay the loot for the Rank Cintel transfer! If you don't believe me, compare *The Dead Next Door* against most other Super 8mm movies. If you think DND looks bad, it only gets worse. Purists will tout that Super 8mm is the way to go because you get "the film look," but few of them ever do. Instead, they get dark and or washed-out footage, emulsion scratches, slice-infested edits, and bad video transfers. So, Super 8mm is to be avoided at all costs. Fortunately, Kodak is quickly laying the format to rest by closing their processing plants and discontinuing film stocks. Now if Super 8 Sound would just go out of business ... [laugh] Seriously, though, save Super 8mm for your training ground. I shot *Robot Ninja, Skinned Alive*, and *Ghoul School* on 16mm using a really old Arriflex BL camera that some old dinosaur here in town has had forever. I think we paid like $2,000 for an entire shoot, which was usually two or three weeks and included the Nagra, mic and support gear. It's a good deal, but the equipment was falling apart! It's frustrating enough to be making a movie with functional gear, let alone garbage that's probably being held together with bubble gum and a prayer! When we started making those S-VHS movies for Cinema Home Video in 1991, I went out and bought a "prosumer" camera, the JVC GRS-707U, a pretty darn good one-chip. It only takes S-VHS-C tapes—up to 30 minutes, but it's got some really unique features like real f-stops. Plus it's big enough to look semi-professional and small enough to do just about anything you want with it. JVC discontinued it shortly after I bought mine; I think I spent like $1,400 for it. And I've shot everything on it—nine movies, plus some special interest videos like *Basic How-To Halloween Makeups Vol. 2*. Of course, the greatest disadvantage to this is the extreme prejudice with which shooting on video is viewed! Even lepers are viewed with some pity, but not us poor shot-on-video guys! But you know what? Format really doesn't matter all that much. The bottom line for anyone making a movie is whether or not the audience *enjoys* it. If the movie's not entertaining then people start blaming format, which is bullshit. I was involved with eight pretty bad video movies before *Ozone* was made, which went a long way toward people taking me seriously. The problem seems to be that most of the "serious" moviemakers frown upon shooting on tape, so when people think of "shot on video" they think of lunkheads like David "The Rock" Nelson and Carl J. Sukenick and Todd Cook instead of Scooter McCrae and Kevin Lindenmuth and myself who obviously have craft in what they are doing. Video can be a viable medium as long as the movie is good. We're not just picking up a camcorder and aiming mindlessly at some bad gore effect or locking the camera on a tripod for 15 minutes while our friends pretend like they're kicking each other's asses. We're really trying to sell the audience a form of legitimate entertainment, to tell a story and play ball with the big boys. None of us *want* to be shooting on video. But I'd rather have a really good-looking shot-on-video movie like *The Sandman* than a really bad-looking 16mm flick like *Robot Ninja* to be remembered for. They both cost the same to shoot, but *The Sandman* gets more bang for its buck. I think a lot of these new guys with talent like need to stop preaching that "shoot on film" crap and show the world that the format *ain't* the thing. For the budgets we're shooting on, it's more important to show that we have skill and craft and talent, and it's hard to do that with a murky-looking Super 8mm or hastily tossed together 16mm film.

CAMPISI: My first films were shot on Super 8mm silent. Next I used Super 8mm with magnetic sound stripes added. I used what I had available to me at the time. I purchased my own splicer and editing tape at the local K-Mart for about ten bucks and begged my parents to buy me a sound projector. Hey, I was a little kid.

A few years later, VHS became available to me. An experimental production, *The Law* went on to win several awards across the country. We are currently shooting on Beta-cam SP, and our next project will be shot on Super 16mm.

The key word for the use of equipment is *availability*. What can you afford? What can you borrow? Who do you know? No two people will have the same resources from which to draw.

The pros and cons of working in the separate formats are varied. What works for one person doesn't work for another. If you've got no money or little resources, then you're going to have to make due with whatever you have available to you at the time. Super 8mm is a great training ground, as is VHS. If you've moved on, and are looking for distribution or more exposure, a superior format is preferred. Betacam SP works for video, but beware that some of the premier film festivals—Cannes, Sundance—won't show *video* movies and many distributors won't even *consider* films shot on video.

Then there's film. Sixteen millimeter is a noticeable step up from Super 8mm, and Super 16mm is even better because of its ease to transfer/blow-up to 35mm. Of course, if you've got the financial backing and or can afford it, shoot on 35mm from the start. Now, of course, you're talking about big bucks and larger budgets.

The different formats also have their pros and cons when it comes to editing. The cost for video editing can range anywhere from $50/hour to $175/hour. Shooting on VHS, for example, can be fairly inexpensive, but then you've got the costly editing to contend with. Sixteen millimeter film has comparable costs.

Many companies and individuals will lend their equipment and facilities for nothing—or next to nothing—if you are trying to get started. There are many ways to negoti-ate this, and you should always take care to have contracts written up should a dispute arise later. The trick is to entice the people with your knowledge and enthusiasm. Show them the script, show them the storyboards, production design drawings, paintings and props. Whatever it takes to get them excited.

Be prepared with adequate paperwork. Most people will want some kind of guarantee that if you make money, they will be compensated on the back end. There are many books at the bookstores with legal paperwork for the film and television industry.

If you've got little or no money, trade-out work is something you should consider. Essentially, trade-out work is the trade of equipment and or facilities for your labor. For example, you might ask an equipment or production company to let you borrow their cameras and lighting in exchange for you working for free on one of their upcoming projects. You can negotiate the same deal for editing facilities.

For me, I was working in the industry and had access to the many production houses in town. I knew the producers, the owners, and they knew me. It was fairly easy to ask to borrow their cameras and lights and editing suites. Many times, trade-out agreements were worked out far in advance.

CRAMER: I still use the 16mm Canon Scopic I started with. I once rented a "sound friendly" camera from the University of Colorado and it ruined thousands of feet of film and wasted several days of shooting—never could afford anything as sophisticated as "dailies," so the problem went unnoticed for a while. They wouldn't even reimburse me for the rental cost so I told them to fuck themselves with their piece of shit camera and I've shot everything MOS [without sound] since then.

FORD: I have only made one feature at this point, *Alien Force*, and it was shot using state-of-the-art digital video equipment. We used a Panasonic DVC camera, which is about the size of the average Hi-8 video camera.

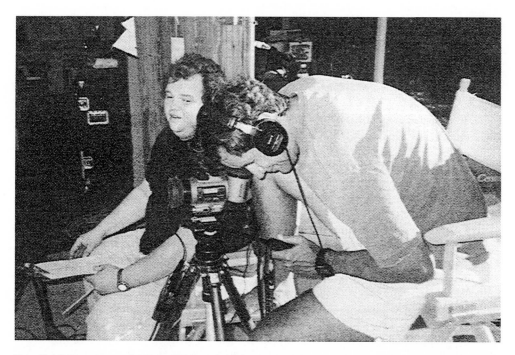

Ron Ford directing and Mark Gordon shooting with a Panasonic DVC camera on the set of *Alien Force*.

But the image is broadcast quality, and just slightly lesser than professional Betacam SP. The camera is so small that it is possible to get a tremendous amount of coverage very quickly, and so it is an excellent choice for low-budget action movies. We almost always just used available light and the camera was hand-held 90 percent of the time. We were able to use lots of locations, too, because we didn't have to haul trucks of lights and camera equipment from location to location. That gave the movie a more expensive look. It also has CD quality sound in the camera, so a separate sound deck is not necessary. The footage was transferred to computer hard drives and the movie was edited on the D/Vision system. We also did all the sound work on the D/Vision. Then the footage from the original digital video tapes was edited directly onto a Betacam master at an online facility. The reason I chose this format and equipment was because it was what was used by Wildcat Entertainment, with whom I teamed to produce my first feature. They brought the production machine to the board, and I brought the financing and creative elements.

GALLAGHER: I shot all my movies on S-VHS. It seemed like the middle of the road. It was better than consumer—and I feel, better than ¾"—yet it still didn't have the price tag of Betacam SP. I was able to build my own editing setup over time without having to take out a second mortgage. And it's great having all the stuff at your disposal anytime you wish. I'd love to do more stuff on it.

We worked with a company on *Exploding Angel* which allowed us to use Beta SP equipment, elaborate lighting, sound and other fringes. But then you become totally reliant on the person in questions, especially since I'm a difficult person to communicate with—most people read me totally wrong. *Exploding Angel* was going to be our biggest movie yet, and what we have looks really elaborate ... but it's yet to be finished. I'm currently working with another large video production house making the *Draculina Video Magazine*. This is a little different since I'm more or less gathering material from many sources and only the *Draculina* segment will be shot at the studio. It's different than making a real movie. It's much more relaxed and not near the pressure or money involved.

GINGOLD: As I've mentioned, the format I used to shoot *Mindstalker* was Super 8 film, and I swear I'll never do it again. At the time I began production, Super 8 seemed to be the best way to go, and it probably was; video technology hadn't advanced to the point where you could turn out something professional-looking without investing in a lot of expensive equipment. I owned all the Super 8 gear I needed and film and processing were fairly inexpensive. Plus, I—like many others—had a bias against the "cheap" look of video.

Things changed quickly, however. Super 8 was on its way out even as I was filming *Mindstalker*, manufacturers stopped making the equipment and labs ceased processing the film. A month after I finished shooting, the photo store I used went from charging $2.35 a roll for overnight processing to more than $8 a roll and a minimum of three days wait to get it back. There was a potential disaster when my camera broke down halfway through filming, and I couldn't find anyplace to fix it or rent me another one. Not that I would have wanted to, necessarily; with so few people using Super 8, there are only one or two companies still making cameras, and since there's no longer a need to be competitive, the quality has really suffered as a result. Thank God I was able to hook up with a couple of guys who lent me one of their old cameras for the rest of the shoot and earned coproducer credit as a result.

Super 8 also meant higher costs involved in postproduction, what with having to make a Rank Cintel video transfer of my footage and so on. Nowadays, I've lost my bias against video, and the form has advanced to the point where you can get something that looks almost as good as film at a much lower cost. I've seen "filmlooked" video movies that only a trained eye could distinguish from the real thing, and until I find the backing to

work in 16mm or 35mm, that's the way I'll be going for my future projects.

HOWE: I've been lucky enough to work in practically every major format, from VHS to 35mm. Here's how they break down in order of quality. Coincidentally, it's also how they break down in order of price: 35mm; 16mm (Super and regular); Broadcast Video (Betacam, D-2); Super 8mm/Industrial Video (¾", S-VHS, Hi-8mm); Consumer video (VHS, 8mm).

Thirty-five millimeter is the tops, but it's expensive and hard to work with. The cameras are heavy and because it's a larger format you have very limited depth of field, meaning you need an assistant cameraperson who really knows how to pull focus. This can really slow an amateur down and lead to a lot of unusable, out of focus footage. Even if you have the money for a 35mm shoot—$80,000 minimum—don't just jump in unless you or at least your D.P. knows what he's doing.

Sixteen millimeter is also expensive but twice as cheap as 35mm. Focus isn't a big problem in 16mm, because you have a wider depth of field to work with. Cameras are lighter and generally easier to deal with. I know that a lot of people think that "filmlooked" video can look as good as 16mm, but that just isn't true. Sure, "filmlooked" video tends to look more like film, but it doesn't look as good as well-shot 16mm. Also, 16mm gives you the option of making a 35mm blow-up, which would give you access to proper theatrical distribution. Try that with filmlooked video.

Sixteen millimeter is also taken more seriously by distributors than video. Most festivals show few movies not originated on film. Imagine where *Clerks* would have gone if shot on video. Probably nowhere. So for someone with a healthy budget, say $30,000–50,000 range, 16mm is the way to go.

Broadcast Video. I know the Super 8mm mavens are going to kill me for this but I believe the next step down the chain is Broadcast Video. I make this claim because the lenses are better and it's easier to get good sync sound with video than with those noisy Super 8mm cameras. Shooting on video has several advantages, you see the results instantly and can play them back on-set. The cameras have high effective ASAs and the image is really starting to look nice, especially in some of the later model CCD cameras. "Filmlooking" can also help to make a shot-on-tape feature look more like film.

We shot *Original Sins* on Betacam SP and made time-code window dubs to VHS for the off-line edit. We transferred each 20-minute Beta SP tape to its own 20-minute VHS tape. Why not just gang a bunch of reels up on one 120-minute VHS tape? Because of all the time you waste searching for your material. Trust me. Scrolling back and forth through a VHS 120 can turn the simplest edit job into an endless nightmare. It also gunks up your video heads and leads to machine failure.

Always off-line on the cheapest system you can find. Our VHS cuts-only system cost us 500 bucks for three months. That was from a friend of mine who owned the system, but even if you can't get a deal that good, it will be cheaper to rough-cut on VHS or 8mm than to go into an on-line studio at 50–200 bucks an hour and do your first cut that way.

Once the off-line is done, you can use those time-code numbers to make an edit decision list for your on-line, and match back to your original tapes.

One thing we did with *Sins* that worked out great was to impose another step between off-line and on-line. When we had the cut pretty much, but not quite locked, we took the original tapes to a facility that had a nonlinear editing system. Nonlinear editing employs a big computer to "word process with video and sound." Your footage is digitized onto hard drives, and then you manipulate it any way you want, 50 times faster than you could with any linear editing system [all videotape edit systems, VHS to D-2, are linear systems].

We did our fine cut on the nonlinear system, in this case a D-Vision Pro. Other systems you might encounter are AVID, Lightworks, or EMC. Once finished, the system made an EDL list for us. Instead of having to go through and make our own edit decision list by hand, the computer generates it on a floppy disk, formatted to whatever edit controller you're using for your on-line. This disk goes into the on-line room, pops into the on-line edit controller. The edit controller then autoassembles your movie. In other words, the computer does all the cuts on its own, you just sit there, put tapes into the machines, and watch it happen. Pretty cool. And it saves you hours of expensive on-line time.

Sound is a big problem on low-budget productions, and once again, D-Vision saved the day. When we on-lined, we only cut picture and dialogue. That cut was then redigitized into the D-Vision where we laid our music and effects, all in sync to the on-lined picture. D-Vision had the ability to mix an unlimited number of tracks, mono or stereo. We had over 30 tracks going in some scenes. Once the mix was done on computer, we outputted the sound to a Betacam SP tape, took it back to the on-line edit room and dubbed it over the cut picture. Sync was perfect and we were able to do a multitrack music and effects job that could have cost thousands and taken months in less than three weeks and more or less for free—more favors.

I was lucky to have access to such a system, but many small video companies are buying them. See if anyone around you has one, and will rent it cheap in the off hours. Anyone who's thinking of setting up their own studio should definitely consider nonlinear. With the advent of MPEG technology, soon every PC in the land will have nonlinear editing capabilities. It's definitely something to check out.

Super 8mm/Industrial video. Well shot Super 8 can look as good or better than industrial video. Lack of good stocks used to be the biggest problem in Super 8, but Super 8 Sound in Massachusetts sells Super 8 stock that's cut from rolls of 35mm Kodak Professional Motion Picture film. Thus any of the fabulous emulsions you can get in 16mm or 35mm you can now get in Super 8mm. I know no one who's used this film yet, but I do know it's expensive and probably somewhat risky.

Plus, Super 8 cameras are still noisy and make shooting dialogue a pain in the neck. If I was doing a picture like *Darkness*—mainly voice-over dialogue and action sequences—I might go Super 8, otherwise I'd stay away. This is just my personal take; people who hate video and would rather work in Super 8 should go right ahead and do so.

Industrial video has the same disadvantages as broadcast video over professional film formats, only you're getting further down the image quality food chain. Still, some very nice stuff has been done at this level and once again, "filmlooking" helps. The big advantage is that these formats are cheap and easy to work with.

I'd avoid consumer video if at all possible. If you insist on going this route, 8mm is definitely superior to VHS, especially over the long haul. Dupe VHS to VHS once or twice and you'll see what I mean.

As for rental houses, camera rentals can be expensive, but you can usually get a deal by pleading poverty. I was lucky in that I'd been working with a number of houses for years before shooting *Sins* so I could get a great deal on the gear. Anyone out there with fewer contacts might not fare as well.

Lighting and grip rental does offer some room for compromise. Most big lighting and grip rental houses have a ton of crummier gear that just sits in the shop. Any money they make renting it is money in their pocket, so they'll often make you quite a deal. Again, plead poverty and ask what the lowest price you can get is. Play one house against another, if you get a low bid from one place, see if another house will beat it.

A final note, most cable companies have a Public Access Station; these stations often have pretty good gear that is available to you, free. Getting the gear for long stretches of

time is usually the biggest problem. Still, check it out.

With all this said, what format is the best for your movie? None of the above; when it comes right down to it, all the arguing about one format being superior to another is stupid. Sure, 35mm is best, but if you don't have any money and really want to do a movie, go right ahead and do it on video. I would have loved to do *Sins* on film, but given a choice between shooting on tape or not shooting, we chose tape. And we'll do the same with our next project if we can't raise money for film. If you want to make a movie, make it, regardless of whether it's Panavision or VHS. Ideas, intelligence and energy are always more important than format.

JACOBS: I shoot on a ½" VHS video camera. My format is determined by my editing system. All I have access to is a JVC ½" editor. It may not be the best but it's in my house, and I have twenty-four hour use of it. The smaller 8mm video cameras look nice but I find that you need an 8mm editor to effectively edit with them. Without one, the loss of generations, especially on ½" tapes, is enormous. That's how I shot *Walking Between the Raindrops*. I shot on 8mm then bumped it all up to ½". It didn't look as good as I wanted it to, but that's what filmmaking is—a learning process. So I learned which format would be more appropriate come editing time. I'd love to shoot on Betacam, edit on great equipment, and do it in a great studio. This just isn't possible right now. I don't have that kind of money; I have a weird work-school schedule; and I don't really know how to use the state-of-the-art systems. This being the case, I have to use what I have. I edit when I edit, on tapes that I can afford. It may not give me the best results and I may be compromising some things, but I'd be compromising even more if I didn't make my films because of these factors.

LEGGE: Up until recently I worked in Super 8mm film. I've gone through many

Evan Jacobs (right) with Chris Lohman (center), and Sean Soderlind.

cameras since 1978: Sankyo, Elmo, Nizo—the absolute worst—Chinon, and finally Canon. I made films to be final products as films. I recorded dialogue with a single system, and edited it all on a Goko editor, with Wurker splices. Editing sound Super 8 is a bit of a trick at first, because of the eighteen frame distance between sound and picture. So if someone gets whacked on the head in the film the sound is eighteen frames ahead of the actual picture of the event. So if you cut purely by picture under these circumstances you'd screw up royally. You basically cut for sound at the head of a shot and picture at the end. Eventually I discovered how the dialog can overlap this way into the next shot, which helped disguise the splices. On the up side, film is film, nothing really looks like it. We all grew up accustomed to the photographic image, and the electronic image looks so "live," it's harshness is displeasing to our eyes. Hence the search for the perfect "film-look" process. I labored long and hard with Super 8. Film is expensive and it's so easy to waste. Splicing it is tedious and doesn't allow you to make mistakes if you work on the original only. If you can afford workprints in

Super 8, why bother? Make it 16mm! The reason you work in Super 8 is to avoid all the trappings of big productions. The workprints, the double system sound, the A and B rolls, the answer prints, et cetera. To make film even more frustrating, you can't really be sure what you got until you get it back from the lab. Even if you did it right the lab may demolish it—and they have—or the post office may lose it for a few months—and they have. Most Super 8 equipment was made to break down and they all did so with astounding regularity. All of these annoyances, and an empty wallet, finally pushed me to switch to video. I am making my first feature in S-VHS, and editing it with an edit desk system, all from JVC. Video has its problems, too, but so far I have no regrets switching.

McCleery: In 1988 I invested ten thousand in a S-VHS camcorder—Panasonic AG-450—and a cuts only S-VHS editing set-up—AG-7500, AG-7300, and AG-750. I bought this equipment to make my movies, but in order to justify the expense I started using it to do industrial videos, weddings, and so forth. Since then I have purchased more equipment and have an a/b roll S-VHS system. S-VHS is a decent format but it is probably as low as you want to go as far as shooting movies go. I've seen a lot of VHS camcorder movies and they just don't hold up. I shoot my current stuff on a Panasonic AG-460, which is a good camera and I would suggest it to anyone who wants to go the S-VHS route. You can pick them up used for around two grand. Editing prices have come way down and there is a lot of used equipment out there that still works good and can be bought for decent prices. Always shoot on the best quality available to you. I know a guy who shoots on VHS and then bumps the footage to ¾" for editing. Believe it or not this holds up pretty well. And there is a ton of used cuts-only ¾" systems out there for under two thousand. Just look around, get the trade magazines and you'll find them. Now Sony has a new camera out that uses digital videotape. The camcorder goes for under $4000 and has specs as good as Betacam SP. As soon as they get editing equipment on the market this will revolutionize the industry. Lastly, "filmlook" your video. There are a lot of processes you can use to take that "video" edge off of your stuff. What I use is a Videonics mixer called the MX1. It runs less than a grand and does more than just "filmlook"—it's a pretty good switcher. To get technical what it does is a field strobe which in effect gives you thirty, rather than sixty, fields of video per second; this much more closely mimicking the frame rate of film—twenty-four frames per second—than video played at sixty fields per second. Videonics is also putting out something called the Video Palette which will do the same thing. So, as far as equipment goes, my advice is to get the best you can for the money you have and don't overlook used stuff. There's a lot of it out there that still works well.

MCCRAE: I shot *Shatter Dead* on the Betacam SP format because I wanted the best possible video image I could obtain. Betacam SP is a professional video format that will very soon be supplanted by digital video, but it is currently the acquisition format of choice by most major television networks and more upscale cable stations. One thing that film and video have in common is that no matter which one you originate your image on, you always make sure that the on-set materials you obtain are the best possible images you can photograph. In other words, whatever stuff you want to do to muck up the image—i.e. excessive grain, solarization, et cetera—should be accomplished in postproduction during the editing process, and not on-set.

I work at an industrial video production facility that sells, rents and repairs video equipment. This is a great job to have if you are patient and willing to work hard enough to establish a level of trust and credibility with your employer to get a cheap or next-to-nothing deal on renting the equipment you need to make a feature-length project. Without this kind of arrangement, I never would have been able to make *Shatter Dead*. It's not a very glamorous job but a person does whatever is necessary to achieve their goals—short of robbery or murder, of course.

The biggest drawback to shooting on Betacam is the cost. My situation made it affordable to me. Normally a broadcast-quality Betacam package rents for nearly $500 a day—(a weekend is usually considered a one-day rental; the best time to be shooting anyway. But you pay extra for a reason. Think of all the shot-on-video stuff you've popped into your VCR and wanted to immediately pull out and throw across the room while searching for the damn head cleaner! In video, every generation you lose for editing or electronic special effects is immediately noticeable when compared to its previous generation—yeah, I know digital video is going to make this a thing of the past). And then when you're done, you lose yet another generation when you finally have to "filmlook" the damn thing.

Oh, and by the way, that's the other thing that sucks about shooting on video; it's not film. Be prepared to hear that shit a lot

(Left to right) Scooter McCrae, Sasha Graham and Kevin Lindenmuth, 1997.

from people who have nothing better to complain about. Just spin around and tell 'em it's not the format you work on, but the story you are telling that counts. Only a *Waterworld*-loving idiot would disagree with that sentiment.

There are many distributors who believe that their potential audience is turned off by the "video look" that people attribute to soap operas and B.B.C. productions. But I've met a lot of people who don't want to watch those old black-and-white movies, and some others who hate those stupid black bars at the top and bottom of the screen which they think are cutting off at least half of their favorite movie! Are these the people we are making these projects for? I don't think so. I know that I would rather have a smaller core-group of viewers watching *Shatter Dead* who, when they say they enjoy it, I know are speaking to me from a shared level of knowledge concerning the history of cinema. You can't please everyone all the time, especially at our low-budget level. Are people really going to hate our shit less if it looks like it was shot on film instead of video?

MURPHY: Every project is different. I used to be a real film snob. But video is so quick and inexpensive. It really depends on the individual project. As far as making deals and all that, all filmmakers should be prepared to reduce themselves to begging, borrowing, stealing, whatever it takes. Die, and let your crew die, before letting your film not get finished.

POLONIA BROS.: We have shot on Super 8, ½" video, S-VHS, ¾" video and some 16mm. As I stated earlier we have been fortunate enough to acquire all our own equipment and I work at a college as a technician so we have access to a fully operational studio with lights and the whole works. We have also acquired 16mm equipment and can make deals with some local postproduction houses to supplement anything we may lack. Most places will work out deals or take services out on trade, so don't be afraid to ask anyone for help if you need cameras or editing equipment, which is where most people run into trouble. You could argue the advantages and disadvantages of formats until the cows come home. Work with what you can afford and do the best you can with it. If you can do that then you're doing okay. If video is all you can afford, by all means use video. You may dream of 16mm and 35mm but a day will come when you can move up the ladder. Just be patient. You have to learn to crawl before you walk. The same applies in film. Start with the basics and as your skills and financial situation improves, you will, too. But don't sit around and wait to shoot on film if you can't afford it right now. Do it on video.

RITTER: I shoot in whatever format I can afford. If I have a story I feel I need to tell, the format is the last thing I think about. It's the creative impulse to do it that pushes me forward on a project.

For *Day of the Reaper* in 1984, all I knew was Super 8mm film, so that's what we shot it on. We edited it on Super 8 film, transferred it to video, and added all of our dialogue, sound effects, and music. Keep in mind that this was silent film, so the dubbing job was atrocious. But this was financed with a dishwasher's paycheck, for under $1,500, so the end product fit the bill. *Reaper* was then actually sold to video stores in South Florida, New York, and L.A. at the end of '84.

For *Twisted Illusions*, an anthology movie, we shot on ½" VHS video. Again, Joel Wynkoop and I just wanted to do something and we had no money, and it was great to finally get sync sound with a picture! The stories were the important thing, I just had to show people what was on my mind. We edited at a TV station and in a real editing bay, so it was exciting to learn all about that in the process.

Truth or Dare was a baptism of fire for me. From Super 8, to ½" VHS ... to 16mm and a $250,000 budget. For that movie, we used Arriflex 16mm cameras and transferred the negative to videotape and editing on ¾"

video, a system called Envision, which the editor, Jack Behrend, created. I wasn't there for the editing but I know they had big problems with the system, from syncing to actual cuts.

Killing Spree was again shot on 16mm. The best way to get a movie shot on 16mm if you don't already own your own equipment is to hire a cinematographer who does own the equipment and you get the operator and the gear for one price. This is what we did on both *Truth or Dare* and *Killing Spree*. Sound gear was either borrowed from a local college or rented at a discount from a company who wanted screen credit. Never forget the importance of screen credit when making a deal for equipment leasing or editing. A lot of companies only do commercial work most of the time and the prestige and publicity they can get by having their name on a feature film will give you great bartering power with them. Tell them you want half-off on the rentals in exchange for a big credit. This usually works—I've gotten free use of a lot of things this way.

Also, the word "student film" helps get you discounts on rentals, sound syncing, and other postproduction needs. All you need to get this discount is a student ID. And hey—we all can't look like students forever, but on every movie I've ever made, I've used college students in varying capacities, and they're always willing to help you out by showing their student IDs to a company!

If you need lighting gear go to a local college with a filmmaking department, tell them what you're doing. Lots of times, if you give their people credit in a real movie, they're willing to lend you lots of their stuff on the weekends as long as one of their people is with the gear. We did this very successfully on *Killing Spree*—we actually hired the local college film teacher as editor of the movie in exchange for free use of all the equipment in the filmmaking department! It worked out great for everyone involved.

Postproduction on *Killing Spree* was done off-line first on time-coded ½" VHS tapes. We used free editing facilities for that at a local place that shot weddings and stuff; they were just glad to help out. The actual Beta SP and 1" on-line edit was done at a local television station. This is a very expensive part of high-end postproduction and can run $300 an hour at a commercial facility. We did our editing for a flat fee of something like $700 as long as we kept it quiet and worked on the graveyard shift unnoticed. The producer struck a sweet deal with an understanding station manager and we ended up there working for two weeks—80 hours—for $700. We did all our final editing, music and sound effects dubbing and made our final 1" master there. So always look into local TV stations as a way to finishing your movie. Phone calls never hurt.

For *Wicked Games*, I had very little money, only about $12,000. Again, for me it was important to make the movie, so once the script was in line I researched the video market heavily and concluded that Hi-8 video was the way to go. Film was out of the question—16mm negative transferring on *Killing Spree* ran over $8,000, so I knew there was no way this time around.

I used Hi-8 because of the positive write-ups it received. Also, the cameras are small and you won't attract a lot of attention while filming in public places with little insurance. Hi-8 is okay, but I had big problems with my camera. I purchased it and ended up having to shoot the movie almost twice over due to technical problems. Dropouts, radio frequency interference, blips, and eaten tapes were only part of the problem. I went through three cameras, all of which did the same thing, so it was a faulty system altogether. I eventually got a total refund on the camera, so I can't go into specific models, but I'll tell you this much—they took the camera off the market!

For any kind of professional use, I wouldn't recommend Hi-8. The tapes shed. They haven't perfected the durability of the tapes. My camera original tapes for *Wicked Games* are no longer good—some of them don't even play! Fortunately, I transferred all the best takes to S-VHS right away and edit-

ed on that format. I think 8mm video is too small a tape to hold all of the analog information needed for audio and video—you should go with ½" all the way, S-VHS at the minimum.

S-VHS is what we edited *Wicked Games* on. Again, we hired a local facility that did commercials and stuff to do it. I supervised the process, but we hired editor Rusty Durham to bring a new viewpoint in on the project, one that wasn't so close to everything. It ran us like $20 an hour to edit on S-VHS. That's not a bad price, but you can shop around for deals that may be better. Again, find a company that specializes in weddings or commercials that would love to be involved in a feature and make a deal.

Wicked Games lost a generation of clarity by being transferred to S-VHS from Hi-8 for editing but its "grainy" look never hurt sales. Some people thought it was shot in 16mm with a Bolex or we "filmlooked" it. So it worked out cool in the end.

Creep was shot with Beta SP, industrial S-VHS, Hi-8, and some 16mm footage. I used all the formats just to do the project—whatever was available. It all cut together pretty flawlessly—most people can't tell what was what format in the final project.

The term "industrial S-VHS" refers to the new breed of cameras that are hitting the market, replacing ¾" video at TV stations. The new JVC three-chip cameras have 700 lines of resolution and cost around $10,000. These are the new thing right now. And trust me—they are awesome, the best semiprofessional stuff you can get short of Beta SP.

For *Creep* I made an excellent deal with a local TV production company that supplied all of our lighting and sound equipment for basically credit and percentages of any profits down the road. We got a crew of five and all of the best gear we could ever ask for, and these people were really enthusiastic and professional to work with. After doing *Creep* they're now doing their own feature film because they loved it so much! That's the type of people you need to work with.

Tim Ritter (standing) on the *Creep* set with actor Joel D. Wynkoop.

Creep was mastered on 1" video. I ended up editing most of the movie myself with producer Michael Ornelas, just to save time. It's important to log all of your footage before hitting the editing bay, so you're prepared. We had about 30 hours of raw footage for *Creep* and it took me three weeks, 120 hours, to log it all properly. You don't want to be on any time clock trying to figure out what goes where! You'll go broke.

Editing is a creative thing—you learn that by working in smaller formats and by watching TV and movies. To edit *Creep*, Mike and I took a little crash course for eight hours on what buttons to push and we sat down and cut the movie! It was that simple— it took twelve days or so, long days, some of them eighteen hours, but we just did it. It was exciting to actually cut the movie together myself. That's really where it all comes together, so plan that stage carefully.

STANZE: I have shot on VHS, Super VHS, ¾", and Super 8mm film. I have edited to Super VHS, ¾", Betacam SP, 1" and D3 digital video tape. Mostly, I feel you should simply shoot with what you have available. At my budget level, there is little room to be choosey.

I am very serious about making my movies and progressing with each project. Therefore, I have gone to extremes to remain employed at a job that offers me the most in terms of needed postproduction, some production, and even duplication equipment. Though my job is not very prestigious or high paying, I have passed up promotions and job offers to remain in this position that gives me access to the video equipment I need and lets me take time off work to go shoot my movies. While such sacrifices may seem drastic, I would be miserable if I had to give up making movies because another job did not offer the same access to the equipment. It all depends on how serious you are about making movies. You have to decide for yourself what sacrifices you consider "worth it."

If you are unable to gain and hold employment at a job that gives you access to the equipment, find someone else who does work around the hardware. Ask them to join your productions as a prominent team member in exchange for their access to and knowledge of postproduction equipment. There is the obvious alternative to wheeling and dealing your way into cheap or free editing: Pay for it. This is a last resort. The number of hours required to post a feature length movie can balloon your budget immensely if you pay full price. You are better off putting those dollars *on the screen.*

Getting back to format: Let's say you do have a choice on what to shoot and edit on. I try very hard to make the shooting format, the budget, and the script work *together.* Don't try to shoot a mainstream story on grainy Super 8mm film. Don't try to shoot a feature length movie on Super 8mm film if your budget is only $2,000. If you know you need a high shooting ratio, shoot on VHS or Super VHS. If you don't have the money to shoot on Super 8mm film, but you think you can get away with a narrow shooting ratio, try to shoot Betacam SP. The more mainstream the subject matter, the better off you are spending the money on higher-end video tape or even 16mm film. The mainstream audience is very distracted by grainy, less-than-Hollywood image quality. The more artsy, nonmainstream movie crowd actually *likes* the grain of Super 8mm. All of these variables are important to consider. Here is an example of how to coordinate all the elements:

I sat down with a few other guys on my team to discuss what we could do as a next movie project. First, how much money could we scrape up? Probably $11,000 or $12,000 if some investors kicked in some cash to supplement my own financial input. What format would be most appropriate to shoot on at that budget level? Super 8mm film would work. A 3-to-1 shooting ratio for a feature length movie on Super 8mm should cost around $4,000 for film stock and processing. Not only do we want to shoot a feature on film—we have not experienced this yet—we know that film, even Super 8mm, will make the movie somewhat more marketable.

Okay, so we're shooting Super 8mm film. Now *what* do we shoot? Super 8mm is too grainy for anything mainstream, dramatic, or dialogue driven. We would be aiming for an audience that would most quickly discard the movie due to its grainy image. In many cases, Super 8mm is much more grainy than low-end video. So let's go to equal extremes and shoot something *very* experimental and "artsy" so that the grainy image enhances the subject matter instead of being something the audience has to "deal with." The movie should be ultra-intense horror or extremely surreal. We decided to go surreal … and we began preproduction on *Ice from the Sun.*

If you have the luxury of actually choosing a shooting format, here are some tips based on my past experience:

(1) Avoid 8mm video tape and Hi-8 videotape. While the picture quality of Hi-8 is quite good if lit well, 8mm and Hi-8 video tape are very thin. Because it is a tiny strip of tape, even the smallest amount of crud on the head or on the tape causes big nasty glitches. Also, I've found it the format most likely to be "eaten" by decks and cameras.

(2) If you edit Super VHS to Super VHS video tape, find out if the editing system keeps the Y and C component video signals separate or if the signals are combined into a composite signal carried by an RCA or BNC cable. The higher picture quality on Super VHS—compared to VHS—is due to the format's separation of the Y and C signals. If the edit system combines them, your Super VHS picture quality is greatly reduced.

(3) Run your edited video movie through a "filmlook" process if you can afford it. This can be used to deceive people into thinking you shot on film. I prefer it simply because it separates my movie from the same image attributes seen in Uncle Bob's camcorder family videos.

(4) If possible, edit to a higher format you shot on. I have had great results editing from Super VHS to Betacam SP and then

"filmlooking" the image. On *Savage Harvest*, I edited Super VHS to Super VHS and then filmlooked this edit to D3 video where we added the graphics and did additional sound effects and music editing—which all sounded beautiful going from DAT to a digital video format. We then mixed *Savage Harvest* down to a stereo 1" dub master. You can get great picture quality and save money by shooting on a lower end format and editing to a higher end format. The tradeoff: Lower-end formats shoot with lower end cameras that may not give you as much technical versatility.

THOMPSON: When I was young I shot on standard Super 8mm film. As the "film look" processes became better and more affordable, I have used video and disguised it. Every video format has pros and cons, but I found with *Contact Blow* that ultimately no one felt the difference between them. I used whatever I could get that weekend. I shot on Hi-8 for one scene, I shot on ¾" for most interiors. I like the durability of the tape and the sound was the best. A good unbalanced microphone sending an unbalanced signal into a professional ¾" deck without any audio limiting going on gave us better sound than the other scenes shot with balanced audio conversion. Most of the outdoor stuff was wild shooting—hanging in trees, off cliffs, windmills, et cetera. For this stuff I used a Panasonic AG-450 S-VHS. I cut it all directly to a ¾" SP Master. There are variations in the image but there are variations in the image of every set. I just never mixed shots from other cameras

The S-VHS image is really colorful and that helped in maintaining saturation when the piece went through a "filmlook" process. The Hi-8 looked great but the tape is really weak. I suggest transferring it immediately to another format. The actual tape is just so small that any drop-out really cripples the moment. I didn't have access to Betacam or I would have used it.

As far as editing, the last two movies were done on linear systems. This is troublesome when in retrospect you want to really change something. However, tape to tape maintains the best image quality. I work with nonlinear equipment and I have concerns about the image going the long distance of generations. I know that the recent AVR output qualities of the Avid and the new Stratosphere—upgrade from the Videocube/TurboCube world—are both being used by news stations, albeit quietly, going right to air. But there are other problems. In my work world, we have encountered transmission problems with long distance sending of signals that were compressed. Digitizing an image involves compression. When it goes out on the air it's getting recompressed. This problem is kept quiet in the industry and is being addressed but it is there. Even without that issue, the stations doing it are going right from their raw footage to computer, then to air. You won't be doing that. You need to go to tape first. In the advertising world, we work nonlinear but we go back to linear to conform.

Having said all that, I confess that I will be doing my next piece nonlinear. Two other elements come into play for me. One is that at the last minute on my last movie, I was forced to make some changes and that caused great grief for everyone involved. The other thing that draws me into the computer world is the potential to use third party programs. Programs like AfterAffects and Photoshop filters offer all kinds of special effect options that can work well in the nonlinear world. When you put a Photoshop filter on a shot, it's digital and clean until it's out on tape. Some inputted video even looks better after it's affected. When you are done, you can output to any format you want. Every copy is a master copy.

THOMSON: *No Resistance*, our first public feature, was shot in Houston on S-VHS with a budget of around $7,000. The budget was spent mostly on tape, costumes and props, and getting people to town, putting them up and feeding them during production. Of course, no one on a project this small got paid; everybody donated their time and attention. We wrote our script to settings we knew we could get, and situations we knew we could pull off. Remember, we could do this mostly because we did it on cheap, consumer grade S-VHS and we had the means to finish it that way and only that way. The main overriding principle was to just get out and create something. Oh, we had an idea that we would produce something that could be justifiably shot on tape, a street-level, available-technology story for which the electronic look would be an asset … and we hoped we could make it so good no one would notice the format. That never happened … consumer grade video is just too crappy to be taken seriously by most people. But then, that was the only way we could produce something at that time, and you have to do it or it never gets done. I'll never do it that way again but I wouldn't have done it any other way at the time. Don't believe anyone when they say there's no sense doing anything on video … it's a cheap and available way to make your own mistakes and learn the visual language.

If you have a job in the film or TV business you can usually swing some help in the equipment area. Or again, schools give you great access to hardware. I owned the video camera myself, but when it came time to edit, the only thing that saved me was that I worked for a video production house. Paying for editing can easily cost scores of thousands of dollars. I did my editing at night on a deferred basis and therefore got free cuts. Public Access Cable has done the same thing for other folks I know.

The format situation again comes down to, for the most part, what you have on hand. We had S-VHS in 1989, and at the time that was underused. What an original idea, we thought, to pull off a whole feature on that cheap format. But a funny thing happened … in the four-five years it took us to get it all done, "camcorder crap" had already boomed and gotten a very bad rep. And in the end that

worked against us. There's nothing wrong with video for first or other low-budget flicks, but it's always a good idea to look into "filmlook" processes, just because it can go a long way to gaining acceptance. A distributor has told me: it's far better from his angle that he get a "filmlooked" video—in a pro format like Betacam SP—where money has been spent to keep the quality on the screen, as opposed to spending all your money just to get film, but then not having the funds to do a quality product. Because as he saw it, his customers couldn't really tell much difference between "filmlooked" Betacam and 16mm in a home video sales environment. He would get the same money for it either way. The only problem then is, you forego any theatrical ability and have to limit yourself to the home video market … but let's face it—that's the most available thing to go for as a starting filmmaker.

ULRICH: I shoot on Super VHS format. If I had the money I would shoot on 16mm film but film is just too expensive. I shot my first movie back in 1993 on standard VHS and the quality was just too poor. So I figured if I was going to continue to make movies I needed to upgrade in quality. I got a Panasonic AG-455 Super VHS camera and a Panasonic AG-1970 Super VHS editing deck. The camera cost around $1,500 and it was worth every cent. You can get a Super VHS-C for a little over $1,000 and the quality is the same or you could get a three-chip camera that has even better quality, but it also costs a lot more. I also invested in a Videonics MX-1 digital mixer, which cost around $1,000. It has four inputs, over a hundred transactions including dissolves. If you use the eight-speed strobe on number one you get a kind of "filmlook." It makes the 30 frames per second look like 24 frames per second, just like film, but most people can still tell it's video. The big advantage in shooting on video compared to film is that you can shoot two hours of footage for $10 on the S-VHS tape. If you shoot on 16mm film it will cost well over $2,000 for two hours of footage.

Tim Thomson directs "freemasons" Flo and Joe in *No Resistance*.

Also, on video you can immediately review the footage. On film you'll have to wait until it gets developed. Of course, the big advantage of film over video is the superior quality.

VOLLMANN: *Dead Meat* was shot on double system Super 8 film. To get the best quality we purchased our equipment from Super 8 Sound in Burbank, California. Rental was out of the question because we all lived in Chicago and it would have cost twice as much to shoot. We purchased a new camera costing $4,000; a used sound recorder for $1,100; used flatbed editing bench, $2,200; film projector and four-track portable mixer, $1,000. Our lighting man, Wes Dodd, already owned lights and a tripod. The new equipment worked fine for us. However, the used equipment broke down shortly after shooting wrapped. We ended up trading in our camera for another used sound recorder and editing bench.

The reason Super 8 was chosen over video or even 16mm was simple. Our film and processing costs were one-third the cost of 16mm, a savings of $8,000. If we would have chosen 16mm our rental costs would have still equaled what we paid for our Super 8 equipment. The advantage over using video was also simple. We all wanted to learn how to make a film. S-VHS would have been cheaper and quicker but we felt shooting on film would help us in securing a distributor much easier.

If I had it all to do all over again I probably would have saved more money and shot on 16mm. There are two reasons for this: (1) In renting 16mm I could have dealt with a rental house and processing lab locally as opposed to a company located a few thousand miles away. It took ten working days to get my film back from Los Angeles—their lab was the only one I could trust. Using a local lab would have also saved a lot of time. When I had a problem with equipment I was down for weeks until it could be rectified. (2) 16mm can be blown up to 35mm much easier that Super 8. A good thing to consider when trying to get your film into distribution.

GARY WHITSON & W.A.V.E.: We shoot on S-VHS and edit using JVC S-VHS machines. We have a Videonics MX-1 mixer which allows for some neat effects and a "filmlook" for video. Advantages in using video are obviously: the cost and ease of use. And for what we do, it's ideal. Not too many people could afford to have their script done on film. Video offers a good alternative.

5. Budget and Funding

With your first self-financed movie the idea is to spend as little money as possible. The best way to do this is itemize everything beforehand and allow a portion of the proposed "budget" to allow for emergencies. You have to be prepared for the worst-case scenario so that when it happens you can deal with it—and if it doesn't happen the shoot went that much easier. You have to be slightly paranoid. Limit the amount of actors, shoot in locations that are readily available or than can easily be substituted, and if there are any special effects, try to shoot them all in the same week. First-hand experience has taught me setting up effects shots tends to slow things down.

Vampires & Other Stereotypes was funded by depleting my savings, borrowing money from family, and maxing out my credit cards and ended up, by the time I completed all the editing and putting it through a "filmlook" process, $30,000. Originally, its budget was $10,000, which only lasted through the actual *shooting*.

Here's what didn't cost:

(1) Equipment. I worked at a video production facility in Manhattan and one of the perks of the job was to use the equipment as long as I did it on off hours. Without this benefit I could not have made the movie.

(2) Tape stock: I recorded everything on used Betacam SP tape stock, which is okay. New stock costs around $25 per 30-minute tape. I used a total of 45 tapes that were basically going to go in the trash.

(3) Studio Space: One by One was gracious enough to allow me to take over their studio for a month. In return they'd get 10 percent of the movie when it made money.

(4) Actors: It was contracted that they'd get a deferment after I made back all the money that was put into the movie.

Here's what did:

(1) Putting up cast and crew in a hotel, since they were from New York and we were at a studio two hours away.

(2) Feeding everyone. Fortunately I was able to do this through the help of my uncle, Joe Timko, who did all the food shopping and cooking. It was still around $250–$300 a day.

(3) Car rental. Unavoidable since I did not own a car in the city.

(4) Special effects: This cost $5,000 for all the effects in the movie, in retrospect far too much money for what was delivered in the film. They were still making props while we were shooting and much time was spent waiting, particularly for the giant rat. Granted, they

didn't have half a year preproduction time but they did promise everything would be ready before shooting. Years later I learned that many of the effects were the result of their students that they taught a class for and that the bulk of the money they received went to paying a dumping fee for the toxic materials they accumulated in their studio the past few years. It hadn't all gone into the film!

(5) Editing: I had free access to an off-line editing system but to do my final edit I had to pay two days—nine hours—at $150 an hour, plus cost of new Betacam SP tape stock.

(6) As this was shot on Betacam SP video I had to put it through a "filmlook" process to make the finished product look like film. I had come across the demo reel for the official "filmlook" process and it was pretty incredible. I always had it in mind to "filmlook" the movie and to me it justified shooting it in video. This process was $5,000, which included the 1" video master.

(7) Publicity: (A) Sending out screeners to distributors, giving tapes to cast and crew, which were hundreds of tapes at around $4 per tape to send out. I think I sent out around 400 tapes total. In fact, I still send out screeners for review to magazines! (B) I had a hundred T-shirts made up and this ran about $500. It was a cool thing for everyone to have but I shouldn't've spent that money.

(8) Creating boxes when I had to go the self-distribution route ran just under $1,000 for the design, layout and printing: an absolute bargain when compared to most design-graphic places.

As I said, the entire budget for the production was originally set at $10,000, which literally grew as more people became involved. My director of photography, though he did an excellent job lighting and shooting, didn't quite understand the expediency, which was a little frustrating because I knew my money and time constraints. Also, the special effects team was extremely understaffed—as the week went on more of them disappeared—to other jobs, prior commitments I didn't know about—until it was just one guy busting his ass. This guy was putting in as many sleepless nights as I was and there was no good reason for it other than lack of planning. I assumed that during the production the special effects team would've coordinated their schedules. *Never assume anything.* Another significant thing, which dragged things on a bit, was the sound recording. The guys I had doing sound were perfectionists— if they heard a footstep in the background, plane overhead during a really good take they'd interrupt and say they had to do it over. I explained that I could redub this in postproduction but they were insistent and this caused some bad feelings. I didn't have time to get the thing "perfect"—I only had two weeks to finish the film! If it came to getting the scene recorded with bad sound or never getting it recorded at all, I'd take the bad sound and fix it later. Also, since all the actors were shipped out there, two hours away from their apartments in the city, many waited around for hours while others did their scenes.

This didn't provoke a lot of enthusiasm, a reason why I chose to shoot *Addicted* almost entirely in the city. By the time I was done with just the shooting my entire budget was depleted. My solution? Borrow more money and charge up my credit cards to rent out the editing system and for the "filmlook" process to finish the film. (See Chapter 6.) This turned out to be three times my original estimate! In addition, it took exactly one year to finish editing the film, mostly because of the added expenses, and another half-year before I was able to "filmlook" it.

In contrast to *Vampires, Addicted to Murder* was entirely self-funded by using my credit card. It cost $4000 because nothing— absolutely nothing—was left up to chance. The cost was affordable to me—it wouldn't put me in the poorhouse.

Here's what cost money for *Addicted*:

(1) Special effects cost $1,000.
(2) Feeding cast and crew, which wasn't nearly as large as the other movie. Keep your production crew small! $500.
(3) New Betacam SP tape stock for the final editing—$200.
(4) Sending out screeners for review and to actors and crew people—$500.
(5) Creating and printing boxes for the final product, total of around $1,000.

The biggest difference between the two films is that I knew exactly what *not to do* from the first movie, which saved countless hours and dollars. I didn't have to put people up in a hotel, have tons of special effects, and I had free access to editing equipment since the place I work for bought an edit suite. And I think the biggest factor was that there was no wasted time—there was no sitting around, deciding things on the set, no making big decisions while people stood around. It was all thought of beforehand. For hours, days, and weeks of time beforehand. In those four years between productions I also came up with my own "film-like" process.

But although *Vampires & Other Stereotypes* cost nearly thirty thousand and *Addicted* cost only a fraction of that, these are by no means "real" prices. If I paid the going rate for equipment, for actors, and for postproduction the budgets of these films would easily be ten times what they were, which would, in effect, make doing them impossible. They were completed because I used every resource at my disposal and put myself in the position to call upon these resources when I needed them. Basically, it took over five years working *hard* in the video production industry to make this happen.

THE INTERVIEWEES WERE ASKED,
How do you handle your budget and funding?
What costs money, and what doesn't?

ARSENAULT: My films are a combination of self-funding and private investments. My first film, *Night Owl*, was about two-thirds private investments and one-third self-funded. I can't believe I actually put up that much, but then again I had a good job at the time, and that film was spread out over a period of three years.

The secret of private investments is that there is no secret. Just ask everyone you know; someone is bound to say yes. My second feature, *Domestic Strangers*, was funded almost entirely from private investments, with only a small amount self-funded.

I have never approached a production company or distribution company for funds, and I have never gotten one of those government grants that all the liberals are whining about these days.

BALLOT: What I can shoot or produce is determined 100 percent by my budget. I'm not going to write a scene that takes place at the gaming tables on the French Riviera. My thoughts are: What can I do with what I have? How can I utilize my existing resources?

I'd love to be able to pay Kevin Costner $200 million to stick a fin up his ass [*Waterworld*] but until then I have to stick to what's within my grasp.

BERGER: I have been incredibly fortunate so far. *Original Sins* was financed by a lifelong friend of mine, David Siegel, who also wrote the musical score. He got involved with me for one major reason: I'm honest with him. Anyway, never try to trick or cheat your investors. There's no point. If

Angel (John Leguizamo) confronts his brother Tomas (Yul Vasquez) in *Night Owl*, a film written, produced and directed by Jeffrey Arsenault. Co-Producer June Lang. ©1993 Franco Productions.

you are in the micro/no-budget videofilm biz to make tons of cash, then you are definitely in it for the wrong reason! There is an opportunity to make your money back and maybe even a couple of thousand here or there, but don't delude yourself or your investor. This level of production is strictly nickel and dime—not that it doesn't have its advantages. Just be aware that there are no get rich quick schemes hidden here. Always treat your investor with respect and appreciation. Without him or her you would be nowhere. Besides, I don't prescribe to the "Other People's Money" theory—I'm in this rink to learn as much as I can about my craft and to progress with each endeavor, not to rook a sucker into throwing his money away. The more projects, the merrier; and you won't get those made through smug attitudes and arrogance. Investors don't mind putting up a little extra as long as the communication lines are open and you give them the opportunity to decide a budget's validity for themselves. Keep good track of any

lessons learned through misbudgeting or compulsive spending so as not to repeat the errors on future ventures. A good idea is to let your investors in on these, again, so as to cement a trust and to let him know you're on top of things.

BONK: I have self-financed my movies so far. To pull this off I saved every penny from other jobs, have charged against my credit cards, have begged off relatives—basically whatever it took to get the flicks done. And so far, I have always been able to pay that money back.

I have three things going for me that definitely work to my advantage:

(1) From working in the antique business with my father for so many years, I have a good work ethic. I will literally wake up at 8 A.M. every morning and not quit working until midnight that day. If I didn't have to sleep, I certainly wouldn't!

(2) Also because of the antique business I have a skill for negotiating for the best price, and reading others in these negotiations, that helps me to get the best possible deal when securing such things as talent and locations.

(3) I have a strong ability of stretching money to its farthest possible potential. For instance, on *Permanent Waves*, I cast actors who were hungry for work, and who also shared the same fervent passion for filmmaking as I did. I only paid the four leads, and it was a preset amount, which probably only averaged out to fifty cents an hour! I spotted an abandoned house that I knew was on rezoned industrial property. Basically, this meant that this house could no longer be lived in. Talking to the owner, I knew he was having difficulty selling because of a conflict with a member on the town's board. He also had inherited the house and so he had nothing into it. I needed a place that I would have unlimited access to and would be able to arrange it how I like it, and then leave it like that for days at a time. The owner told me $500 for a month's time. I got it for $250. I never pay crew—I offer them the experience, as well as promise to provide the same hard work on their productions. In the past, I have been the entire crew on some of my other movies—not a good idea! I warned the actors about their clothes ahead of time—telling them which outfits would get ruined, and asking them to supply something that could get ruined. I supplied furniture and props needed from local garage sales, and even sold some of it off after for a profit. I scheduled short, leisurely shoots, so no one would have to take any serious time out of their work or school schedules. Having unlimited access to the place allowed for late night and early morning shoots. Time of day wasn't a factor—nighttime scenes could be shot during the day with the windows blacked over. Daytime shoots could be shot at night with a little extra light. It was also shot on S-VHS so we didn't have to deal with the high cost of film or the heavy duty lights for film. We did plenty of rehearsing to keep down on the number of takes on set. In addition, I also used the place to stage some scenes for an additional special-interest video I was shooting.

Now all that was pulled off for $500. Less if you consider what I sold off later. And in the end I had a 65-minute short, which I would cut down heavily for the anthology *Dark Descent*. But if I had never released it—well then, I wasn't headed to the poor house.

On future productions I would further utilize people who were as passionate about making movies as me—like with *The Vicious Sweet* and *Strawberry Estates*. *Sweet* ran about $3,000—complete with forty zombies and monsters and blood effects and an incredible performance from the lead Sasha Graham. *Estates* unbelievably came in under $1,000—and it stars my good friend and popular B-movie actress Debbie Rochon. And the location was incredible! Jerry O'-Sullivan brought *Gut-Pile* in under $2,000, and he even had a cool robotic head for the possessed scarecrow, along with numerous gore effects—including a severed head in a wall and a gutted man on top of a car hood. And even though little money was spent, every penny went into the set design. And in the end the production values are quite nice!

BOOKWALTER: Well, this is probably where my experience will be useless. I'm sure most of the people reading this will know the boring old story of how eighteen-year-old J.R. Bookwalter went traipsing up to Detroit, Michigan, to meet with Sam Raimi [*Evil Dead*] in the hopes of being a production assistant and instead walked away with a deal to make *The Dead Next Door*. Well, that was 1985 and things like that just don't

Director Ron Bonk (second from right) and the cast from *Strawberry Estates* (1997).

happen these days. I had the good fortune to have it happen a second time in 1989 when I was in Los Angeles finishing *DND* and met David DeCoteau (*Creepozoids*), who hired me to make a 16mm feature called *Robot Ninja* for him—and we subsequently made eight more movies after that together, six of them on S-VHS video. When I finally became tired of being a "hack for hire" in early 1992, I decided to make *Ozone*. That project was initially going to be directed by David Wagner, who had written the original script. He and partner Doug Snauffer approached me for help with it and instead I wound up talking them into letting me make it. Dave Wagner even tossed in the $1,500 he had! I matched it with my own money, and Ron Bonk (*City of the Vampires*) kicked in another $500 down the road. So, we made *Ozone* on $3,500. It's funny, because I figured when I added up all the receipts that it would total around $6,000. But I'm very good at sticking to a budget, and I suppose that came from working with DeCoteau. It certainly wasn't from Raimi, who initially was only going to kick $8,000 into *Dead Next Door* to

shoot on VHS video and wound up with a $125,000 investment into a Super 8mm feature that took four years to make! After *Ozone* I produced *Midnight 2: Sex, Death, & Videotape* for John Russo [*Heartstopper*] which was made for $10,000 of Russo's own money. Most recently I finished *The Sandman*, which was entirely funded out of my pocket. I began it with no set budget—I decided I would spend whatever the movie dictated and whatever was within my means. I haven't added it up but the final budget is probably in the realm of $15,000. I had two line producers who each had to get paid, an all-new cast who had to get paid, a trailer park to rent, computer equipment to obtain, et cetera. We also paid the bucks to license the song "Mr. Sandman" for the opening credits. That cost $2,300—with a finder's fee—but I think it's worth every dime. It adds the sort of "legitimacy" that your talent alone cannot! It was also shot like a "real" movie in that we had six weeks of full-time preproduction and three-and-a-half weeks of full-time shooting. It's interesting to note that we did originally go out to seek investors for *The Sandman*, but

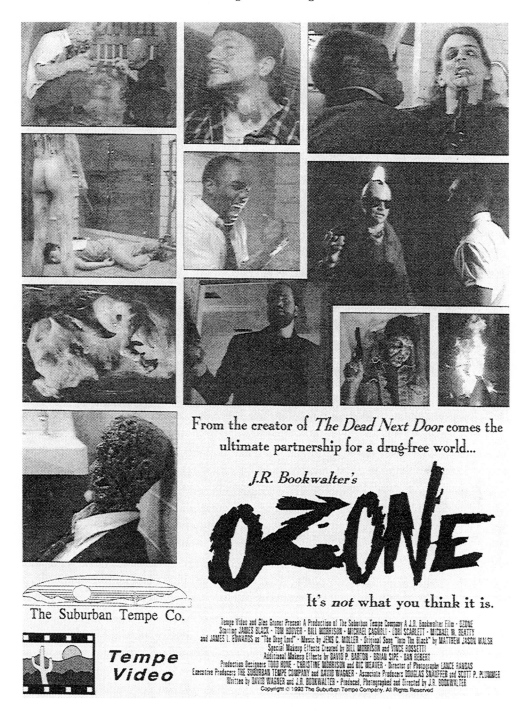

From the creator of *The Dead Next Door* comes the ultimate partnership for a drug-free world...

J.R. Bookwalter's

OZONE

It's *not* what you think it is.

The Suburban Tempe Co.

Tempe Video

Tempe Video and Glen Gruner Present A Production of The Suburban Tempe Company A J.R. Bookwalter Film · OZONE
Starring JAMES BLACK · TOM HOOVER · BILL MORRISON · MICHAEL CAGNOLI · CORI SCARLETT · MICHAEL N. BEATTY
and JAMES L. EDWARDS as "The Drug Lord" · Music by JENS C. MOLLER · Original Song "Into The Black" by MATTHEW JASON WALSH
Special Makeup Effects Created by BILL MORRISON and VINCE ROSSETTI
Additional Makeup Effects by DAVID P. BARTON · BRIAN SIPE · DAN BEHENT
Production Designers TODD HONE · CHRISTINE MORRISON and RIC WEAVER · Director of Photography LANCE RANDAS
Executive Producers THE SUBURBAN TEMPE COMPANY and DAVID WAGNER · Associate Producers DOUGLAS SKRIFFER and SCOTT P. PLUMMER
Written by DAVID WAGNER and J.R. BOOKWALTER · Produced, Photographed and Directed by J.R. BOOKWALTER
Copyright © 1993 The Suburban Tempe Company. All Rights Reserved

Trade advertisement for J.R. Bookwalter's *Ozone*, shot for $3,500.

only raised $2,000. I try very hard not to find investors because there's a 99 percent chance that they will never see their money back, let alone make a profit. This is especially true now, when B-video product is the scourge of the industry! To me, finding investors is akin to just stealing somebody's money. I've never felt good about taking people's money.

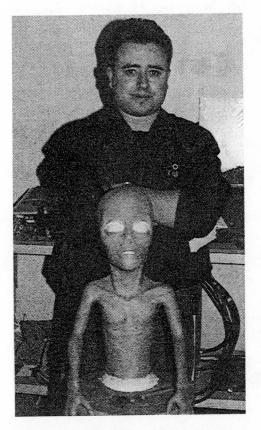

Gabe Campisi with an alien from *Shadowdance*.

Working with DeCoteau was cool because he was just hiring me to do a job and in the end of the day it's up to him to sell the movies. Kind of takes the guilt away. So, I recommend that you guys stick with your self-financed flicks or shack up with a distributor that will hire you to make some in-house product for them.

CAMPISI: Plenty of side jobs got me the financing I needed for all my early projects. They were cheap projects, mind you, but self-funded nonetheless. More expensive projects went on my credit cards, and our current projects are mostly being funded by outside sources.

Outside funding is the most difficult thing to do for a filmmaker. You're forced to leave the world of make-believe behind and go into the world of corporate strategy and finance. Sometimes it seems you've either got

to have a rich uncle with millions of dollars to spare—or you've essentially got to have a business and finance degree from Harvard to pursue financial investors.

I'm not saying this to sound pessimistic. It's just a realistic view on an all-too-familiar situation. Investors didn't get wealthy by giving away their money. They will ask plenty of questions, and put you in the hot seat if you're even lucky enough to get that far. You'll hear, "Why should I give you money, and not the next filmmaker in line? Who will handle the money? Which accountant? Which attorney? Can you guarantee a return? Show me statistics on similar films, and their financial performance. Show me something *wonderful* you've shot."

This is where a calling-card project comes into play. You can show off a produced project, and prove that you know what you're doing. Publicity and awards you've received for the project should be exploited. But even this won't guarantee an investment, since investors want to deal more with a *business* person than a *creative* one. Having a strict, knowledgeable business partner is ideal in this situation.

What it all comes down to is no *film project* alone will get you the money, and no *business plan* alone will either. A combination of the two, however, stands a superior chance.

In my situation, I was fortunate enough to know enough people in the industry to assemble a "team" of financial, corporate and creative experts. Each individual handles a unique responsibility. As an example, a State of Nevada government agent highly trained and skilled in management and corporate matters became our VP of operations. A corporate bank account representative with years of experience under her belt at Bank of America became our VP of finance. A former UNLV English and marketing professor of mine became our executive in charge of public relations. And, of course, the creative end was left to me and my fellow *filmmakers*.

So you get the picture. Together, over a period of about one year, we created a 300-page business plan that has captured the

Marlene Shapiro and Monica McFarland discuss their cash supply problem in Ronnie Cramer's
Back Street Jane.

attention of several financiers, attorneys and studio executives—and led to our current negotiations. I should also mention that because of our combined venture, we retained three of the most prominent entertainment attorneys in Los Angeles. One of them represents Steven Spielberg and Robin Williams.

If you're going to do a small project, or if you're just getting started, by all means find the money with friends and family or put it on your credit cards. When you're ready for the big time, there is no set road of cultivating success.

CRAMER: I raised a lot of money—in no-budget terms—for *Back Street Jane* and it was a depressing, humiliating experience. I went into countless homes clutching my little prospectus, explained the film and told my life story countless times—begged for money and came up empty more often than not.

Most of the people I talked to were keenly interested in hanging out—learning about the film business, et cetera, but balked

when it came time to sign that check. I shudder to think of the hours I spend groveling for nothing.

When I was offered a straight salary to direct my next film, *Even Hitler Had a Girlfriend*, I jumped.

FORD: My movie was financed entirely through an inheritance. The money fell into the laps of my wife and myself, and I allocated a certain small portion of it to make a movie. I knew I had to make a commercial movie and make a profit the first time out or I'd probably never get the chance to make another. I decided that aliens were the hot trend, and so I proceeded to develop a cheap action movie with an alien in it. Although I felt I understood the language of film very well, I had never gone to film school and had no real practical technical knowledge about filmmaking. So I had to find a production entity to align with. I had been very impressed with Wildcat Entertainment when I wrote *Blazing Force* for them. Mark Gordon, who runs the company, seemed a

Trace (Tyrone Wade) fights Gorek in his true form (Mark Sawyer) in Ron Ford's *Alien Force.*

straightforward and honest guy who knew how to make a movie. So that's that. I put up the cash and the creative stuff; he put up the production machine and the sales force. The movie was budgeted by Mark's father, executive producer Albert Gordon, using computer software, and we stuck to that budget very tightly. We actually finished under budget and I was returned part of my original investment. I can't really say the exact cost, since we are still marketing the movie. But let's say it cost considerably more than the average Kevin Lindenmuth production but considerably less than the average David DeCoteau.

It's possible to make movies very cheaply, but you have to consider every cost ahead of time if you want to keep the costs to their absolute minimum and also make sure that every cent shows up on the screen. Prepare a budget. And then stick to it.

GALLAGHER: My first movie that I sold, *Gorgasm,* I found a guy to put up half

the money, and I put up the rest. On *Gorotica* I formed another company called Ill-Tex Productions with Robert Walters, and once again we shared the expenses. *Gorotica* made a decent amount of money, enough to buy us additional equipment and fund our next movie, *Gore Whore. Gore Whore,* in turn, funded our third movie, *Exploding Angel,* which has yet to be completed.

GINGOLD: There's not much for me to say regarding the money issue; it all came out of my own pocket. I never drew up an actual budget, but simply planned to spend what I needed to while striving to do as much as I could as cheaply as possible. Of course, things would end up costing a lot more than I had planned, and I even stopped work on the film at a couple of points to build my finances back up. I still don't know exactly how much I've spent on *Mindstalker*—I dread the day when I add up all my receipts—and I don't entertain any fantasies about making it all back. Spending too much is one of the mistakes I hope I'll have learned from when I embark on my next project.

HOWE: My friend Chris Ingvordsen, who's directed over a dozen 35mm features including *Virtual Hell*, had a rule he calls "O.P.M., or Other People's Money." Sure, if you have some excess capital laying around that's not earmarked for food or rent, go out and do your movie, otherwise try and get someone else to pay.

Producing on credit cards is a bad idea that can fuck you up for the rest of your life. Sure, we've all heard about the Robert Townshends [*Hollywood Shuffle*] of the world, but what about the fifty other guys who tried financing on plastic and ended up in debt and losing everything. Only one in fifteen indie features ever gets finished. Less ever make any money. Think about that before whipping out your Visa.

Get your money from investors; doctors and lawyers are a good place to start. There are all sorts of legal rules which vary from state to state when you're doing this, so check your state's rules and be careful. Get a lawyer to volunteer his or her time, if you can, to help you sort all that stuff out.

And most importantly, even in the most casual investor relationship—say your Uncle Joe is giving you the cash—make sure the investor understands that everything he invests is risk capital. His chances of getting it back are slim. Make sure that losing all of it will not send Uncle Joe to the poorhouse.

We were lucky with *Original Sins* in that we found an investor who was willing to pay for the movie. I was also able to barter my services—shooting, gaffing—to some production companies in exchange for free services.

In order to show our investor our gratitude we structured our deal so that he gets his original investment paid off first, before anyone else sees a dime. That's a pretty standard arrangement in the micro- and low-budget film world. It's a good way of making your pitch easier for an investor to swallow.

JACOBS: All of my projects are self-funded. I work for a marketing research company part-time and that is how I get all my gravy. Since I'm working on video the cost of my films isn't that expensive. It'd be nice to be funded by someone else and just be a "director for hire." However, at the state I'm at I tend to shy away from investors. People sometimes offer money but I don't think I'll ever take them up on their offers. First of all, I can't guarantee that my films will turn a profit. What do I do when I can't pay my investor back? Secondly, most of these investors are friends of the family. Money is a very crazy thing and I'd feel bad about owing people. I like taking the risk, losing or making money, finding or not finding distribution, et cetera.

I have two ideal situations for funding. One is that I'm making enough money off my films to keep on making and distributing them myself. As it is I keep putting money in. It'd be nice to have my films pay for themselves. My second scenario is to work for a production company and I'm just making the films. They handle funding, distribution, and promotion. I'm just concentrating on the movie.

LEGGE: When I was doing short films, all the funding came out of my pocket. For the feature films *Loons* and *Cutthroats*, I was lucky enough to get partial funding with a regional fellowship grant administered by the local media arts center. I probably would have been unable, or at least very slow to complete the projects, since even being as frugal as possible, Super 8 is expensive.

McCLEERY: As far as funding goes ... it's good to have a day job to support your filmmaking habits. *No Lie!* It's hard to make money at this. Sure, a few guys have been able to do it but not a whole hell of a lot. I do fund my films out of pocket and because of that there are times when I have to stop shooting so I can amass more funds. I'm no marketing genius. In fact, my business sense is for shit and this is a part of filmmaking that I continually ignore. But don't do as I do, do as I say! It is really important to get your product out there. Publicity is the key. If no one sees it, nothing will happen with it. But ultimately, I think you should plan on losing money on your first production. The object is to make sure it isn't that much. Come up with a marketing plan before hand and a marketing schedule and stick to it. Send the film out to all the magazines for review. And remember the old saying, "If you are only doing a film to make money then make a porno." You may not be able to show your grandparents but you probably won't lose money.

MCCRAE: I'm functioning in an unusual way right now, as concerns the funding of projects. *Shatter Dead* was every week's take-home paycheck cashed in at the bank and put in my pocket to rent equipment and feed the crew, et cetera, for an entire summer. This is not a healthy way to live but currently it is the only way I know how.

I have no idea what advice to give concerning this subject, except for the usual cry of "keep your day job." Being an independent filmmaker means having the funds to do whatever you want to do with those funds.

MURPHY: It's weird. You almost profit the most from the mistakes you make, because those are the things that you save so much on in the next film. You don't make expensive mistakes twice. Instead, you get even more creative in ways to save money. Go at it making ten dollars look like a hundred.

I haven't gone the investor route yet. So far, I like self-funding. You don't have to answer to anyone. But it's all on your head. The hardest decision is the decision to commit to the project in the first place. Once you say "Go!" you have to ride it all the way. It's like jumping off a cliff. You can't quit once you start shooting. You just have to keep finding new ways to keep going forward.

With *Jugular Wine* I borrowed money like crazy. I just went out of my mind with credit cards and loans and all that. One ac-

tress, my friend Rachelle Packer, lent me eight grand! And she didn't have the money to lend. That's how much people were pulling for me. And after the fact, not being able to pay them back for a long time really killed my spirit.

Pay off your debts! My big "after the fact" budgeting advice. Pay off your debts or you'll find it even more difficult to summon money for the next film. Not to mention you're a shit if you don't. If you pay people back and show a respect for the money that was never really yours in the first place then you will gain respect and maybe even be able to borrow from that source again.

POLONIA BROS.: All our pictures have been self-financed so we could retain creative control. We make our films very, very, very—did I say real—cheaply. We have learned to make every dollar count and utilize existing locations and props to elevate a film's budget. Money should not be a concern to a certain degree. If you have to, and you have the intuition, you can make a little look like a whole helluva lot! Of course, if you can find a partner to help chip in cash and work with you, this is also a viable route.

RITTER: I have self-funded projects and have raised money for them. For *Day of the Reaper* and *Twisted Illusions*, I washed dishes and was a short order cook, putting all my extra money into those projects. But they only cost $1,500 each to produce! Those were first feature efforts.

Truth or Dare—A Critical Madness was actually financed by a Chicago distributor. I put together a prospectus—a budget, artwork for the movie, time frame, and materials relating to me and my partners. What really sold the project was the visual stuff—*Truth or Dare* was done as a short story in the anthology movie *Twisted Illusions* and that helped show what I wanted to do and how that would work. We also produced a video that showed all our key personnel at work, sample scenes from movies of a similar nature and how much money they made. This visual

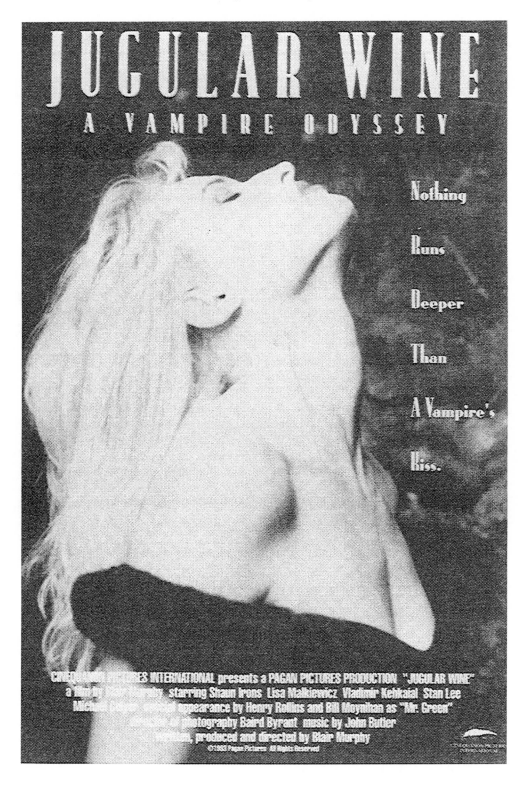

Trade advertisement for Blair Murphy's *Jugular Wine*.

representation was really what sold the project, because no one in the business seems to read anything. They're more liable to *watch* an idea than read it. That got us in the door and eventually the $250,000 budget it cost to make the movie. This is the ideal situation for filmmakers—have a distributor finance and release your work. But this was back in 1985–96, when the market was different.

For *Killing Spree*, I capitalized on the success of *Truth or Dare* and went around locally in South Florida to raise the money. In addition to family and friends, we got local real estate owners, video store owners, and others to invest in the $75,000 project. Again, we made a videotaped sales presentation pitch of the movie, showing clips from *Truth or Dare* and other ideas that we had for *Killing Spree*. We also got a foreign distribution contract set up before the movie was made to help satisfy investor questions on whether the movie would sell or not. The videotaped presentation really excited investors and got them interested again. It still took about a year to collect all the money, set up the partnership, and weed out the players from the pretenders.

Both *Truth or Dare* and *Killing Spree* were set up by lawyers so the investors were involved in a limited partnership. Basically, when the movie is done and sold, all first moneys that are made on the project go back to the original investors until their investment is paid off. From there, it's a 50/50 split between the investors and the film production company and those you may have given out percentages to for participation in the project. To do a limited partnership you must have a company, so it's important to incorporate as early on in the game as you can. You have to be ready to show investors that you are a real business—a film production company. Having a company also protects you from certain personal and financial liabilities if a project doesn't earn money at some point or goes sour for reasons beyond your control. You need a company in case of lawsuits, basically. You want to protect personal assets as much as possible.

After *Killing Spree*, the market for independents changed and sales for independents were really declining. This was in 1988–1992. It was a rough period.

I was trying to get funding for *Truth or Dare II*, which eventually became *Wicked Games*. I thought it would be easy to get a sequel to a successful movie financed.

I fell into what I call "the venture capital trap" during this period. During this time, I researched all kinds of different organizations in Florida which supposedly financed business projects. These "venture capital" sources are located all over the country—just check your yellow pages. Basically, they take a big fee that is built into your budget for the work of raising funds. Primarily, they fund businesses like ice cream shops, video stores, whatever. But I managed to sell one big company on the idea of moviemaking.

I spent about a year budgeting, lining up deals, putting together figures, signing letters of intent, and getting ready to set up an operation that would produce and distribute horror films. After all this effort, I went into this big meeting at an expensive restaurant with their head venture capital dealmaker, and he told me that he would need $10,000 from me to cover the legal costs of getting the tail end of this million dollar deal in place! It turned out to be a con—the guy was stinging a bunch of other people at the same time, luring them into the process for about a year, saying that the "millions for their dream businesses were only $10,000 away in legal fees." Needless to say, I told him that if I had $10,000 I would be starting a movie now, not jerking around with him.

So I wasted a lot of time with the venture capital procedures, although in retrospect it was a good learning experience. I had to pitch my ideas to lots of big money men, and I really got that down pat. One of the first money meetings I went to involved all these oil tycoons who were interested in investing in the movies. I pitched them my first movie idea for *Truth or Dare II* as a "Western with chainsaws instead of guns"

FROM THE CREATOR OF "TRUTH OR DARE"
COMES A NEW KIND OF MADNESS...

TIM RITTER'S

KILLING SPREE

TWISTED ILLUSIONS INC. presents **"KILLING SPREE"** Starring Asbestos Felt •
Courtney Lercara • Raymond Carbone • Joel D. Wynkoop • Rachel Rutz. •
Director of Photography- Mark Pederson • Music by Perry Monroe •
Special Make-Up Effects by Joel Harlow and Mark Pederson• Film Editor-
Bob Williams • Assistant Director- Vincent Miranda • Produced by Al
Nicolosi • Written and Directed by Tim Ritter
Un-rated • A Twisted Illusions Release • Soundtrack available on Twisted
Illusions Cassettes.

Home video artwork for Tim Ritter's *Killing Spree.*

and they all got up and walked out of the room! So I learned … the hard way!

Eventually, one venture capital group came up with $5,000 before going out of business and I decided to go ahead and do *Wicked Games: Truth or Dare II* with that money and my own money, including credit cards. So that was how *Wicked Games* was financed—basically myself. It ended up costing about $12,000 and the venture capitalists that put in the $5,000 were paid off in the end. But at that point I just had to make a movie, so I sunk every extra penny I had into the project.

Creep was the easiest movie to finance. It had a good hook—the star was "celebrity scandal" favorite Kathy Willets, known as "America's Favorite Nymphomaniac," and I adapted a script for her and said, "We're making this movie." I just started using my own money to begin production and producer Michael Ornelas did the same. Also, lead actor Joel Wynkoop started to pitch in, and we just did it. I think Francis Ford Coppola once said that "if you just start making a movie and doing it, other people will believe it's happening and join in and it'll get done." That's what happened with *Creep*—the money was always there. Eventually, executive producer Tony Granims joined in and pulled together lots of financial resources for us, but *Creep*, like *Wicked Games*, was made for the passion of doing it and putting a "name talent" in one of our small movies. *Creep* was the easiest project to put together financially because it just happened. I'm still amazed that it all fell into place. It was a $10,000 production and we spent probably half of that in actual cash; the rest was deferred. And we got lots of great stuff for that money, including wrecked cars and exploding buildings. The actual limited partnership papers on *Creep* weren't even formulated until after shooting was completed! That's a real rarity—and a gamble, if you're not dealing with people you trust, but I trusted everyone on *Creep*—to do it that way, kind of backwards. It worked out fine, but again, it was the circumstance. Each project

is different and it depends on your passion for the material and who helps you set it all up. It's important to surround yourself with a core group of trustworthy colleagues.

STANZE: My movies are usually about 80 percent self-funded. My last movie, *Savage Harvest*—$4,000—was 100 percent self-funded. When I am spending someone else's money, I make sure each investor is already attached to the project in some creative or production aspect. I do this for two reasons:

(1) If I am already in a friendship/working relationship with the investor, there is a mutual trust and respect. They know I'm going to make a movie with their cash and not rip them off. Investors who do not know the producer have a tendency to get cold feet and yank away the promised funding just as you're getting ready to shoot. Also, I am familiar with the investor's interests and intentions, reducing my risk of someone getting upset and trying to sue me for something later. I would feel very uncomfortable, especially at this budget level, spending money invested by someone I do not know very well.

(2) Everyone knows that movies made at any budget level run a healthy risk of never going into profit. If I have spent someone's investment on a movie that does not break even, I at least want the investor to have gained personally from the production. If an investor loses all their money and has not shared in the rare and exciting experience of making a movie, the investor has lost out entirely. My investors feel that if they don't see a penny of their money back, they have at least spent it on a rewarding personal experience.

THOMPSON: I've talked about what I know of these things in the context of the other questions. I don't have much to offer here. I'll just say I have never succeeded in getting funding for a project. For me the only

Home video artwork for Eric Stanze's *Savage Harvest*.

Kevin Shows, Tim Thomson, David Rains and M. Gary Miertschin on location in Houston for
the shooting of *No Resistance*.

real advice I might have is don't let that stop you from your work. Some people respect your budget; everyone respects your work. Do it with what you have rather than wait for money to come. Your talent, time and method will show through on any format. If someone sees what you have done and decides to fund it, the biggest loss is that you have an opportunity to it again with hindsight. If you are waiting to "do it right," you could be waiting a long time.

THOMSON: Basically, I wish I had rich parents. Barring that, you gotta work for your cash. *No resistance* was funded entirely out of my own pockets ... and the total of $7,000 it cost me to make was spent mostly on tape, costumes and props, and getting people to town, putting them up and feeding them during the production. Of course, no one on a project this small got paid, everybody donated their time and attention. We wrote our script to settings we knew we could get, and situations we knew we could pull off. We kept it as simple as we could, and you know ... it all still managed to bare-

ly survive disaster. But I think that's par for the course.

Remember, we could do this mostly because we did it on cheap, consumer grade S-VHS and we had the means to finish it that way and only that way. The main overriding principle was to just get out and create something. Oh, we had an idea that we would produce something that could justifiably be shot on tape—a street-level, available-technology story for which the electronic look would be an asset—and we hoped we could make it so good no one would notice the format. That never happened ... consumer grade video is just too crappy to be taken seriously by most people. But then, that was the only way we could produce something at that time ... and you have to do it or it never gets done. I'll never do it that way again, but I wouldn't have done it any other way at the time. Don't believe anyone when they say there's no sense in doing anything on video—it's a cheap and available way to make your own mistakes and learn the visual language.

If you have a job in the film or TV

business you can usually swing some help in the equipment area. Or again, schools give you great access to hardware. I owned the video camera myself, but when it came time to edit, the only thing that saved me was that I worked for a video production house. Paying for editing can easily cost scores of thousands of dollars. I did my editing at night on a deferred basis, and therefore got free cuts. Public Access Cable has done the same thing for other folks I know.

Mostly because of the script, *No Resistance* got some attention despite the less-than-acceptable format, and that'll be our ticket to bigger and better means of filmmaking. So there's no substitute for having a done product.

For the next project we are looking at having to raise money from investors. To get a superior looking film, we're going to try to get money to shoot and process film stock, get some real lighting equipment and skilled folks to run it, shell out for a committed sound crew—nothing sinks a film faster than bad sound—and other niceties. The funny thing is, that since I made *No Resistance*, I've proven to a lot of people who do these things that I'm serious about doing something original and fun ... and so I've gotten commitments from people to help me out for less money than they would ordinarily expect. So the no-budget project helps out in yet another unexpected way. In addition, because I do commercial films and videos as my day job, I've made friends and contacts who will be a big help when the time comes.

But as for how to actually get money from investors, I don't have the experience yet to say anything. I've simply done everything I can do to make the process easier.

ULRICH: I self-fund my movies because it's hard getting investors to fund your film and it's very risky filming with other people's money. If you self-fund a movie and run into problems finishing it or can't get it sold then you've lost a few dollars and a lot of hard work. But if it was funded by investors you owe somebody some money. I know a few

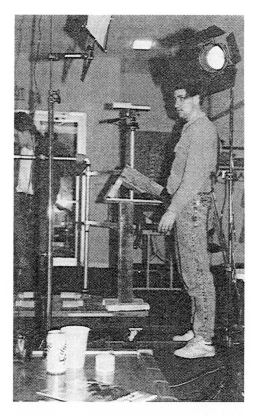

Director Tom Vollmann on the set of *The Clinic*.

filmmakers who have tried to make a film with investors and would have the film come to a halt because of problems with the money from the investors. Don't get me wrong, if somebody was willing to invest in one of my films I'd probably do it if I had a good script to work with.

VOLLMANN: Financing for *Dead Meat* was quite simple. I took an ad out of the classified section of *Fangoria* magazine looking for people interested in collaborating on a horror film. The response was overwhelming. I then organized a meeting, calling only the serious minded people. My proposition was simple; if anyone wanted to be a part of the project they would have to invest what money they could reasonably afford. Since I was putting up half of the $20,000 needed to complete the film we were able to raise most of the rest of the budget among crew members. We were still short a few thousand, so two garage sales and help from my family took care of the rest.

This way of financing seemed to me the best way to make a film. Since I was shooting professional Super 8mm, I needed people who were experienced. Among my crew I had two film students, one of whom shot my film and the other helped with lighting. I also had a lighting specialist who handled the cinematography as well as two experienced sound people. Three special effects artists donated their time and makeup supplies to help fund the project. Having ten crewmembers invest in *Dead Meat* helped insure that this film would be completed. It also gave them hands-on experience as well as a say in how *Dead Meat* would turn out. The crew knew right from the start that making a profit was remote at best. They all invested because of their love of filmmaking.

The reason I did not seek outside funding was simple. With such a small budget I felt that it was better to have a handful of filmmakers decide the outcome of *Dead Meat* as opposed to doctors, lawyers, et cetera.

WHITSON & W.A.V.E.: Most of our tapes are what we call "custom" tapes. That is, a customer sends us a script and or story idea and we produce it for them for a set price. We then turn around and sell it, paying them a small royalty. That way the cost to them of the movie is less than if we couldn't turn around and sell it. I used to do "custom" artwork for clients and I thought this was a natural extension of that. If people wanted comic strips drawn to order maybe they'd like to see their scripts taped to order. It's proven to be an excellent way to make a variety of movies while having someone else pay the costs.

6. From Preproduction Through Postproduction

Let me talk briefly about some things everyone thinks you need—but you may not really need—in order to do a movie. This is simply my opinion and is based on how I've made three feature-length films. As with about anything else in low-budget filmmaking you are doing this at your own risk.

In low-budget filmmaking, particularly on a first film, you usually don't need to get production insurance or location permits for the shoots because you aren't going to have a big crew and you aren't going to be blowing up any buildings. If anyone asks you what you're doing, say it's a student film, which isn't far from the truth. Don't go on about how it's a direct-to-video feature because people, jaded with Hollywood products, automatically assume that you have a huge budget and that, perhaps, they can get some of that money going their way.

If you're worried about not having insurance or permits by all means check it out, though you have to incorporate as a business to get the production insurance. Most states have a film commission and you can get their number from information. This is all up to you. I just base this on having done three video features in this fashion.

If you choose not to go with insurance and permits, make sure that you have contracts for the locations and for the actors.

Locations

If you are shooting on city streets and aren't doing anything too conspicuous you can usually get by without any problems, though police seem to stop by at least once during a production. If anyone asks what you're doing again tell them it's a home movie or a student film. Public buildings and public areas, such as streets, are also okay. With *Vampires & Other Stereotypes* I shot primarily in a studio in New Jersey and for scenes shot in New York City I simply went out on the streets and winged it. Usually you'll end up using houses and places of work, since those are the easiest to get.

To prevent worry about a location disappearing, such as someone telling you you can shoot in their house and then on the day of shooting telling you "Oops, I forgot I have to have a root canal today," have the owner of the house or location sign a contract that states you have permission to shoot there on such and such a date. This isn't exactly legally binding but it does put in writing, very clearly, when you will be shooting there.

Production Insurance

A low-budget production in the under $5,000 range cannot afford production insurance to cover the cost of equipment and people. This is somewhere in the neighborhood of $1,500–2,000 dollars for a month period. Instead, this is what I have done:

(1) When you hire the actors you must have them sign a contract stating that you are in no way responsible if something happens to them, which has to be okay with the actors as well. This doesn't mean you can go ahead and make a snuff movie but it does protect you to some degree to have it in writing. I've never had any injuries on any film but accidents do happen.

Also in the contract it should be stated what they're getting paid, if anything, and whatever else is expected of them.

(2) If you are renting equipment from an equipment house they are covered by their own insurance and if you don't have any they may add a 10 percent fee to cover you under their insurance. If you're using your own equipment, just be careful.

Crew

Making a low-budget film involves a great deal of trust between you, your actors, and crewmembers. I find that putting everything in writing, and going over it with each and every individual, makes it clear what's in store. Although there should be flexibility in shooting—let's say a certain scene is taking a little longer than expected—you shouldn't throw your crew or actors any curveballs such as totally rearranging schedules at the last minute. People don't like surprises and this organization of locations and scenes should have been thought of weeks, if not months, in advance. Get all your agreements and understandings taken care of beforehand so you don't have to think about it during the actual shooting.

You only need two or three people for crew and by this I mean to shoot, light, and haul equipment. On my last two projects my assistant—not to mention 90 percent of my crew—was Michael Velasco, who I worked with on my then day job, and who also was interested in making films. Make sure you trust your crew and make sure they're interested in the project almost as much as you. Enthusiasm is what fuels the low-budget production. Also, a small crew is less likely to bail out, they're quicker to communicate with, and are ultimately cheaper, as you don't have to feed a dozen people. On *Vampires & Other Stereotypes* I had as many as fifteen crew people and it only succeeded in complicating things and added time because I had to individually talk to them for every one thing I wanted done.

Make sure you have a sound person, one person who only deals with recording the sound for your movie. This is as important as the camera person. Get someone who knows what they are doing and who knows the equipment.

As I think very visually I've found it easier for me to be the camera person as well, which enables me to see how the actors are in the frame. Once I see a good take I know it, then on to the next. I usually act as the gaffer as well.

For assistants or for any of the above use college students—they'll work for free and they need the experience.

Actors

For bit parts, nonspeaking parts, and extra bodies—as in crowd shots—you can use friends and even relatives. But for your main characters, use professional actors. How do you get them? Whether or not you live in a big city or in a small town put an ad in the local paper or local actors paper, citing the types needed, call the local stage theaters and college theaters to see if anyone is interested, and have them send you headshots and resumés.

To cast *Vampires & Other Stereotypes* I put an ad in *Backstage* and received over 1,000 headshots for actors. I had to go to the post office in a van to pick up three garbage bags filled with photos and it took me two weeks just to open and go through all the mail, then two solid weekends to have auditions and a following day for callbacks. In retrospect I think I spent a little too much time doing this and saw too many people. I even said there would be a deferment for pay when the movie ever made any money, since I was so sure I would get a distributor as soon as it was completed.

To cast *Addicted to Murder* I had several people cast for parts while I was still writing the script. Mick McCleery of One by One, who also played the demon "Eric" in *Vampires & Other Stereotypes*, was in mind for the main character, Joel Winter, from the film's inception. Laura McLauchlin, who also had a small part in the first movie, was cast as Rachel, the vampire friend. Rick Poli, another veteran of the same movie, was given a cameo as a building manager. Other assigned parts went to novelist-editor Gordon Linzner for the "expert on serial killers" and screenwriter-reviewer Ron Ford as true crime novelist Polonia. For the other parts I put another ad in *Backstage*, though I didn't receive nearly so much mail. This time I kept the auditions down to one weekend since I eliminated many people from the headshots and resumes they sent. Everyone chosen from the auditions fit the characters very well, from Sewell Whitney as the tabloid TV host to Sasha Graham as Angie. In fact, as soon as Sasha walked in and started reading the lines for Angie I knew she had the part; it just clicked. And I think she did an exceptional job as the evil vampire.

As far as payment I was very upfront and told them that there was none. This wasn't to scam them or be cheap. It's simply because I didn't have the money and didn't want to promise them any that I didn't or may never have. I said that in return for being in the movie that they'd get a copy of the finished video to use on their reel and that they'd get publicity in the various genre mags, which they did. Lots of publicity. Almost every magazine article, whether published in the United States or England, Spain, or Australia, used a photo of Sasha or Laura. Sasha even made the cover of two magazines, *Shocking Images* and *Samhain*, a notable English horror magazine. Subsequently these actresses got more auditions for other movie projects and were cast in a few New York plays.

In making your first few films I don't think it's necessary that you pay the actors, though do have them sign a contract with what you agree to do, so that it's in writing. For any agreements or deals also have a written contract so that there's no confusion about anything. Remember, you're starting out your film career, you're probably investing all your own money and there's a chance you won't make this money back when the film is completed. So why should they be making anything if they're also starting out? You're all in the same boat. Also, money seems to distort things. You can pay them when you make your "Big Budget" movie down the line.

When you have auditions it is best to have "open" auditions and tell the actors to show up between this hour and that hour. This will save you hours of needless scheduling. If they have to wait a few minutes, they have to wait. They're used to this.

Rent a space or get a space where there's enough room to accommodate you, an assistant, and all the actors who show up. Check into local theaters for rehearsal space. They charge hourly rates.

Do not give your home phone out to actors while you are still making casting decisions. This is a mistake—you'll get calls all hours of the day and night. You call them and tell them the "when" and "where" of the audition and what it's for.

Videotape the auditions and before each actor auditions have them state their name and phone number. Also, have them write this down while they're waiting.

Type up a synopsis or description of what your film is about, approximately when it will be shot, and maybe some details about yourself and your "production company," and if there's pay or not (this information should be in the newspaper ad) all on one page. Then make a hundred copies of this and stack them where the actors are waiting. This will save you hours of time explaining the same thing over and over, not to mention saving your voice box.

Have the actors either do a monologue of their own or read a page from the script. No more than ten–fifteen minutes per person.

Hopefully you can keep the auditions to two days. Just call the people back who you are interested in casting. It is understood that if they do not get a call back they did not get a job. Such is the lot of the actor.

After you cast the people you want to play the characters give them all a copy of the script to read because some of your first choices may bail out for various reasons. That's why you videotaped the auditions, so you'll have backup choices.

What should you expect from your actors, and what do they have a right to expect from you? First, the actors will memorize their lines—and they will come up with their own interpretations on how to perform and

have plenty of questions about the characters. You should know all the answers to all their questions because you created these characters. Even though it may not be written in the script, you know that such-and-such character was probably picked on in junior high school and that is why he is a serial killer—and so on. Actors will look to you for answers, which you, as a director, must have. Actors should also do things the way you want them to, how you envision them saying the line in that "movie in your mind"; match the reality to how you pictured it when you were writing the scene. My favorite thing to say on *Vampires & Other Stereotypes* when an actor suggested something for a character that I didn't agree with was, "That's a good idea but that's a different movie." If they were persistent I'd shoot one take of the scene their way—tape is cheap—and when it came to editing I usually ended up using my version. Sometimes, though, actors' suggestions can greatly improve a scene. Go with what feels right but don't be overly influenced by other people. Ultimately this is your film, not film by committee.

THE INTERVIEWEES WERE ASKED,
How did you get your actors?

ARSENAULT: I always place an ad in *Backstage*. No matter what you're looking for, you're likely to get a flood of responses. *Night Owl* was a SAG (Screen Actors Guild) film, so I had to pay the actors SAG scale in accordance with the Limited Exhibition Agreement contract. One major advantage to using this contract is that I was able to hire non-SAG actors as well. The disadvantage was not the money—$75 a day—but the paperwork, payroll fees, overtime, pension and health payments, et cetera.

Domestic Strangers was nonunion. It was a little more difficult finding the right actors, but they are out there. Getting a good

performance out of a trained, competent, experienced actor is not a problem. Getting a performance out of a nonactor is a challenge, but it can be very rewarding. On *Domestic Strangers*, I cast the part of "Danny's Mom" with a friend of mine who had never acted before. I had to shoot a lot of takes, sometimes one line at a time, but she was so perfect as the character that some people regard her performance as a highlight of the film.

BALLOT: *The Bride of Frank* features a cast of real-life characters that play exaggerated versions of themselves. Most of the actors in the movie are the real people that

Jake (James Raftery) eyes Zohra (Karen Wexler) in *Night Owl*, a film written, produced and directed by Jeffrey Arsenault. Co-Producer June Lang. ©1993 Franco Productions.

work at the warehouse and trucking company where the movie was shot. We did, however, need a few actors that couldn't be found at the warehouse. There was a scene that called for a 300-pound woman to dance naked and another scene that required three women to play prostitutes and expose themselves on the street. For that, we took out ads in *Backstage*, a trade publication for actors. The response was surprising. We got over a hundred calls from people interested in the parts.

Our philosophy was that at this level, without paying people, without real professionals, we'll just try to find people that come off natural on camera and people whose real-life persona closely resembles the character they'll be playing.

BERGER: Our script for *Sins* was so extreme and off-putting that we mainly went with friends who understood our sensibilities pretty well or acquaintances who considered the script a challenge. Our *Backstage*

roundup was pathetic. A few good choices for one of the more difficult roles, which always turned into the same story: an actress would read; we'd like her; she'd accept the part; two days later we'd get the call telling us she's backing out. We almost used a blow-up sex doll for the part. It's tough to convince someone who reads a graphically sexual/violent script that you are going to film it "tastefully." So it took a while, but luck ultimately dragged our actors to us. Once you get them you have to play the appreciation game once again. You've always got to remember how much a person is willing to go through for your movie—especially if it requires nudity or sexual situations—most of the time for little or no pay! This is a big sacrifice for most people and must be eternally appreciated by the filmmaker.

BONK: I have, so far, secured actors mainly in two ways—by placing ads in local papers, or by casting friends. I have managed to get a couple actors thanks to referrals from

Director Ron Bonk and actress Sasha Graham on the set of *The Vicious Sweet*.

friends in the business. All of these means have lead to mistakes but also some great successes. For *Vicious Sweet*, I did it right. I used a friend's business on a Sunday when it was closed to hold the auditions. I videotaped the auditions and had others there for further input. After that, we had as many rehearsals as humanly possible to make the performances as smooth as possible. The only problem was that the lead, Sasha, wouldn't be available until she actually showed up for the production. She was coming from New York City and there just wasn't the money to pay to haul her back and forth for rehearsals. But I had seen her work, knew she was good, and got her an advanced copy of the script. And she more than amazed me! Her acting in the movie is incredible. Can someone get nominated for an Academy Award for a S-VHS movie? This method worked just as well on *Estates*, where we shipped Debbie Rochon and Tina Krause in with no rehearsing and they responded with strong performances. Basically, I knew what I needed and just worked at getting them to comply with it.

BOOKWALTER: Hmmmmm. Well, acting is not something that my early work would be remembered for. Living in Akron,

Ohio, and being surrounded by community theater talent has always meant that the cast is the weakest part of my movies. *The Sandman* is the first movie since *The Dead Next Door* where I concentrated so much on the acting, reason being that *Sandman* is basically a drama with a monster in it. Most of my other movies were gore showreels or they were made on the cheap on insane deadlines where casting was the last thing on our minds. I've been crucified over the years for having terrible actors, but I think *The Sandman* is a turning point. I think as far as getting good performances that it's a matter of casting the right person in the role and the rest is easy.

CAMPISI: Real actors are a scary bunch of individuals, or as they're commonly referred to, "A Strange Breed." There are two ways to find actors. If you've got the money, you should tap into the SAG (Screen Actors Guild) pool of talent. SAG has a number of producer contracts available, including deferred and low-budget agreements.

If, however, you're shooting independently and are financially limited, there are several ways to go about locating decent actors. But locating them is just the beginning.

Word of mouth always works great.

Promo for Gabriel Campisi's *The Law.*

Spread the word. Go to the local universities, colleges and theater groups and ask permission to post up "posters" of what you're looking for. Put an ad in the paper and hold an open cast call.

Screen test everyone, or at least have them go over lines in your presence. This of course is the director's job. You as the director must work with the actors in order to get the best performance out of them. There are no set guidelines for this procedure. Every director works his or her own way, and possesses his or her own style.

If you have even less time or money, you should turn to friends and relatives. This oftentimes can be difficult if they're not *real* actors. The director can attempt "overnight" lessons, and create Oscar-winning material by the next morning. You might be surprised at the multitude of natural talent that exists with your friends or family.

If you're shooting with little or no budget, you should make sure you personally take care of your cast. This goes for your crews as well. They should be well-fed and you should pay for their gas if they have to drive out of their way.

The pressures of shooting a motion picture are difficult enough when there's financial backing. If you're shooting with little or no money, and your cast and crew are unpaid, the pressure doubles. You should at the very least make sure they are comfortable with food and drinks. A good sense of humor is always a prerequisite to shooting an independent feature.

CRAMER: There are a lot of very capable performers right here in Denver and I've had the good fortune to have worked with many of them. The downside is that many are "too good" for such a small market and eventually move on. Of the six principals from *Back Street Jane*, five left soon afterward for New York or California.

FORD: I'm lucky with actors in that I am involved fairly heavily in the theater. I love to act in plays. It's the most enjoyable thing I can think of; way more fun than making movies. So anyway, I have lots of theater friends who I have done plays with, all of whom want to be in movies. So I wrote a lot of parts for *Alien Force* with friends in mind. Tyrone Wade, who played the action hero lead, was the star of the previous movie I wrote for Wildcat, *Blazing Force*. I always had Tyrone in mind for the role. I could not possibly have found a better guy for the part

in this level of filmmaking if I had looked for twenty years. Our name actor, Burt Ward, was chosen from an agency. We decided to hire Burt because he has a camp appeal amenable to our project. And he was in the range of what we could afford—barely. Other roles were cast through auditions. In L.A. you can put casting ads in *Dramalogue* and *Backstage West* for free. You get deluged with hundreds of head shots, even for parts which offer no money—be upfront about that in your ad. Then you schedule auditions. That easy. I'm sure there are similar casting publications in most major metropolitan areas which have active theater scenes. Otherwise, don't hesitate to recruit from community theater and college theater groups. Generally, stage actors do very well. They are very serious actors and they care more about their performance than about how they look, which is more than I can say about a lot of film actors I've worked with.

GALLAGHER: Once again, *Draculina* played a big part in my getting in contact with 95 percent of the people I used in my movies. *Gorotica* was actually made because a reader contacted me and wanted to work with me on a movie. I sent him my most bizarre script, *Wake the Dead (aka Gorotica)*, figuring it would send him running. Six months later we were shooting the movie.

GINGOLD: All of my actors were friends of mine, or friends of friends. I deliberately wrote *Mindstalker* to have only a few key characters so I wouldn't have to worry about getting more than two or three actors together at once. And even that sometimes became a problem; there are places in the movie in which two people who shared a scene filmed their shots up to a year or more apart! In cases like that, it helps to cast people who know each other well in real life, because they can imagine the eyelines they have to match.

In casting my leads, I was looking for people who had enthusiasm for the project and whom I felt I could trust to stick with

Promotional artwork for Ron Ford's *Alien Force*.

it through the many months of unpaid filming. Many of them had been involved with everything from local theater productions to *Rocky Horror Picture Show* floor shows, so they were already into acting in some form or another. In some cases, their performing interests worked their way into the script; one of them dabbled in standup comedy, which became a facet of that character. And in general, since I knew most of my cast already, I was able to tailor the roles to suit them. It has been said that 80 percent of getting good performances out of your actors is casting the right people for their parts, and when you're working on a very low budget, writing roles you know you'll be able to cast means you'll have half the battle won in advance.

But remember what I said about trusting people to stick with the production? One thing I've found, through my own experience and talking with others, is that every filmmaker working on this level has or will have to deal with an actor who proves untrustworthy in this regard. In some cases, it will be the person who seems most enthusiastic in the beginning, but will quickly find better things to do with his time once production begins. Without mentioning any names, one of my actors made it nearly impossible to finish shooting; he would blow off filming days, either giving me an excuse beforehand or just not showing up. Naturally, I couldn't give him a hard time about it because he would almost certainly walk for good if I did, so I just gritted my teeth and filmed him when I could, and finally got all the footage I needed in the can. And he gave a good performance, too, so I suppose it's a good thing I stuck with him.

When it came to casting the smaller parts—the indie equivalent of "day players"—things were much easier. Either I or one of my crew would ask friends if they wanted to come down and shoot a scene, and we rarely had a problem finding someone. In situations like these, the allure of "being in a movie," without any serious time demands, can work in your favor. In the case of the girl in my library scene, a friend who was still in high school went through his yearbook and pointed out girls he thought would be interested. The one I wound up choosing did a good job and proved to have a hell of a scream to boot. Also, casting interesting people you know, and adapting their idiosyncrasies to a scene, can add extra "color" to your movie and make their scenes more interesting.

HOWE: Casting is almost as important as the script. A bad actor can sink a movie pretty damn fast. And it is very hard to find good actors who will work for free.

The drill in the New York City area goes like this: A $30 dollar ad in *Backstage* magazine will get you more resumes than you ever thought possible. You have to weed through these hundreds of headshots, set up auditions usually for 40–50 people, and then spend several days doing readings until you can pick the people you want. And just as likely as not, when they see your script they may suddenly lose interest. This happened on *Sins* more times than you'd believe.

Whenever possible, cast with people you already know and have a relationship with. Since I work on a lot of shoots, I was able to find most of the actors for *Sins* from people I'd worked with before. This made it much easier on everyone concerned, because we all knew each other and liked each other.

Try and stick with professionals or semipros. Casting your friends from school can lead to real problems as they lose enthusiasm for the picture. You may not just lose cast members; you may lose friends. If someone doesn't seem 100 percent committed to the project, drop them immediately.

Local theater groups are another good source of talent that may not have the stuck-up attitude of a lot of struggling "professional" actors affect.

Actors and actresses can be huge pains in the ass. Let attitude be a factor, though not as important as performance, in judging actors. Sure, maybe someone does give the best read, but if they're going to bog the shoot down with their prima-donna bullshit, you're never going to get that performance on screen.

There are as many types of actors as there are people, and every director has his or her own way of coaxing a performance from a cast member. Each situation will be different, but here are some general guidelines to think about.

Get your actors excited about the project. Let them have a hand rounding out their characters. Consider seriously any suggestions they make. But always remember, you are the director and you must have the final say.

Many actors are naturally lazy and will often take the easy way out with a character or performance. Challenge them to go further, to do more. Don't be obnoxious about it, but be firm. If someone isn't giving a hundred percent, let them know. But have that conversation in private. Never chew out an actor—or anyone—in front of the rest of the cast and crew. It's bad form and makes you look like an asshole.

Never give an actor line readings. First of all, it may sound to you like you're saying the line perfectly, but if you recorded it and played it back, you'd see what an ass you're making of yourself. Plus, it's obnoxious, a real insult to a professional actor and is sure to generate hostile feelings almost instantly.

And most important for the low budget guys, rehearse. We didn't do nearly enough of this and it hurt us in a lot of ways. Not only will rehearsal make shooting go faster, it helps you with your script, identifying dialogue that's overwritten—our biggest problem—or not working.

Finally, never tell anyone, cast or crew, that the shoot is going to be easy. If you do, you're lying. The smartest thing we did when prepping *Sins* was tell everyone who wanted to get involved that it was going to be a total fucking nightmare. It was. This way we were sure that everyone coming on board was up for it. We literally tried to scare people off, and did scare a few, so the ones that remained were troupers enough to put in for the long haul and get it done. The three leads in *Sins* went through hell with us. If anyone likes that movie, those three women deserve as much credit as anyone.

A final note: try not to do a weekends-only shoot. The more breaks you take between shoot days, the more opportunity your project has of falling apart. Figure out how many days you need and then try to schedule those days in five- or six-day blocks.

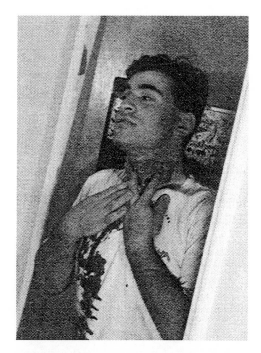

Michael Troetti, minus part of his throat for his role in Mike Gingold's *Mindstalker*.

Shoot fast and shoot hard. Then maybe go back for a weekend and pick up what you missed. With 90 percent of the film in the can, that will seem like a walk in the park.

JACOBS: One thing that I'm quickly finding out, as I embark on my second video-movie, *Safety in Numbers*, is that everyone wants to say they're involved, but saying and doing are two different things. People often said to me, when I was filming *Walking Between the Raindrops*, "Hey, if you ever need me for anything, just ask." Then, when it comes time for line memorization, rehearsing these lines, and just generally committing, people seem to fall somewhat short. They won't show up, they'll be late, they'll have other plans and the filming will have to be cut short, or they just won't take the movie seriously. This is a problem, and this is why I'm trying to work with smaller casts and crews. The less people, the less problems, the less head-aches. To get the best people and performances, I usually write with an idea of who I want to play what parts. I

Promotional still from Mike Legge's *Potential Sins*.

imagine how they talk, their speech, tone, mannerisms, and I just go from there. Then I usually approach them about playing the part. *Walking Between the Raindrops* was written about me and the two guys who play my friends in the movie, Mike Vogelsang and Chris Lohman. The script was derived from actual conversations that we had. It also served to document that time in our lives, when we hung out all night, slept in all day, and then hung out again. I also try to be very supportive of the other actors' performances, and very flexible with their schedules. I always try to remain calm, even when I'm ready to slug someone. Of course, I never would. For me, friends are the best way to go as far as actors. They may be flaky, they may not be as good as "real" actors, but they're my friends. I know them, I know what they're capable of, and they know me. It makes the filming process more comfortable, and that makes a huge difference. As long as I can get them to where they need to

be, and we get all the shots and takes that I need, I'm fine.

LEGGE: I've been very fortunate with actors since I act and direct on a freelance basis in the local theater scene. From seeing so many people playing different roles I am able to judge whether I think they're suitable for the parts I have in mind, and if they are amiable enough to work with. I can't stress the second part enough. Talent is fine, but if locked in with an overwhelming ego and temperamental personality, I'll pass them by. I like most actors, but shake a tree and twenty-seven actors will fall out. They are everywhere, and you don't have to saddle yourself with a problem. Over the years I've formed a repertory company with my people, using a core group of about twenty actors that I enjoy working with, and I always like to add one or two new people with each production to keep myself fresh. If you're looking for actors, start local. If you have a community theater, don't be a snob about it. They're still actors, and in my experience amateur doesn't mean "no talent," and professional doesn't mean anything special. Most aspiring actors will work for free food, just to have a movie on their resumé, and other actors will do it for the fun. But it won't be fun if you don't make it fun. Don't waste their time with sloppy scheduling. Don't try to talk them into doing something they feel uncomfortable about. Don't turn into a screaming goon, belittling the people you work with. I've seen such people and they are unbelievable. Don't make the mistake I've seen in countless indies, which is to turn on the camera and let the actors "act." Very few actors, especially inexperienced ones, can act without direction.

If you are the author of the script as well as the director, then you certainly must know what you want the characters to convey at any given moment. If you don't know how to direct for acting, then read about it. Study the basics of delivery, subtext, finding the "spine" of each scene, and learn that less is more. In movies you act primarily with your eyes. Many stage actors initially will come across too "big" on film. You have to tone them down, and make sure they stay natural. My preference for shooting days is to tell the actors what pages we will be shooting, but I don't insist they learn their lines ahead of time. Stage actors will be disoriented with shooting a movie, because they are used to continuity of action, not with the scattershot way a movie is made. That's why they need to establish their character before the first shot is made, because it is their responsibility to maintain the choices they've made for their character. If you are lucky enough to get experienced film actors, you won't have to worry about some aspects of this, but you still have to direct them. For an independent producer I say *stay away from unions*! I dealt with AFTRA on my first movie, *Working Stiffs*, because the lead actor I wanted was a member and a friend, but the nonsense and bullshit I went through with them was not worth it. The requirement they had just to use one actor was ridiculous and unreasonable. From my experience with them I can see how they keep actors *from* working, by making it extremely difficult and arduous. There's plenty of talented people out there; you just have to look for them. Go see local shows, advertise, talk to actors, they're bound to know other ones. And do your directorial homework.

MCCLEERY: Actors. They are my biggest problem. The proverbial thorn in my side. During the writing process you are working by yourself and only have yourself to blame if it sucks or praise if it's good or come down on when you don't spend enough time working. But then the job of shooting comes and you have to deal with people and their individual schedules and hang-ups and problems. In my experiences I've worked with two types of actors: semiprofessional actors and novices who are just interested in acting as a hobby or an experience. The good thing about professionals is they tend to show up on time and are somewhat ready to work. The problem with professionals is they

are sometimes not interested in your input as a director on their acting in a scene. The good thing about novices is that you can mold them to how you want to do the scene. The bad thing about novices is that they are a little less likely to be on time because after all, "this ain't their full time job." I've been lucky in the way that I've surrounded myself with a group of people who tend to act in each of my projects and on any new projects there is generally only one or two new actors working with my six or seven old actors. This makes it very easy for the new actors to assimilate with my old group. I've done projects where 75 percent of my cast had never before worked with me and it added a lot of time and stress to the project because I had to break in these new folks. Being an actor myself I have my own theories on acting. My theory when I do a part is this: "Be honest, while you are in the part, convince yourself that you are the character, and then play those emotions with honesty." As a director I just try to get the same honest performances out of my cast that I would give. Sometimes it works, and sometimes it doesn't, but in film-style shooting there are ways to make even the worst actor look passable. Well, maybe not the very worst but with creative cutting you can do a lot with poor acting.

MCCRAE: In college, I used to take out advertisements in *Backstage* for actors. They would send a headshot and a resumé to my mailbox and I would call back the ones with interesting looks and some solid experience. The next step is renting out a small studio space for a couple of hours and setting up appointments with your top choices; usually fifteen minutes is enough for a reading and a discussion of the material. Always bring along a camcorder to videotape the performance. Hell, tape is cheap; let the damn thing keep on running the whole time. Sometimes someone who appears to suck thirty-six inches from your face because you have gas from drinking all that soda or because you're in a shitty mood from six hours of smiling and being polite will appear to be

Mike McCleery on the set of *Vampires & Other Stereotypes*.

an Olivier on playback the next day. And that really is the most important thing in the end; you don't care how this person smells, as long as they can deliver the goods on-camera. *You* want to capture a good performance as much as *they* want to give one.

Videotape is a great format to learn on if you want to get good performances from your thespians. You just keep on rolling until you get the line reading just the way you want it, and then you always do one more for safety. Don't let anyone tell you otherwise; "Safety Scooter" says it's the way to go! Also, when you're trying to get good reaction shots out of your performers, always keep that camera rolling. Sometimes the most interesting things happen in between the things that you are looking to pull out from the deepest part of your actor's soul. An itch, a muscle spasm, confusion from your nebulous direction can give rise to the most fabulous expressions; it's surprising how many times this works better than "you're sadder than you've ever been"—huh?—or some such request. Everyone knows what it's like to feel hungry or cold and other human basics. Many of my favorite reaction shots in *Shat-*

ter Dead are the moments that I stole from in between the actual moments.

Although most of the performers in *Shatter Dead* have acted before in other film projects or stage productions, only Flora Fauna and Robert Welles are professionals who actually have headshots and resumés. A roomful of actors is like a roomful of directors; everyone has something in common and gets along great—as long as they're not all trying to get the same job that day! Having one or two professionals mixed in with your young cast can be a wonderful learning experience for the less experienced actors you have obtained. Playing an inexperienced actor against one of your friends can result in a better level of performance for the friend as the learned thespian can be very helpful in establishing a professional and relaxed environment. For example, Stark Raven only had stage experience before she starred in *Shatter Dead*, and her broad gestures and clear voice worked wonders all the way to the back row of the theater I saw her in. But she occasionally had difficulty toning down her stage performance for the camera, so I always made sure she was playing opposite a camera-trained person in her dialogue scenes. This always gave her a reference point as to what was an appropriate level to play the scene at.

I also had the advantage of knowing everyone in the cast. I didn't have the time or the money to take out an advertisement and hold proper auditions for this project, so I wrote all the parts with the people who would play them firmly entrenched in my mind; this was a wonderful and unexpected luxury which made the writing experience that much faster for me. This should not be taken to mean that the people playing the parts are anything like the characters they are portraying. I simply mean that knowing the strengths and limitations of the acting talents of the people involved made some of my dramatic choices easier to make. Also, knowing a person's natural speaking rhythms and the tone of their voice makes writing dialogue that sounds like it would be coming from their mouth much less difficult. And sometimes it means knowing when not to give a person dialogue; Stark Raven's face and mannerisms were to me far more revealing than anything I could have given her to say, and I kept on cutting more and more of her dialogue as the shoot progressed.

Part of the director's chores is knowing when to admit defeat when all else fails and find another way to film something so that it does work; that can mean changing the close-up to a wide-shot or an over-the-shoulder shot for a dialogue delivery, or relying on the reaction shot of an actor giving a stronger performance that day to sell the scene. A director who works well with actors is one who creates an environment in which a viable performance can be obtained and sustained throughout the duration of a shoot.

MURPHY: Cast who you can. Roll the dice. Good luck. Remember to at least feed everyone on the set. That's a given. It's part of your job, maybe the easiest and most important aspect of keeping everyone happy. Don't skimp on food.

In low, low budget your actors can be-

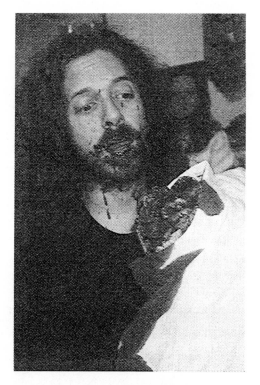

Scooter McCrae takes a lunch break on the set of *Alien Agenda: Out of the Darkness.*

come a liability. Be careful not to cast someone who may walk on you halfway through production. Once you start shooting footage of them, you have to finish the movie with them—even if they hate you.

Do auditions. Hunt everywhere. Use strange people.

If a performance is only so-so, don't blame their acting. You're the filmmaker. You are in charge. Before you even begin to dream about yourself as a filmmaker you should accept full responsibility for everything: earthquakes, stampedes, police, butt cancer, low budget performances. It's all your responsibility. Everyone is a fine tool. It's your job to figure out how to use them correctly. Figure out why they're fine and bring that out of them ... or cast someone else. But don't blame them. Make decisions and then celebrate them.

POLONIA BROS.: We use many theater and college majors as actors, people with an

Comic book legends Frank Miller (left) and Stan Lee had cameos in Blair Murphy's *Jugular Wine*.

interest, ourselves, and sometimes friends. I believe the best performance is when one is sincere and natural, and you can get great acting from nonprofessionals. You use who you can.

RITTER: I get calls all the time from filmmakers in "Nowhere, U.S.A." asking where they can find actors for their low-budget movies.

When I did *Day of the Reaper* and *Twisted Illusions* I was in high school so I drew from the high school drama department, including using the drama teacher. He even later had a major role in *Truth or Dare* he was so good. Anyway, if you're in high school or college, actors are available right there in the drama department.

For *Twisted Illusions*, Joel Wynkoop and I also made up flyers saying, "Actors wanted for low-budget horror movie—auditions coming soon," and we listed a hotel room and a time where people could come and audition. We put these flyers on cars in shopping malls and passed them out everywhere! Kind of crazy, but we met some cool people

who wanted to help out in front of and behind the camera that way. Also, for victims and zombies in horror films, everyone qualifies. As George Romero says, "Everyone wants to be a zombie." We also used waitresses and bartenders where I washed dishes in several roles for *Twisted Illusions*.

For *Truth or Dare* we had open auditions and used local talent agencies, drawing on the local Burt Reynolds Playhouse actors. It's important to have open auditions—sometimes everyday people in a role turn in great performances. To have an open audition for a movie, all you have to do is go to the local papers and news stations and tell them what you're doing. Everyone loves to do stories and get involved with local filmmaking. Then, set a time and place, videotape all applicants reading scenes from your scripts, and do this until you find what you're looking for. We did this same method for *Killing Spree*, casting most of the movie through open auditions. You get lots of serious-minded people interested with minimal expense on your part.

For *Wicked Games*, I teamed up with

Tom Karr (left), producer of 1972's *Deranged*, on the set of *Creep* with director Tim Ritter.

Kermit Christman, who ran the local Palm Beach Shakespeare Festival. He had an endless supply of actors and actresses. All cities and towns have dinner theaters and local plays. Do some research, find out what's going on in your community, watch some plays, and make yourself known. Interested people are always around you, believe me.

I've been lucky in one respect—my filmmaking partner and friend Joel Wynkoop wants to be an actor, so that always helps me in any casting predicament. He's dedicated and not concerned with money, which are qualities every actor or actress needs to have. But it's tough to find people like that all the time.

Once you do so many features people start to come to you. For *Creep*, I wrote the whole movie for actors and actresses I already knew and had previously worked with. I get resumés and phone calls from actors all the time now, so once you build up a reputation in your area, finding decent actors will never be a problem again even if you aren't paying them with anything more than experience and a nice meal during the shoot. The star of *Creep*, celebrity Kathy Willets, actually called me up asking for a role in my next movie! Of course, you have to pay celebrities and your best actors—it's just a matter of professionalism once you get to a certain level.

Getting the best performances out of an actor ... that's tough. In the beginning, when you first start making movies, you just want to get people to show up. But when you really start to direct and write characters I believe the biggest responsibility a director can have is casting the right person in a particular role. Then you have discussions with that person on the character. One on one, you answer questions and give out information on your creation. Then you have read-throughs, individually with each cast member of importance and then all together as a group. That fine tunes everything, makes you sure of everyone's ability, and saves you time on the actual shoot.

I've done this on every movie except *Creep*. *Creep* was made very fast, and as I said, with particular people in mind that I knew could handle the material.

Sometimes you get into trouble with bit players, though. On *Creep* I had one actor who kind of froze when the camera was on him. Auditions and read-throughs went fine, but when the cameras rolled he couldn't remember anything. I sat off-camera and actually fed him lines, the way I wanted them said, and he repeated them after me as we rolled tape. And I was able to coax a decent performance out of him in this manner. It was tough, but in the end, it worked. It costs time and money in editing to fix a problem like that, but you improvise and adapt.

When an actor or actress is good, you do little as a director except make sure they hit their marks. Sometimes I'll act out the scene or show them what I'm looking for by doing the action myself so they are better able to understand what I might be looking for. Also, recommend they view movies with similar scenes or tones that your project might have. This is great inspiration and good homework for your actors. Patricia Paul played a "female Dirty Harry" type of character in *Creep*, and she had never seen a *Dirty Harry* movie! So naturally, her assignment was to watch all the *Dirty Harry* movies for inspiration!

I had Joel Wynkoop, who played the titular creep in *Creep*, watch *Maniac* (1980) and *Henry: Portrait of a Serial Killer* for tips on how to partially act as a tormented serial killer.

If you want something said a certain way, you say it that way so the actor can hear it and imitate in his own way what you want. Actors are very creative and can bring to life your creations in their own unique way. Therefore, I let them sometimes improvise and let them try things in different ways. Nothing is ever written in stone when I direct a script; everyone is a contributor. As a director, your job is to tell the story in the best way that you can. Take people's ideas into consideration, use them if they're good, but don't be weak, either. If you know the way you planned a scene to unfold is the right way, then by all means do it your way. Stick to your guns. But if you have extra time, and are shooting on video, maybe film alternative ideas that your actors may have had. Some-

times, in editing, you discover they were right after all!

It's a hard line to be firm yet open to ideas and stay focused, but it can be done. That's why it's important for read-throughs and character discussions with actors before you film. But always let your actors act. Sometimes they'll bring new dimensions to the role that you won't believe! Remember, it's a collaboration of creativity and you'll be calling the final shots in the editing bay anyway.

STANZE: When working on low budgets that do not allow you to pay your actors, an actor's enthusiasm is just as important to me as acting ability. The best actor you audition is not going to benefit your movie if he or she decides not to show up when scheduled. Or if the actor has an ego and wants to stir up trouble on the set, no amount of acting ability makes up for it. A troublemaker slows down the shoot and upsets all your other actors, weakening their performances. An average actor with high enthusiasm will get a part in one of my movies a lot easier than an actor with a crappy attitude. Teamwork is an extremely important factor in my productions. I don't have time for actors who need to be stars. Actors who can't grasp the concept of teamwork do not belong on my set. I do cast "friends of mine" and use some of the same actors over and over again because of their reliability. If they are team-oriented and dedicated, casting them is a very smart move.

A note about cast and crew members: While it is a director's job to give the orders and the cast and crew's job to follow orders, it is best for a director to not let this go to his head. Being abusive to an actor or crew person is not constructive at all. It will piss people off or make them quit the production. This is not worth the ego-stroke you just gave yourself by being abusive toward them. The atmosphere on a set can be tension-heavy from time to time due to the pressure that naturally exists when trying to pull off a movie shoot. Tempers may flare and voices

Actor Todd Tevlin (left) and director–writer–executive producer Eric Stanze of *Ice from the Sun*.

may rise. It's okay if everyone knows that it is caused by the situation and not because of someone's ego. I don't get abusive with my cast and crew. I feel they are the best people in the world for devoting themselves to my movie production. I am *extremely* lucky to have such motivated, talented, hard-working people around me contributing to my movies. A director should never forget the importance of everyone involved in the project. A director leads a team. And the team makes the movie, not just the director.

When casting actors, I do not believe experience is the key to good performances. I often cast actors with no experience. They are usually much more natural than a stage actor with a mile-long resumé. It is hard for stage-trained actors to come down to the subtle acting needed for performing in front of a camera. I've seen movies made at my budget level that went to the added expense of hiring paid, professional SAG actors. I honestly found their performances to be no better than those of most inexperienced actors cast in my movies. Don't spend the money on these people just to say you've used "professional" actors! Most of the time,

the viewer watching at home will be unable to tell the difference. I have auditioned and cast SAG actors, but not paid them. If the SAG actor gets a part, the other actors who are just "friends of mine" pretty much hold their own and perform just as well as the "pro."

Even though I lean towards using actors I've worked with on past projects, I still always hold an audition. Auditions bring in new possibilities who could end up benefiting the movie. Also, even if an actor has been in a past movie of mine, I still have them audition. This educates them as to what kind of movie we are making next and helps me match up actors to characters.

THOMPSON: To date I haven't run an ad anywhere. But that's for a few reasons. One is that I live in New York City. There are a lot of hungry acting people in every major city. The more important reason is that I need to work with people I trust. That involves getting to know them. Most of the directors who I listed as inspirations to me picked a crew and drew from it again and again. One guy came and volunteered to help

Christopher Mack and Spencer Ross star in Nathan Thompson's *Contact Blow.*

on the set. In a low budget piece it is not unlikely that you will get to make an appearance of some sort sooner or later. But as it happened, during the making of *Contact Blow*, I saw the guy on a TV show. It wasn't a huge part but it was enough to start me thinking about how I could use him. Then someone couldn't deliver for me and a lead role opened up. The crew already knew and liked him and it was a natural progression. Another of my leads I saw in an off Broadway show (way off) and just approached him. Actors are used to this and he was very nice. I got a phone number and two years later called. He was surprised I had kept the number that long. But I had gotten a good feeling in our brief time together and asked if I could buy him a beer—or ten—and lay my script on him. By the end of the evening we knew we'd get along. I also tend to look for people who are real characters in life. If the role is not too demanding emotionally, then a novice who just is the guy you want can be a great addition to the cast.

Working in an advertising agency I get to meet a lot of acting people at audition time. I have yet to use one as they are all union and afraid to break the rules. I hear stories of people changing their name, et cetera, and pretending someone else did the work but ultimately my experience has been that working union actors don't want to mess with the program. If they are caught working in a nonunion piece, punishment can range from expulsion to having to write an apology letter to the union newspaper. That could be pretty humiliating.

THOMSON: It's a simple and unavoidable fact that on low-budget films, you have to draw in a lot—if not all—of your acting talent for free. Friends, family, neighbors, schoolmates, et cetera. Which is not hard, because most people think it's fun to help out on a movie, but the drawback is that people are less than reliable when they're not getting paid. So stick with people you know and can trust—and this goes for crew people, too. When money is at its tightest, getting an Academy Award–winning performance should be less on your mind than "I just need someone here at this place at this time." And then, when you can raise more and more money, you can start to afford some better talent here and there. Of course, having connections with theaters and drama departments offer no end of people looking to hone their skills, get a break, log some set experience.

Try to avoid having to do a lot of crowd scenes; concentrate on smaller groups of people, it's easier to pull off. And mostly just put people in a comfortable position where they can act like themselves.

One interesting thing that happened with *No Resistance* is that because I was the cameraman, the acting wasn't as good. Sound strange? The fact is, I shot *NR* as well as directed because I had the equipment, couldn't pay anyone else to run it, and I thought that's the way I wanted it. But as the director, I was spreading myself too thin. Most of the time, when I should have been paying attention to how people were acting, I was too involved with the lighting and the exposures and the composition and the movements. Had I gotten someone else to shoot, I could have spent a lot more time thinking about how people were talking and moving ... and it would have helped out a whole lot. So getting a good DP [Director of Photography] involved is always going to help you.

Get releases from absolutely everyone— pay everyone $1 in exchange for their signature on a release. Again, it protects you, but more importantly, it looks good to distributors.

ULRICH: I usually get actors from other filmmakers' movies and by putting an ad on the Maryland Film Commission Hotline, which is free. So check your area for a film commission. And because I work with tiny budgets I get actors who are willing to work on a volunteer basis. I've found that a lot of actors out there, who are just getting started, are willing to work for free just to get some experience, exposure, and something to add to their resumé. Unfortunately, it almost seems that for every ten actors out there there's only one *good* one. Occasionally you might come across an inexperienced actor with raw talent and if you're a good director you can get a good performance out of them.

VOLLMANN: When we had our first meeting on *Dead Meat* it was decided to use friends and family for acting roles. *Big Mistake*. Our first rehearsal was a disaster. Always, whenever possible, look for people who have acting experience. I took out an advertisement in a local performing arts publication looking for actors. This cost $17. Next, I secured a rental space at a local park district to hold auditions—$14. This was the best money I ever spent. Over fifty actors showed up. We approached this audition as if we were big-time producers. A handout containing the who, what, where, why, and how was distributed to the actors as they entered the building. This saved me from making a big speech and wasting time. Our script was dialogue heavy and required actors who knew their craft. I was nervous about this because usually horror films are not that talky, and I was unsure if I could get enough good actors to play these critical roles. I was pleasantly surprised. The actors were so good that there were at least two good choices for every major role. All of our first choices agreed to work for nothing. The script and the complex characters that we created were the reason. A good actor will relish the opportunity to deliver good dialogue.

Since paying actors is usually not an option on a low-budget movie we always encourage actor's input. Be flexible with ideas they might have; try different types of approaches to certain scenes. Remember, they're not being paid and you need them more than they need you.

GARY WHITSON & W.A.V.E: We've gotten our actors from several different sources including local model agencies, advertisements in local papers, and *Backstage*, as well as using friends. We try to make things as relaxed as possible on the set. We try to have as much fun as possible and allow the actors to make suggestions for improving the script or their particular character.

* * *

Director Tom Vollmann (right) on the set of *Dead Meat*.

You've got your actors (for better or for worse). Your crew is ready to go. Now what? Here are some tips that might make your life easier when you are shooting and editing your movie.

Storyboarding

Drawing out your scenes and putting your thoughts down, visually, on paper, can be very helpful in blocking out scenes and coming up with a "look" and style for your movie.

Before I shot one frame of *Vampires & Other Stereotypes* I had drawn out, in comic book style, how I envisioned the scenes. Yet, when it came to actually shooting, and I was dealing with actors, crew members, and special effects—and the schedule started to get far behind—I ended up throwing away these storyboards. This was because each picture I had drawn, each "shot," would take hours of setup time and time was not on my side. In this instance, where I was making my first film, dealing with everything at once as well as trying to do everything at once, story-

boards were a hindrance. I found that they had locked me down too much.

In contrast I didn't even think of storyboarding *Addicted to Murder*. This was because I had specific locations in mind and knew, in my mind, everything that I had to shoot. Because I had spent so much time with the script the storyboard was locked in my head and ultimately the movie turned out 90 percent how I envisioned it.

I think storyboarding is an individualist thing—some people need to plan everything out, some are better and more creative when they're improvising. Try storyboarding—if it doesn't work it doesn't work.

Shooting

I usually go through a scene a few times to figure out the blocking—where the characters are standing and moving while they are delivering their lines. Then, I'll shoot the wide shot a few times, then go in for close-ups, making sure the actors keep the same positions and movements so they'll match when I cut to one to the other. Also, get close-ups of their hands, if reaching for an object, them walking into frame, and so on, so you have something to cut to in editing in case you need it. You'll be thankful for these "cutaways" while editing, believe me.

Also, use lots of motion—zoom, pan, tilt, hand-held following the actors—these all help to make it more visually interesting and become very effective if there's a reason for the motion. For example, if someone is being stalked, maybe you'll shoot hand-held, running after this person, from the stalker's point of view. If you didn't go to film school, read some film theory books and take notes when you watch movies for the things you like.

Recording and Editing Sound

I would say that sound is more important than your picture. For example, people are more willing to watch bad television reception as long as they can hear it, but will refuse to watch anything where the picture is crystal clear but the sound is messed up. Use microphones when you are doing dialogue on your production. Do not use the camera microphone as your main recorder of sound, only as a point of reference. Preferably "boom" all of your audio. By this, I mean have a microphone at the end of a boom pole so you can keep it just out of the frame—it doesn't get in the way, you can move it, walk with it, and so on, and there's only one cable going from it to the camera. I prefer not to use clip-on mics because they are too sensitive (they pick up scratching on shirt, and so forth) and there are too many wires.

With *Vampires & Other Stereotypes* I had several audio people who would "boom" or clip on the mics of the actors and make sure the sound was okay. Unfortunately, the studio we were working in was near some train tracks and every twenty or so minutes we'd have to stop and wait for the thing to pass. This really slowed things down because we tried getting the sound "perfect," time we could have used better by just concentrating on the scenes and worrying about redubbing

or looping the voices later in editing. Next to special effects I think recording sound "live" takes up the most time.

With *Addicted to Murder*, I shot the entire movie here in New York City and New York City is *very* noisy. I knew I was going to have to redo the sound because, even though the microphones I was using were very good, I still picked up extraneous noise such as phones ringing in other people's apartments, traffic noises, and so on. So, we recorded all the sound with a boom mic during the shooting and I was resolved to use whatever I could use and worry about dubbing or looping the unusable stuff later.

Here's how I did this: I edited the entire movie together, bad sound sequences and all. Then, after I was finished with the picture, graphics, and visual effects, then and only then did I set about fixing the dialogue. I would have the particular actor come in one evening when I was on the edit system, sit him down in front of a good microphone that was hooked up to my record deck, and have him watch the segment they're redubbing several times. Then, I'd have him say the lines while they were watching his image or scene coming from the master tape that was playing on the play deck. While he is repeating lines you are making a copy of the film with him repeating the lines on the record deck. Keep on doing it until you feel he gets it. Also, have him do this sentence by sentence. Make sure you are recording on your record deck the entire time. It doesn't matter if you record rewinds, et cetera. If you do this for all the actors you may end up with four to seven tapes of repeated scenes but this will make it easier when you're trying to sync it all up on your master.

When you're all done with recording all the dialogue that needs to be done, you're ready to put this on your master.

Since you've recorded everything chronologically and have a choice of which "take" is the best—and can even adjust it better by plus or minusing frames on the edit system—you can sync up voices exactly. It will take a while but it's the best way to do this. Don't do this on your master tape, though. Do all your sound editing on a copy or submaster (see below).

To avoid this sounding like it's been dubbed over, I kept all the dialogue on channel 1 of the video then added the appropriate ambient noise (room tone, and so on) on to channel 2, which covers up any spots where there isn't any dialogue at all. It doesn't bring attention to itself.

To add all my sound effects, I'd end up with three tapes—one tape with the dialogue and ambient noise, another with all the sound effects (crashes and auto sounds, whatever) and a third with the music. Then, I'd take the dialogue and ambient noise tape and insert it on channel 1 of the master tape. After this I'd mix the other two tapes (sound effects and music) onto channel 2 of the master, riding the levels so that it never interfered with the levels of the dialogue.

For any foreign sales you must have your dialogue and f/x/music tracks separate.

Editing

Logging footage. Going through it and deciding which takes are the best saves you much time in editing. This may take you weeks to do but doesn't cost you any money. You just need your TV, your VCR, and a pen and paper.

Editing Equipment. Once you know where everything is, it is time to edit—on Super VHS, 3/4", or Betacam or a nonlinear system such as Avid or D-Vision, depending on what you have access to. (See the chapter on equipment and format for some ideas about what might work best for you.)

If you go to school, use the school's equipment. If you work at a production house, work out a deal and or barter. If you have to rent a VHS or ¾" system, they are around $150–$200 for a weekend, $300–$400 for Betacam and nonlinear. So you can conceivably get 30-plus hours on the thing between Friday and Monday. If you have no clue how to get access to equipment find someone who can get ahold of equipment.

Off-line and On-line Editing. Off-line editing refers to everything from you logging your tapes to cutting a "rough cut" of your movie.

For example, if you are editing on Betacam SP you usually do a rough cut on S-VHS or ¾" copies first, in order to save money if you're paying for a Betacam edit. Getting access to S-VHS and ¾" editing systems is easier and far cheaper. Copies on S-VHS or ¾" are made from your Betacam masters, with vis code, or visible time code, on the tapes. This appears as a numbered box at the bottom of the screen. These vis codes, or window dubs, can be made at most duplicating facilities. With Betacam, time code is recorded on the tapes for this editing purpose. So, the idea is to edit with these vis code tapes, decide how you're editing the movie without paying huge costs. While you're doing this you have to write down all the numbers on the tapes, making sure to keep track of which tapes the vis code belongs to. When you're all done you will have a list of your edits and the tapes they correspond to. So, when you go to edit on the Betacam system you take your camera originals and know exactly how to put it together. This is referred to as the on-line edit.

With *Vampires & Other Stereotypes* I did a rough cut because I had free access to a ¾" edit system. Then, I did the on-line edit, which I had to pay for, when I had the final cut. This probably saved me a few thousand dollars. By the time I did *Addicted to Murder* I had access to a Betacam SP edit suite and didn't bother to do an off-line. I simply watched, and logged, all my footage beforehand, which took a month, and went directly into the on-line. Since I had no time constraints other than doing this on the system's off hours, I could take my time.

Nonlinear editing. Familiar systems are Avid and D-Vision. Your footage is downloaded onto computer discs and you can edit your system there for the rough-cut. With nonlinear you can easily swap scenes, extend scenes, and generally have more control over editing. Most people use this for an off-line, and once they have their ETD— Edit Decision List (these are all the numbers you wrote down on the ¾" rough cut system, which now are automatically recorded by the nonlinear edit system)—they are ready to do their edit. Other people simply output this computerized image to S-VHS or Betacam and use this as their final edit, as the digitizing of the footage does give it a rather unique "filmlook."

Graphics. The title sequence is very important because it sets the mood and perhaps look of the subsequent movie. I've found the best equipment that's accessible to a low-budget filmmaker are MACS, with programs such as Titleman and Adobe Photoshop. Most on-line edit suites (Betacam and ¾") are equipped with computers. If you are unfamiliar with the technology, find someone who is through all the usual resources. A good title sequence immediately sucks your viewer in.

Filmlook

"Filmlook" is one of those vague terms currently floating around the low-budget world of independent film (should we say video?) making. Through this process, video is somehow transformed into a supposedly more expensive-looking medium, thereby making it more saleable.

While in the past few years this term "filmlook" has referred to any method of making video look like film, it is a name registered to Wood Holly Productions out in California, the company that came up with one of the best methods of this process. It is also the most expensive, so only the professionals can afford it. Some television programs that use this process are *America's Most Wanted*, cable's *Not Necessarily the News* from a few years back, and FOX's *Down by the Shore* and *Herman's Head* from a few years ago. A recent low-budget feature is my own *Vampires & Other Stereotypes*. Yes, video run through this service looks great, but it's not economically feasible for the low-budget filmmaker.

There are a few companies that have come up with cheaper services—some better than others—and my recommendation is to get a demo reel of just what they can do. Prices range from $500 to $1,000 to do a 90-minute feature.

Yet, even if a lump of money is put aside for a film-as-video process, there are certain preparations for it to work to its best advantage. Videos shot in 1", ¾" SP, and Betacam SP work the best, while Hi-8 and S-VHS are marginal. Also, when shooting, the camera lens must be diffused with a nylon stocking or diffusion filter to take the hard edge off the video and quick left to right motions for actors or objects must be avoided or they'll appear staggered. In other words, don't "filmize" your martial arts epic or it will look a little crazy.

But if you're limited as to how you shoot, and have to pay this extra expense, is it really worth it to run your video picture through a filmizing process? Is it really going to make it easier to sell to a distributor? I think it will. What it will definitely do, from the best process to the mediocre, is make your video more watchable. There's just something annoying about watching a narrative shot on video—it's like watching an afternoon soap or something on the BBC. It is much more accepted that narrative be shot on film. In fact, it's expected.

How do these processes actually make the video look like film? First, it's taking the video's 30 frames per second and changing it to film's 24 frames per second. Video is much more "real" than film because the 30 frames make everything so much clearer— the eye is taking in more information. Film, usually projected at 24 frames per second, has a slight strobe—and when you're watching a film your mind accepts this sense of motion as part of it. When the video image is changed from 30 to 24 frames per second your mind registers it more like film, what it is accustomed to watching in a narrative.

Graininess is also added to the video. All film has some grain to it—Super 8mm more than 16mm and 16mm more than

35mm—which gives the medium a particular texture. Video only appears to be grainy when shot under low light conditions, a time when video conditions are poor and the footage unusable. Because video cameras need light to have a good image, the only way to get this grain is to run it through a film-as-video process—and further the film illusion.

One of the reasons for shooting video with diffusion on the camera lens is that video, shot at 30 frames per second and needing much more light, is far crisper than film. Film, on the other hand, tends to be a bit blurred when it's projected. For example, the sharpness of film depends on its size—with Super 8mm the blurriest as the smallest; 35mm and 70mm the sharpest since a much larger frame, and more information, is projected. The filmizing process also blurs the video.

There are other film and video differences considered with the film-as-video process, such as color and contrast. Film colors depend on lighting and film stocks. With video it is simply pressing your white balance button on the side of the camera with whatever light you're using. But unlike film, video is limited to the colors it can reproduce. The worst color on video is red. I've seen title sequences in red that are so blurry and fuzzed out they're unreadable. By adjusting the chroma so that these video sensitive colors are muted and don't "bleed," the filmizing process makes the video colors resemble those shot on film. It also simulates film contrasts. Film works very well with contrasts, particularly black and white. Video handles contrasts poorly. You never videotape a man in a black shirt against a white background or shoot window blinds or a striped shirt without getting that tell-tale "humming" on the picture. Many of these film-as-video processes make the video more film-like by increasing the contrast ratio of the video, making these contrasts darker. This trick succeeds, like the others, in deceiving your eye that it is watching film, not video.

So, if all of this stuff has been done to the video, basically changing everything video is, why not just shoot the feature on film? Again, cost. Film stock alone will probably be twice that of the best film-as-video process and still everything you shot may not turn out, from bad film stock to a jammed film gate. Even if all the film does turn out, there is the added expense of doing a film-to-tape transfer, an addition of several thousand dollars. In contrast, video is extremely user friendly for the low-budget filmmaker. You don't have to worry about what you taped turning out—you have the immediate gratification of knowing that what you see is what you shot. The video camera frees you up, things can be done quicker and cheaper, which is really the reason these film-as-video processes are around to begin with.

7. The First Film: How Long Does It Take?

In my opinion it shouldn't take more than a year to write and polish the script, a half-year for preproduction and organization, and no more than another year from the time you first start shooting to the time you edit your last scene.

You have to be stubborn and persistent, not easily dissuaded from making your movies. And you have to be out there *doing* things—not just talking about them. Since graduation from college I've come across dozens of gaffers, editors and camera people who will talk endlessly about how they're putting a "deal" together for a million dollar movie or how they've written a script and it's being "sent around."

What do they have to show for this? Nothing—and the same people who were talking about this years ago are the same people who are still waiting for their big deal. With all the energy and time they've put into phone calls, meetings, and rejection, they could have made a movie. Maybe talking about it makes them feel it has more of a chance of becoming real.

Well, I've no use for talkers. If a million dollars isn't going to land in your lap, I guess you aren't going to make a million dollar movie. Given a choice between making a film and not making one, which would be more satisfying?

Vampires & Other Stereotypes took a year and a half from the time I first started shooting to the last day of editing, and *Addicted to Murder* took exactly six months from shooting to completion. The reason the second one took far less time than the first was because my organizational skills had improved and because *Addicted* was more thought out in terms of blocking scenes and editing. While I was shooting *Addicted* I had in mind how the final project was going to fit together. I also gave myself a self-imposed time limit on the project, which I stuck to, no matter what. I worked on it twenty hours a week, if not more, for four months, sacrificing weekends, editing until four in the morning during workdays.

It will definitely take a year to do your first feature, but try not to let things drag out longer than two years. A project that never seems to end can be depressing, and you'll bring yourself down, particularly if you're one of these people who has to finish a thing or they go nuts (yes, you know who you are).

Making a film can be all-consuming, and even though it's something you want to do, you don't want it to be everything you do all the time for *years*. This is a big reason why there are two- and three-year gaps between my films.

THE INTERVIEWEES WERE ASKED,
How long did it take to make your first film?

ARSENAULT: *Night Owl* took two-and-a-half years to shoot, and about three years to complete. Why? I would raise enough money to shoot for two days, so I would shoot. Then I would stop, raise enough money for another day. And so on. At this rate, I thought the picture would be completed in six months. The first half of the film took only five months to complete. The second half took a staggering two years! Why? I ran out of people to ask for money. *Night Owl* started shooting on December 18th, 1989, and wrapped sometime in April or May of 1992. With the same cast! And the funny thing was, the lead character was a man who hadn't aged in forty years!

I finished editing in the fall of '92, got the first answer print around January of '93, and had the "world premiere" on June 30, 1993, in Hollywood, California.

I learned my lesson with my second feature. I raised enough money to shoot the entire film at once. The downside was I didn't bother to raise the money to edit until months and months later.

BALLOT: It took four years to create *The Bride of Frank*, mostly shooting on weekends and editing at night. Most people aren't in a position to leave their day jobs so they're relegated to working on their movies when they have spare time. I quit my job to finish the movie and the last six months of production was a full-time endeavor.

BERGER: We were careful with preproduction so everything was scheduled pretty tightly. No major surprises. This is because of a wonderful crew—small as it was—and superlative cast. We got *Sins* "in the can," so-to-speak, in twelve days—that's a 108-page script. Plus two or three days for second unit shots and voice-overs. I off-line edited a rough cut inside of a month. It was the fine-tune edit and on-line and sound mix that consumed time. Mainly, securing the equipment for trade of services or special "buddy" fees. It took roughly another full year to finish postproduction.

BONK: My first film actually took about two-and-a-half months to shoot, but it could have been a lot shorter! I originally started with a whole different person in the lead. Our original plan was to shoot four days a week for a month's time. But eventually, this actor started showing up later and later, less and less, and then not at all. Though he was having personal problems, and I was trying to be sympathetic, I was slowly running out of both time and money. And I figured if this movie failed to get made I would never get another chance! So I contacted another moviemaker and brought Matthew Jason Walsh in, whose work I had seen in *Midnight 2*, knowing he could do a fine job in the role, and shot straight for two-and-a-half weeks. Sometimes the crunch shoot involved very early or very late hours, but we did manage to pull it off.

Then it took me five weeks to edit, but nearly a year to box and begin to sell. My first cover was done through a local photo house as a clam-shell design. It took them a month just to design, and then technical problems sent it back in, where it stayed for nearly another month. From there, I finally set about marketing it for a few months, but a friend in the biz suggested I would have a tough time selling it if it wasn't in the professional "sleeve" format. He recommended a friend who worked wonders with the old design, and delivered a much sleeker box. But there was a problem on that layout, too—the cover was $\frac{1}{16}$" too short in front. It was then sent back to be fixed but since that cover guy was now doing another cover for me he waited until that one was ready as well before sending them in to be printed. Finally, it came back, and the movie sold like hotcakes. Then on December 31st, 1996, I discontinued it. I hated it! Someday, when I'm a rich man, I'm going to go around and buy all the copies back!

BOOKWALTER: *The Dead Next Door* was written in August 1985; Sam Raimi became involved in the next month and we didn't start shooting until June 1986. We finished the picture edit in December 1988 and locked the sound in April 1989. So, it was basically four years, and then the movie didn't come out on video until mid–1990. Usually the reason for such delays would be money, but since Raimi was bankrolling it, that wasn't a great problem. What *was* a drag was that we would work to get so far on the movie and then send it to him for approval, which would often take months. During the time it took to make *DND*, Sam shot, finished and released *Evil Dead 2* and developed *Darkman*! I understand that he was busy and *DND* took a backseat to his larger efforts, but that was really the big stumbling block. Before he put up any more cash, he had to approve what was happening at each stage. Usually there were no changes or problems ... I think Sam is just used to being a control freak and didn't want us off doing anything that he didn't approve. Had I known that was going to be the situation in advance, I probably would have went ahead and shot another movie with all of the money we were wasting on an office and the overhead!

CAMPISI: My first completed film took several weekends to shoot. It was shot on Super 8mm film, and a mere five minutes long. My resources were limited, considering I was twelve years old at the time.

In subsequent years, many films took the same amount of time, and some took considerably longer. *The Law* took over two years. I was eighteen years old, right out of high school. The film was shot on VHS, and for what it was—considering the budget of

International film star Caroline Munro on the set of *Night Owl*, a film written, produced and directed by Jeffrey Arsenault. Co-Producer June Lang. ©1993 Franco Productions.

a few thousand dollars, using friends as actors—it didn't turn out too bad. Looking back, it was a great learning experience.

Today, films will take as long to shoot as their budgets and effects will dictate. The standard Hollywood film takes an average of ninety days to shoot. These are the big budget projects. The lower budget films shoot in about half that time due to the financial restraints. Remember, time is money. And the more time you spend on the set, the more money is being spent to keep those people and equipment there.

Then there's the postproduction, editing and music score. This can add several more months to the overall time necessary for production.

An independent film, however, does not have to follow any of these guidelines. If you're just shooting on the weekends and stuff, with limited funds, you can take all the time in the world. Just make sure your actors don't age in between the scenes.

The living dead on the set of Ron Bonk's *The Vicious Sweet*.

CRAMER: A "week" of shooting generally takes about three actual weeks since most often it's done at night and on weekends. It would be nice to set aside a week-and-a-half or so and go for it—but most cast and crew members have "real" jobs during the week and you just have to accommodate them.

FORD: From start to finish, *Alien Force* took about six months. Mark Gordon, the producer, wanted to get something into production very quickly in order to prepare a trailer to sell the movie at the MiFed market in Italy. So, I wrote the script—from a solid outline—in about a week. We were casting and preparing all the makeup effects and wardrobe and props and whatever else while I was still writing the script. We went into production the week after that. We shot for eleven days straight, twelve hours a day. The trailer was cut and we sold a lot of contracts to various foreign markets at MiFed. Then, based on conversation from film buyers at the market, we decided to add our "name" actor, Burt Ward, to the movie. I came up with the concept of having Trace—our hero—converse with his leader back on his planet via a viewer device so that we could integrate Burt into the entire movie, not just have him pasted on at the beginning and the end of the picture. I wanted it to feel like he was actually part of the plot, not an afterthought. I think it worked very well. So, we set that up and shot Burt Ward in a single location in one day and Tyrone's reactions in different locations on a second day. Then editing the movie took a long, long time. The sound editing work, too. Then the on-line. Then we sent a final tape to Texas to have the special effects put in by Tim Thomson. That took some time. Then more on-line. The on-line facility also provided us with a "film-look" process. Finally, we had a completed movie, nearly six months after beginning. Don't know where the time went.

GALLAGHER: *Dead Silence* [first film], which I only sold in one issue of *Draculina*, was shot over a six-month period. We had one problem after another. The lead actress was supposed to come in from California but

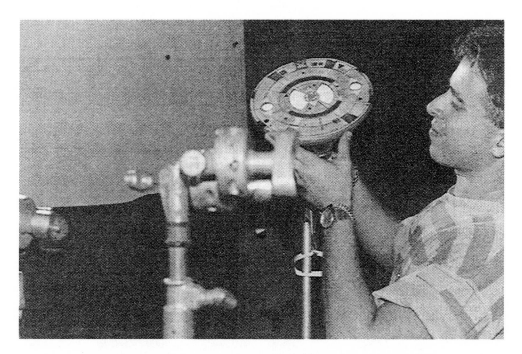

Gabe Campisi working on a miniature spaceship on the set of *The Law*.

backed out at the last minute, leaving us stranded in the airport waiting for her. I then took a local to fill her place and she sucked royally. We kept shooting on weekends and holidays over the next six months. At one point I knew the movie was not going to go anywhere, but I was determined to finish it anyway. Once it was over the lead actress tried to sue me for money, and I just said "fuck it" and put in on a shelf.

GINGOLD: It has taken a long time—too long, I must admit—to finish *Mindstalker*. Filming took the better part of two years, which is not such a bad thing; when you, your crew and your actors are holding down jobs or attending college, and all the money is coming out of your own pocket, it can take a long time to get the footage you need. The real delay came in postproduction, due partially to the way I went about it. After having all my footage transferred to 1″ video, I had timecoded VHS dubs made of all my reels and set about putting together a rough and then a fine cut edit. Because I didn't own VHS editing equipment myself, or know any-

one who did, I had to do this work at a facility in Manhattan, and it took a long time to get the movie into a state where I was happy with it.

This goes back to my comments about my script; since it wasn't locked before I started shooting and some of the scenes weren't completely thought through on paper, it took a lot of work to make them play on screen. And there was something else I discovered while making *Mindstalker* that I'm not sure is true for everyone, but that I feel very strongly: No matter how much you write and rewrite, no matter how much coverage you shoot, you'll never really know how anything's going to play until you've cut it together and watch it on a screen. Scenes that you think will play perfectly don't; things that you thought didn't work while shooting will prove to be great; exposition that seemed vital during the scripting stage will be dead weight; performances will both disappoint and surprise you. I went through several different cuts before I finally arrived at a version of *Mindstalker* I could consider "done"; in the process, the running time dropped from 93 to 78 minutes, minus credits. One of the advantages of working on the indie level is that no one's standing over your shoulder forcing you to finish by a certain date; you can take as much time as you want—though for God's sake, don't take over six years like I did—to get it right.

HOWE: It took Howard and me two years to make *Sins* from when we started writing to dubbing the mixed audio onto our on-lined picture. This kind of schedule isn't uncommon in our world, mainly because we all have to hold down paying jobs as well as making movies. If we were working on it twelve hours a day, we could have done it in half that time, and probably made a much better film. Unfortunately, real life intrudes.

Don't rush. When I first got out of school I had this immature idea that I was so cool and creative that I could write a great script in ten days. And to prove it, I wrote a few. Of course, they sucked and the perspective of a few years showed me that. It takes time to write a good script, shoot solid footage, and edit that into a watchable movie. Rushing out and making half a dozen video features in a couple of years might give you a nice ego boost, but it won't result in good movies. Take the time to think about what you're doing. Quality, not quantity, should be the watchword of the micro-budget filmmaker. After all, how long is the wait between Cronenberg's movies? Or Kubrick's? If you really want to get a career going, making one great movie is going to do more for you than making ten shitty ones.

JACOBS: *Walking Between the Raindrops* took about one month to film and another month to edit. It would've only taken about two weeks to film but Rachel, who played the lead role of Sarah, came down with mononucleosis. So not only was I starting filming at 9:30 P.M., I had to have her home by 12:00 A.M. One night I had her home at 1:30 A.M., and she was too sick to film the next night. Other than that, the filming went fine. The editing would've been done quicker, but I

was at the mercy of the schedule of my friend, whose editor I was using in his home. Appeasing everyone's schedule was somewhat hard, but I did my best. I learned a lot about some people, and I realized who was reliable and who wasn't.

LEGGE: The time it takes to do a feature film under low budget circumstances is almost overwhelming. If you script it thoroughly like I do, going through rewrites, putting it aside, looking at it again with fresh eyes, et cetera, the screenplay can take six months to a year. Then if you have no acting resources to draw upon, that search begins. It may take another few months to find suitable people. Then, once you have that done, you've got to schedule this small army of cast and crew. It is the common rule that everyone has a "real" job they must attend to in order to do things like eat, clothe themselves, and avoid sleeping in shipping crates. Therefore, you usually have to do your shooting on weekends. I've learned over the years to do three things:

(1) Schedule the entire shoot, be it six months, nine months, whatever, but give them definite dates! Don't try to schedule things on the fly, or you're going to hear constant excuses like, "Sorry, I'm getting married that day," "Sorry, I got to go do this stupid family thing or my wife will kill me," "Sorry, I'm shampooing my carpets today." From the beginning, instill people with that feeling of commitment. If you can square away the dates from the get-go, people tend to feel obligated, and only the most obtuse ones will forget to show up, or go ice skating instead.

(2) Don't do long shooting days. If you feel comfortable with it, do a storyboard for every shot you intend to get on a day, and try not to keep your people there for more than three hours at a time. I stagger my scheduling so although I may be there for three hours the actors

are there only when they're needed, and they can leave when done.

(3) Don't forget to make it fun for everyone. There's a fine line to walk here, but some elementary rules apply. Don't yell at anyone, no matter how hard you want to. If you have a problem with someone, take them aside privately and talk reasonably with them. Most people will resent any public humiliation of themselves, so keep your temper. Keep your schedule moving, but don't crack the whip constantly. People need small rests between takes, to get back into gear. Keep the set atmosphere light and cooperative, and you'll have a happy crew who will want to work with you again. So after all that's done, now you've got to edit and soundtrack the thing. In video you're probably editing it yourself, so depending on your experience and knowing what you want to see, it will take you weeks to do this. Unless you already have sophisticated sound equipment, you're probably better off spending some money on a pro sound mix. Many areas have media centers with reasonable rates, and some public TV stations have low rates for their studios. So what have you got here now? Maybe two years of work? Are you sure you really want to do this? Right now, I'm scaring myself, and I've been doing this for twenty years.

McCLEERY: As far as length of time from the start of your production to the end … it really varies on how much work and at what intensity you put that work into it. I've done feature length projects that from start to finish took three months and one that took four years. But what I would say so your project doesn't take four years is to have a plan on how to finish your movie before you start. Don't say "I'll worry about that when I get there." That's what I said on *The Killing of Bobby Greene* and it took me four years to finish. Lay it out on paper and have a plan on each stage of preproduction, production,

and postproduction. You should really go as far with your plan as to have a distribution plan worked out as well. There is no guarantee that it will all go as you wrote it down but at least you will have thought things through and be ready for some of the problems that will arise.

McCRAE: It took me twenty-six years to make my first film; I guess I don't get bored very easily. But if you want to get technical, I shot *Shatter Dead* in ten days—eleven, if you count one day for stunts and makeup effects—over the course of a three-month summer period so I could stagger the shoot money from my paycheck and still afford rent and food. I wrote the thirty-page screenplay—with some drastically different scenes than what ended up on screen—in twenty-four days. The day before I started writing anything down, I called my friend Matthew Howe [cowriter and codirector of *Original Sins*] and asked him if he could shoot a video project for me over the summer if I could write it fast enough so it wouldn't interfere with his schedule as a cinematographer; he gave me an enthusiastic affirmative.

But there's no need to rush your first feature; it's probably going to be your calling card for a couple of years, so you want to make it as good as it can possibly be. Staggering my shoot over an entire summer made it less exhausting for the cast and crew of friends I was stealing the weekends from; ten days straight can be far more tiring and demoralizing when you can't afford to pay the crew. Also, it helps to maintain your friendships this way, which I think is very important. After all, you really can't afford to lose your friends until you're rich enough to buy new ones.

MURPHY: My first film was *Steps*. It was a forty-minute student film. It took forever because no one put a time limit on me. I wanted it to be perfect, too. I think I spent three years at college making it. [Laughs.] I don't plan to do that again.

Hardcore rocker Henry Rollins (right) and Shaun Irons in Blair Murphy's *Jugular Wine.*

My first feature length film was *Jugular Wine*. That took me even longer, about five years, because I never had much money in the bank at any one time. And post took forever. Even after you cut and lock your picture the sound mix is like a big bomb waiting to trap you at the end of all your work.

POLONIA BROS.: It took us about three months, a whole summer, to make *Splatter Farm*, our first film. It didn't see distribution until three-and-a-half years later. Filmmaking at our level is difficult because most of us have the responsibility of full-time jobs, families of our own, access to equipment at limited times—the list goes on and on. The important thing to remember is to always remain passionate about what you do and evaluate yourself honestly. You can brag yourself to everyone you know and meet but the proof is in the pudding: Your films. It is also a good point to make that as a filmmaker you should try and encourage others and offer helpful advice. I have noticed a disturbing trend in many independent magazines for

other filmmakers to feud needlessly with each other because of what one person thinks about this person's films and so on. Who cares! You are always going to find someone who does not like what you do, or thinks that their films are better.... Just concentrate on where you are at and strive to always do better. Sure, it's easy to get angry when someone trashes your movie in print or attacks you personally. It's happened to everyone. That doesn't mean they are right. It's their opinion. Learn to take criticism with a grain of salt.

RITTER: *Day of the Reaper* was my first feature-length film. It took me all of the summer of 1984 to shoot it, and I think I finished in late September or early October with the final shooting. It was edited and released on video in November 1984.

Shooting took all summer because basically I didn't know what I was doing. My cousin Joe Preuth and I made the movie and financed it, pooling our dishwashing money together. As we shot, we got into creative differences over who would direct and what the movie would be. We both thought up the story, so we were both very close to the project. Then effects started not working out too well.... I had that Savini book *Grande Illusions* and we were trying to imitate his effects very unsuccessfully, and we ended up going the H.G. Lewis route and just dumping blood and food parts from work all over the victims.

Also, our lead actress turned out not to be a very good actress, so we killed her character off early and used one of the other girls in a minor role as the lead. The script fell apart early on, and we ended up improvising a lot of scenes, not recording what we were saying at the time! Later, during dubbing, we ad-libbed again, and that's why some of the dialogue is so off-sync; we were saying totally different things on camera than we were during postproduction! The movie was shot with Super 8mm film silent equipment.

I almost gave up on *Reaper*. After all the problems, I just looked at the footage, said "forget it," and started editing it together about three weeks later! I really don't know why—I guess I like to finish things I start.

We had a local guy do original music and it came out real good. It was the first time I had original music in one of my films, so that was exciting. The score wasn't bad, and it helped move the thing along.

When *Reaper* was finished, I actually thought it was really good. I had pride in it, mainly because it was done in the spirit of an H.G. Lewis movie: finished and released no matter how bad or good it was.

I had taken a role in *Reaper* as a cop, mainly so I wouldn't have to rely on another actor showing up on the set all the time. Anyway, *Reaper* played at this sci-fi horror show and I was awarded "the worst actor as a cop" award at this show! Needless to say, I gave up my acting career right there.

The important thing for a first film is to take your time. Get it done at your own pace; there's no rush. Do the best you can with what you have, and then go for it! If you are able to look back at your first film ten years later and see how much you've improved, then you're succeeding. You should feel comfortable with each project being seen, and then each one should get better. But you have to put all your energy, your best shot, into each and every movie. You will always learn from each project.

I thought *Reaper* was a work of art when I was sixteen years old. Now I look at it and laugh at it so hard I could almost cry. But believe it or not, the thing still sells! People ask to buy it all the time just to see how I started out. It's not bad for a high school kid that had no money, I guess.

Twisted Illusions, *Wicked Games*, and *Creep* were all shot on weekends around people's work schedules. *Truth or Dare* and *Killing Spree* had a little more hard cash behind them than the other movies, so they were scheduled and shot in twelve consecutive days straight each.

I think another thing to remember as a filmmaker is that *quality* is important, not *quantity*. These films are going to stay with you the rest of your career, so do the best you can with each one. I'm not embarrassed by *Reaper*, for I know I did my best and took the time I needed to get it the best that I could with the equipment I had access to: Super 8mm silent gear.

I know plenty of film-video makers who shot terrible projects on two or three day shooting schedules. Later, they have to explain why the movies are so bad or they take their names off the projects altogether. I'd rather have my name on a few decent projects than two hundred horrible ones that never improve. You should grow as a filmmaker with each experience and movie. We probably shot twenty to twenty-five actual days on *Reaper*. A feature-length movie should always take between fourteen to thirty shooting days, sometimes more with pickup shots, et cetera.

Remember, give yourself time to lens your vision.

STANZE: Making my first movie took about the same amount of time as my other

Eric Stanze (left), executive producer, writer and director of *Ice from the Sun* with producer Jeremy Wallace.

movies. The organizational aspects of production were pretty easy for me to figure out early on. The only differences in amount of time taken to make each movie result from how much or how little I spread out the shooting schedule. *The Scare Game* was shot over two continuous weeks. *The Fine Art* was shot over three continuous weeks. *Savage Harvest* was shot over nine days of continuous shooting, plus every weekend for four months. *Ice from the Sun* will be shot during sixteen days of continuous shooting and travel, plus every weekend for five months. The reason the shooting schedules keep getting longer is because I'm spreading things out more now. In the past, I would drive my cast and crew into the ground, sometimes having them endure back to back twenty-hour shooting days. I have since realized how much this risks the health of my team. So now I spread things out a lot more. As far as the preproduction goes, all of my movies have been prepared in an average of nine months. This includes writing the screenplay as well as other preproduction duties.

The most important element of preproduction is organization. If you plan out specific dates to shoot specific scenes and effectively communicate these dates to your cast and crew, you will avoid chaos on the set as well as the resulting need to reschedule scenes. Secure and double confirm your locations before you schedule your shoots there. Select your cast and as soon as possible give them a specific shooting schedule. Give as much advance notice to special effects artists, letting them know exactly when and where effects are going to be shot. For effects-heavy movies, an effects unit shoot after principle shooting is advisable. Type up all the information about the entire shoot and give copies to everyone involved. Select a production team member to continuously call and reconfirm all dates with everyone involved in the shoot. While organized preplanning is very important, a good director/producer must be prepared to make spontaneous decisions under pressure. On something as complex as a movie production, everything will not go smoothly all the time. Be ready to think up alternatives when problems arise. All of your cast and crew will be standing there looking at you for answers, so be prepared to handle the pressure.

THOMPSON: Which first film? When I was ten I would crank one out in a weekend. My first feature was shot in fourteen consecutive days. Cutting and scoring took another year. For my first feature I got lucky enough to have Jim Nicholson score it. He was in school at the time and cranked it out in a few days. Some things go so fast and others take so long. Hurry up and wait is the saying of the industry. Money can be a waiting factor. But my personal hell has been more the waiting for a favor to be available or the waiting on someone's schedule. Of course the need to make a living tends to get in the way. *Contact Blow* took a couple of years as well. But there were some mitigating factors. I did a whole rough cut first. I played that for responses from peers so that I could get some thoughts on what worked and what didn't work. This was extremely useful for content and I intend to do it again, but this time on nonlinear equipment so that I can use what worked as is rather than having to start cutting all over again. This will save me months. And every day saved actually saves more days because as time drags, it is harder and harder to motivate towards the finish line.

THOMSON: There's a cute little rule about costs, quality and the time it takes to pull off any type of film or video project. Think of a triangle, and on one corner you have "cheap," and on another corner you have "good," and on the third corner you have "fast." Now, the rule is, you can have only one side. That is, in doing your project, you can usually arrange to have two of the three attributes. You can do something fast and cheap, but it won't be good. If you want good and fast, it takes moolah. Conversely, if you need something to be good and cost less, you have to take your time. The low-budget filmmaker has to take very slow, careful steps to create good material.

No Resistance took over four years. Half a year to gear up enthusiasm, a year to produce a decent script, a year to prepare and shoot it. And a year-and-a-half or so to post-produce it. It was an excruciatingly slow process. But it was worth it.

Most of the early time was spent just gearing up ... lining up people to take part and really have them commit to it ... time to arrange all the locations, build the props, get all the planning in order. The shooting took only seventeen days, total ... but those seventeen days were spread out over almost five months, because of the difficulties in arranging schedules, preparing equipment, and the like. And in the end, editing took so long because we simply didn't have the money to do it right away, so we hung back and waited until it could be done right. Again, at every step, it was more important to just figure out a way to get it done, than anything else ... and that can be time-consuming. If you believe you can do it, and have good people behind you, it will work out.

ULRICH: It took me a year to make my first movie. One of the reasons it took so long was a lack of experience. When making a movie you're guaranteed to run into problems; it's just a fact of life. My advice to anybody making their first film is make a few short films first and learn from your mistakes. And that's another fact of life, you're gonna make mistakes. My second movie only took six months because I learned a lot from the mistakes on my first movie and I had things more organized. The key to a smooth shoot is good preproduction; you almost can't lose.

VOLLMANN: From script to postproduction *Dead Meat* took two years. The script took three months, casting and preproduction two months, and principle photography eight months. The post production took nine months. Since our movie was shot on film, getting the film in the "can" plus postproduction work took a lot longer than something shot on video. For instance, with a shooting ratio of three to one [one good take out of three] we would only average 2–4 minutes of usable footage in a day. The reason for this is:

(1) Lighting is much more difficult for film than video. On video, you set up your lights and check a monitor to see how it looks. On film you must take exposure readings with a light meter, which takes twice as long as video.

(2) With film we would rehearse scenes longer and in more detail so as to not waste precious feet of film. On video, you can see exactly what you're getting by looking on a monitor. Rehearsal isn't as important.

(3) Film needs to be sent out and processed, so it's hard to move onto other scenes before seeing what your unprocessed film looks like.

(4) Sound: When miking for film, camera noise can be a problem, unless you purchase an expensive lead barney [camera cover] to drown out the camera's motor, you must painstakingly try and position your mike so as to eliminate the annoying sound of the camera.

(5) Special effects: These always take long hours to do, especially if you want them to look convincing.

(6) Actors' schedules: Remember, actors have lives as well as jobs. Many times we had to shoot around someone's vacation time or a child's birthday. This adds months to your shooting schedule.

(7) Equipment failure: Film equipment is more mechanical compared to video. It must be cleaned and maintained more than video equipment. Breakdowns are more likely to occur with film than video.

(8) Postproduction: Editing film is time-consuming. First you must sync your sound takes to your film takes. This would go quickly, provided the editing table cooperated with us. Next, we would select the best shots and assemble scenes. Some days we'd be lucky if we'd get one three-minute scene edited in an eight hour day. Since we all had jobs we did the editing at night and on weekends.

After six months we had finished film editing with matching dialogue. Now, we needed to add music, sound effects, and an ambient track to complete the soundtrack. Each track has to be recorded and synced to the almost two hour film. This took months. Mixing, which was fun, added another two to three months. With our film ready for video transfer we carted it off to Los Angeles to complete our postproduction. Now there are two ways to transfer film to tape: one is Telecine, the other is Rank. We chose Telecine because it cost about one-fifth of what a Rank transfer would cost. Telecine isn't bad if you are just using it for dailies; however, for a finished product that you hope to sell, Rank is well worth the extra money. We ended up doing our Telecine transfer twice before we were satisfied. This not only added an extra $600 to our budget, but added three more months of reediting to make our second transfer more palatable. As you can readily see, shooting on film, at least the way we chose to do it, was quite time-consuming. But the experience gained in learning how a film is made using a hands-on approach will benefit me as I move on to other more challenging projects.

WHITSON & W.A.V.E: It took over a year before the movie we first started with was completed. It started out as *Sisters* and became *Stalked* after a few revisions. When we first started it, it was just for fun so one guy played two parts. But when we decided to sell it, we had to change the original idea and rework it. So the original idea using Daylight Savings Time as a major plot point was scrapped and it just became a slasher movie involving twins.

8. Publicity

So, your direct to video feature is done. Before you get boxes made (which you will have to in order to distribute your film) you should send out copies or "screeners" to the various magazines for reviews and, perhaps, articles. Good reviews and publicity always helps. While you may not get coverage in a magazine like *Fangoria* (though they are doing features on underground filmmakers), you will get reviews in the smaller magazines and fanzines such as *World of Fandom*, *Screem*, and *Alternative Cinema*. Also, keep in mind that while one magazine will rave about your film, another may think it's terrible. Remember, you're dealing with individual tastes. Ultimately, what positive reviews will get you are some good quotes for the video box cover or a future magazine advertisement. Publicity is only good in the sense that it gets your name out there to an audience. Publicity does not necessarily generate video sales.

Magazines and Fanzines

I have found it true that editors of magazines do not reply to inquiries. So it's best to go ahead and send that copy of your film for review, along with a "press kit." This includes the list of actors and crew, a synopsis of the film, and any information on the production. Also include two or three slide dupes or photos if you want them to print a picture.

You may also want to put a visible time code or the words "For Screening Purposes Only" at the bottom of the screen of these screener copies. This is a preventive measure against people making copies and pirating your tapes. Most tape duplication facilities provide this service.

The cheapest way to mail your tape is fourth class book rate at the U.S. Post Office. Most of these magazines are published quarterly or only twice a year. Response time may be up to six months.

People never return tapes. If you are sending tapes overseas, make sure you send your tape in the correct format (PAL, SECAM).

See Appendix 2 for a list of magazine and fanzine addresses.

Testing Your Audience

While you are waiting for the reviews and articles you can test your film's response by giving it to a local video store to see how many times it rents within a week. If it rents every day for two weeks this is something you can tell potential distributors in your cover letter. A distributor doesn't have to like your film to buy it—he's just interested in making money.

Magazine Advertising

I have sold a few dozen videos by advertising in various magazines but barely broke even on what I had spent on the ads themselves. Your best bet is to put an ad in a magazine with a higher circulation or find out if a magazine distributes flyers with advertisements with their subscriptions. Some publishers will only charge you $10 to $15 for distributing 500–700 flyers to their magazine subscribers. Even better, include an ad in an issue that you have an article or review in: This enables your potential buyer to know something about the film beforehand. If they're interested in the article, they may be interested in buying the film.

Prices for ads tend to be negotiable to a certain extent. You may be able to work out a deal with the editor where the magazine will not only create an advertisement for you but buy the videos off you for half price (wholesale cost) and sell them via their own ads. This way you don't have to front any money, and you'll still make a profit on the tapes.

THE INTERVIEWEES WERE ASKED,
How important is publicity for your films?

ARSENAULT: I was lucky enough to get some good reviews in some high-profile publications like *Variety* and *Hollywood Reporter*. But this was only because *Night Owl* was screened at a film festival. I think publicity is important and you should start early, but I confess, I'm not very good at it. Most low-budget movies don't have enough money to hire a publicist, but that would help.

BALLOT: Sometimes Hollywood studios spend more on promotion than on production. You can have the greatest movie ever but if nobody knows about it then nobody will see it. Get publicity wherever and however you can. Since we little guys don't have any big time professional PR firms to represent us, it's an uphill battle.

BERGER: Publicity makes your world go 'round. If you slouch in this area then you're a goner. Get your tape to every fanzine or magazine or website worldwide. Luckily, in the case of *Sins*, good word of mouth was instantaneous, especially overseas. And you always have to be grateful when that happens. Also, it definitely humbles this hardened soul whenever a friend or colleague passes a screener on to someone who can make a difference. Any and all press coverage is valuable—if not for that initial project then definitely for the next one! I compile a file of originals just in case I'm ever asked to produce a press booklet. This can happen when trying to entice a foreign distributor who may not be familiar with your work or in acquiring an investor for future projects. Save every word—good or bad—that is written about your film. Better safe than sorry.

BONK: Publicity, of course, is the key. You can have a great looking box, a mini-classic, but if no one sees it, it isn't going to sell! For instance, on *What a Deal*, I sent out a press release to antique magazines and newspapers. I took advantage of free advertising, since most of the publications will print press releases for free. This lead to minimal orders. I then took advantage of reviews, sending copies to related newspapers and magazines, as well as several prominent library publications—being an instructional video, I figured it would fit right in! This again led to a few sales. But I wasn't in a position to place large ads, so I sat back and waited patiently. Now the library publications work very slowly, and it sometimes takes six months to get something reviewed in them. But finally, out came a glowing article in *Library Journal*. That was the one break I needed—sales began to pour in from libraries. More importantly, several new distributors contacted me, wanting to sell my product. Every month I seemed to land a new distributor, and sales have been steady for nearly two years now.

Now, with my horror movies, it's a little different. But there are dozens of B-movie publications—including a few of my own—willing to give what they deem a "cool" movie some press. On top of that, there are literally hundreds of home spun 'zines that will give you coverage and a free ad for a copy of the tape. All it really takes is one glowing review in the right publication for hundreds of fans to come knocking, as well as large scale subdistributors. Or several great reviews in a series of smaller mags.

An alien from *Shadowdance*, directed by Gabriel Campisi.

BOOKWALTER: Certainly publicity is important, but it has to be the right kind. I have this theory that being in *Fangoria* magazine nowadays doesn't mean a whole lot, at least not in the good old days when *Evil Dead* and *Basket Case* were "discoveries." Case in point: I released *Ozone* in January 1994 and made all of my money back—and a small profit—in the same month. The only real publicity up to that point was a piece in *Draculina* and some plugs in my newsletter *The B's Nest*. *Fangoria* finally ran a piece on independent filmmakers which included Leif Jonker, Scooter McCrae, and me in the late spring of 1994, but I didn't see sales jump at all! And very few people commented to me that they even saw the article. Another example: this movie *Sleepstalker* came out a while back. Virtually no coverage in *Fango*, yet it went on to be a big rental hit. It's nice to be in *Fangoria* or other mags and to get an established reputation, but the people who are working on a regular basis are the people we don't hear about much, if at all! So, I'm concentrating less on selling myself to the horror market. Most of the people there either know my name or have heard about or actually seen one of my movies. In the end, it's not about how much press coverage you have, it's about whether or not the movie is any good.

CAMPISI: Publicity is as important as the individual producer dictates it to be. If you're just looking to make films for fun, on weekends, with no commercial or financial gains in mind, then publicity is irrelevant. If you're looking to sell your film or to get notoriety for it, then publicity can make or break you.

My short film, *The Law*, is far from the best film in the world. But because of the publicity it generated, it opened up a million doors for me that otherwise would have been closed. Film festival awards, newspaper and magazine write-ups, and exhibitions all contributed to making the film's success.

Publicity also gives you what is called "a third person endorsement." This means that instead of you telling investors or other producers, "I'm a filmmaker," the articles speak for themselves. The publicity adds clout and credibility to you as a professional. You can gather all your press clippings and awards and assemble a "package" of notoriety to present to interested individuals.

CRAMER: Publicity is very important. *Even Hitler Had a Girlfriend* sold approximately 10,000 units immediately after being praised in the national press. Up until that time the picture had just sort of been "laying there."

FORD: Publicity is everything. Reviews really do help get buyers interested, and they will get you more money. Get people interested in the movie as much as you can. I send tapes to every publication that reviews these kinds of movies. I solicit my friends who are also writers to do features on my movie and send them to fan magazines. I do everything I can to get the word out there.

GALLAGHER: Do I mention *Draculina* a lot? With Draculina Publishing I have a great deal of exposure to the public. I get quite a bit of attention when something is released. I do send copies to magazines that I think might do me some good. We've been written up in a lot of publications with feature articles, and my lead actress from *Gorgasm* is the cover girl and centerfold in *Max* magazine, where they did nothing but talk about the movie. I think it's important, and even bad reviews can work in your favor. Joe Bob Briggs kind of cut down *Gorotica* in his syndicated newspaper column, but he did it in a way that everyone wanted to see it. We sold a lot of copies through that.

GINGOLD: Publicity is important to any film, at least in terms of getting it out there and seen; even if you're not in it to make money, finding an audience is still the ultimate goal of any filmmaker. Of course, I have something of an advantage working at *Fangoria*, so garnering publicity for *Mindstalker* won't be too difficult, but it also allows me to give some advice from experience on the other side.

One of the most important elements in getting your movie covered is providing as much material as professionally as possible. Sending a handwritten letter to a magazine or local newspaper is good, but sending a typed or computer-printed letter, along with a press release and information about yourself and the movie, is better. While you're in production, contact local newspapers and even cable stations; particularly if you're outside the mainstream filmmaking centers, the idea of a movie shooting in the area can seem quite newsworthy. And while you're shooting, make sure you have someone on hand to take photos. Lots of 'em. The more the better, and in color whenever possible. Even if you have to take them yourself in between takes with a little "tourist camera," it's an awful lot better than nothing. No matter how good your film is, or how interesting a person you are, very few magazines are going to run an article on you and your movie if there's nothing to illustrate it with. Also, if you know someone who's an artist or good with photo layouts, have them do up some dynamic poster/ad art to send to people. An arresting image is a good way to get your project noticed.

Still, in the end, the film itself is its own best publicity. Send VHS screeners out to every genre magazine you can track down, give copies to other filmmakers, show it to anyone you think might be interested. Not only will this draw publicity to the movie in question, it can attract people who might want to work with you on future projects, or—in the best of all possible worlds—put money into your next feature.

HOWE: Get all the publicity you can get; anything helps from local TV and newspapers to fanzines and on. We didn't do nearly enough of this on *Sins*. We were lucky enough to get a little piece in *Fangoria* about the shooting of our movie, and it helped us immensely. Call all your local papers and TV stations. Get copies of any and all articles and put them in a package to show to distributors. Try and get favorable quotes from local reviewers or celebrities. Anything helps.

JACOBS: This is of paramount importance. My friend, Mike, who shot *Walking*

Between the Raindrops, said it best—"You haven't done enough publicity until people are calling you to say they're sick of hearing about what you're doing." If you want people to know about what you're doing, it's something you need. If you want screenings, sales, or just notice of what you're doing. However, I am still learning about the best way to achieve publicity. I know a lot of people that do fanzines, so I'm advertising in them, and doing interviews, et cetera. I'm also contacting local newspapers, as well as the big newspapers, and I've had some degree of success. I just think if you want people to know about what you're doing you'll be able to find avenues that are available to you. I didn't know that people really do appreciate video, as in festivals, screenings, organizations, et cetera. I just found them by looking; I wanted to find them. I also think that if you're putting your heart and soul into something, why not publicize? Why not share it?

LEGGE: Somebody said there's no such thing as bad publicity. If your name is out there, good or bad, at least it's out there. If you're an indie, seeking reviews in indie mags, better develop a thick skin fast. Sure, you may think your movie's great but you may find yourself alone in that opinion. When your project is finished, you'll naturally show it to the people involved, but don't go by them. They're prejudiced. If you can show the film in a local venue, do it! Get some complete strangers to see your movie. Find an arts center and see if you can schedule a screening. Rent a hall. Show it. Then show it again. When you feel confident enough, send out copies to reviewers. There's lots of them out there: *Draculina, Alternative Cinema, Video, Cult Movies, Psychotronic*, to name a few. Beware though, because many of the so-called reviewers give themselves a thrill by showing how cleverly they can vivisect your film. You can't let it bother you. Chainsaw reviews full of destructive criticism are worthless. It takes no great wit or insight to say, "this film is a piece of shit."

But, if you get constructive criticism, pay attention. They are seeing things with different eyes. If you hear the same criticism more than once, seriously consider doing something about it. And whatever you do, don't whine about it in print, or worse, send a letter to the editor complaining about it. You're only setting yourself up to be a dartboard again, and they will always have the last word. If you get positive reviews, gather them up and make a press book. If you write and get articles printed about the film, include that, too. Choose photos that convey the type of movie you have. If you don't have a distributor, take out ads. Most classifieds are cheap and display ads are affordable on occasion. Take action. You just went through two years of major crapola; don't keep it a secret.

McCLEERY: Publicity is as important as making the film. I'm sure I don't need to say that you can have made the best underground film in the history of the underground and if no one sees it then who cares. The area of publicity is an area that I am just now exploring because, as a reluctant artist, I would always finish a project and then decide that it wasn't good enough to put out there. I would say that my next project would be the one I would release to the masses. Of course, with this attitude I'd never have anything before the public and then all my work would be for naught. I'm by no means an expert on publicity but it's a matter of getting your name in the underground film press as often as possible. You have to build a reputation for yourself. Actually, my reputation in the underground press has been printed more often as an actor than as a director of my own work. But any mention of your name is a help, because the next time someone sees the name they may be more inclined to give it a closer look.

McCRAE: The publicity for *Shatter Dead* has almost been more important than the film itself; many more people have heard of the film than have actually seen it, which is fine by me if it leads to more work. Initially, one of the reasons I made *Shatter Dead* was not to have a viable product available to the home video marketplace, but to have a completed project that I could present with a screenplay that I was working on at the time to give potential producers a better idea of the kind of style I was going for in my written work. The screenplays I had been writing at that time had seemed so unusual to everyone I presented them to, and I insisted that they were not so strange; I felt that what I needed was a final presentation of a test script so people would better understand the atmosphere I was trying to achieve on paper. As *Shatter Dead* progressed through the shooting stage, I realized that I might actually have something I could show in public without too much embarrassment.

Shatter Dead is now recognized for its "signature" shot of Susan peeking through a bloody hole in a door. This shot wasn't in the script; I storyboarded it the night before we videotaped it, and as we did, everyone gathered around to watch it on the monitor and commented on what a captivating visual moment it was. So when I sent out my first tentative video copies I made a video photo of that shot and stuck it on the bright red box cover with no additional text. When I finally got a video distributor they agreed that this was a great, strong image to have on the box cover. Thankfully, I had saved the door with the bloody hole in it—I *still* have the damned thing!—and redid the image with a film still-camera. That image, with or without text, has come to be *the* representation of *Shatter Dead* in the mind of the public eye.

So after all this, I would have to say that it is very important to have a "signature shot" from a project that produces instant audience—or audience-to-be—recognition. *Dawn of the Dead* has a glowing zombie head on the horizon, *The Exorcist* has the image of Max von Sydow in the night looking up at the bright window of the house, and *Star Wars* has Darth Vader's head floating in space, not to mention the enormously popular

Hildebrandt poster that we all grew up with. I believe that the best "signature shots" are images that are actually in the film and not ones that are created especially for publicity purposes. It's just good old fashioned positive reinforcement to go see a flick with an advertisement image burning in your brain which is suddenly transformed into a meaningful image as it is revealed for the first time in the context of the larger work. One always has to be careful about this kind of thing backfiring, of course; imagine one going to see *Citizen Kane* for the first time after encountering a poster containing a very clear view of a sled with the word "Rosebud" etched across it. Now that would really suck.

You should also not be afraid to send a copy of your project to every possible review outlet in all of creation, from *Cinefantastique* to *Draculina*, and all the letters in-between. Good or bad, a published review is great free publicity. I got lucky in a big way. *Fangoria* was one of the first publications to take notice of *Shatter Dead* in an article on independent filmmakers; normally this is the magazine you work up to after being covered in all the smaller periodicals! It almost made the whole process a little bit anticlimactic. Also, I lost some of the more varied coverage I would have received in other magazines because I had already been "discovered by the mainstream." It's strange to get a response like: "Why do you want us to devote coverage to you when *Fangoria* already has?!" Recently, I've been able to worm my way into some of the other periodicals I like to read, but I cannot deny that it's always kind of cool to see your name in print somewhere.

Did I mention promotional tie-ins like T-shirts or eye-catching flyers that are more than just a Xeroxed order form? Cover the planet with this kind of crap. Rent out a hotel room at the next *Fangoria* convention and arrange a publicity screening in the room for when the show is just ending and people don't know what else to do. Good word of mouth is the best publicity of all; no amount of money or flashy trinkets are gonna buy you that. If your project is as good as it should be to compete in an environment filled with crap, it should be able to withstand the arrows and slings of a group of total strangers with a six-pack sitting down to watch it. Free screenings are a great way to establish to other people your faith in a project and a certain pride at showing off the craftsmanship of it.

MURPHY: It is your job to garner your own publicity for every film you create lest they do not simply reach conclusion and slip away into sad cinema obscurity. Keep pushing it because no one else will push for your work like you can. Even if you do get a distributor keep pushing for your film's publicity on your own. Send a screener copy to everyone—*Everyone!*—and don't ask for them back. Make sure your address and phone number is on them. These free copies are the investment that keeps working. Give them as gifts to magazine editors. Give them as gifts to anyone that might know someone. Try to have some artwork on the cover. A cover makes a big difference—that's the reason why Blockbuster picked up my film. Really, publicity is as much your duty as every other step in the film that came earlier. Just accept it as part of the game—or the job. And if you're shy *get over it!* You're speaking with light, for Christ's sake, at the end of the millennium. You're a filmmaker. Cultivate your voice in every way possible. Put it out there. It doesn't just stop with film in the can. Be loud. Be naked. Be magical already and don't give up. Even if everyone hates your film *still* keep putting it out there. Audacity, boldness, persistence: these are your insane commodities that only you can create. So go nuts.

POLONIA: Publicity is vitally important. You can make a great movie, but if no one knows about it what good does it do? Place ads in magazines, get reviews from other filmmakers and critiques. Stay out there and keep pushing. Eventually you will get noticed.

RITTER: Publicity can make or break your project. If you notice for big Hollywood event films, the *hype* starts months in advance. You start reading about these movies and seeing clips and teasers for them months ahead of time. This is to insure that people know about the films and are hopefully eagerly awaiting their arrival.

The same goes for smaller independent films. Whether you're shopping your film at the festivals or self-distributing it, your only hope of making a dent in your market is to get the film noticed. Now Hollywood can pour millions of dollars worth of advertising into projects to publicize them and, obviously, the independent can't. But what you can do is hype your own movie in local papers and national magazines. Develop a hook, or hook into a controversy with your project that starts people talking about it. Sometimes you do this by accident as you're publicizing your movie. With *Wicked Games* I went on a local talk show to promote the movie and ended up making a comment on how the local film liaison office did not help me out as an independent; and this comment mushroomed into a major political controversy! They edited my comments out of the show in reruns, and then it became a censorship issue. *Wicked Games* was in the headlines all over Florida for a solid month in every major newspaper! That helped put my name out there and sell the movie. *Wicked Games* became "that independent Florida movie that challenged the system." It helped sales immensely.

Reviews help sell your movie in the press, too. If you can get an established filmmaker or a well-known critic to give your movie a good review or blurb before it's released, this can help your cause, too. So always give that a shot. Keep in mind, Stephen King's blurb about Sam Raimi's *Evil Dead* is what put the movie on the map and created all the distribution interest.

When you finish shooting a movie, that is the time to begin mailing out stills and press releases on it to the magazines. These magazines need plenty of lead time, sometimes as

A Current Affair visits Kathy Willets and Tim Ritter on the set of the horror-thriller *Creep*.

much as six months. So by the time they run your story, the movie will be just coming out. It's hard to time these things, but it can be done. Be sure to take plenty of still pictures on your set—you'll need them for press kits and releases.

When I'm ready to release a film, I time my magazine articles ahead of time and go on a mini "publicity tour." I hit the news shows—local and national if possible; my story for *Truth or Dare* got picked up by CNN in 1986 and *Creep* was covered by *A Current Affair* in 1994—radio stations—I ended up being interviewed with H.G. Lewis in 1994 while promoting *Wicked Games*—local newspapers, genre magazines—*Fangoria, Draculina, Film Threat*—and talk to anyone else that will listen. Now I did not *plan* to be on CNN or interviewed with H.G. Lewis or on *A Current Affair*. These things just happened in the process of promoting myself and a particular project. You can achieve this, too, just by getting out there and publicizing. You have to become your own PR manager. No one is going to come to you, so it's a concen-

trated effort on your part to get out there and hustle. It gets tiring and old sometimes talking about the same movie and events over and over again, but try to keep it fresh and exciting. Always be enthusiastic and try to hold back in giving away all your big scoops and stories to one interviewer. Save a little something special for each different story if you can. This will keep people interested each time and give new interviews a fresh slant. That's why I say believe in your script before you make it, because you'll be talking about it for years to come! It's all part of your sales pitch to sell the movie. The whole idea is to get noticed, sell your product to customers, and get on to the next level.

And never forget industry publications like *Variety, The Hollywood Reporter*, and *Video Business*. Being in prestigious magazines like these can help you get noticed by other filmmakers and raise funds for the next project. If you can show an investor that your work has been taken seriously in the film world, it legitimizes you a bit and helps get you into new financial doors.

STANZE: I hate publicity. I understand publicity is necessary to get people to see the movie you've just worked so hard on. Still, it makes me uncomfortable. Often, I am a burnt-out mess by the end of a movie's postproduction, making me a poor spokesman for the project. Usually, I leave publicity duties to people on my team who are not involved with postproduction. That way, when the time comes to promote, they are far less burnt out than I am. Also, I am pretty paranoid of coming off arrogant. I realized that "tooting my own horn" is the only way to get noticed, but it makes me a bit uncomfortable. The best possible publicity scenario is to land a home video distributor that will promote the movie effectively for me. The distribution company I'm currently involved with has done a fantastic job of pushing *Savage Harvest*. I don't have to promote it myself and I am confident in their ability to handle the task. Bottom line, publicity is *extremely* important. However, for me, it is just one of the least enjoyable aspects of making movies.

THOMPSON: Publicity is extremely important. Being in advertising I have a taste of what the right kind of attention can do. Things take on a life of their own when they are publicized well. I did a series of interviews with magazines that acknowledge low-budget work. The next thing I know someone tells me that they came across an interview with me on the Internet. I had done several and didn't know that one of them had ended up there. It actually had color photo scans and a whole page dedicated to *Contact Blow*. It's amazing how publicity can take on a life of its own.

A few suggestions I have for being prepared to publicize:

(1) Take a still camera with you. If you can't get someone to take photos for you on the shoot, make the time to take them yourself. After *Contact Blow* was done I had to go back and recreate scenes. Often the actor's hair was different or we couldn't get into a space to which we used to have access. I regretted not having more photos from the shoot. I have heard recently of movies that used photos of people that weren't even in the movie! Don't get caught doing that. People will be disappointed.

(2) Make it convenient for people to give you attention. If you have access to a scanner, use it. Scan some photos of your project onto a disk and include them with your movie packet. Most of the low-budget magazines are short-handed and an article that comes in on a disk—as well as hard copy—with photos already scanned can be inserted into the overall magazine layout that much easier. A single photo in color fits onto a floppy. Several fit on a Syquest. Include some information on what program you used. Also include the photos themselves. Some people want to do it their own way. One magazine actually preferred a Polaroid to pics scanned at 500 dpi. That's just how they liked to work. Hey, they are doing you the favor.

(3) Don't be full of yourself when you submit your work. One thing is clear to me from reading hundreds of reviews of low-budget work—no one is impressed with the fancy equipment you used. They will be more impressed that you delivered a finished piece with so little equipment. If you act like you have everything a filmmaker could want, the reviewers will compare you with *Star Wars*. If you acknowledge what you had to work with, you will be treated much fairer. In the low-budget world, everything is clear on the screen. There are no secrets from the informed viewer and these guys have seen a lot.

(4) If you can find someone who is in the art world, or in the computer art world, you have scored. If you can't, learn Photoshop or Illustrator. It's amazing how much you can do yourself with either one of these programs. And it's amazing the response and respect you get when

they discover that you already have "art-work"—meaning a poster, box, single page leaflet, et cetera. Almost every reviewer of *Contact Blow* printed the box artwork.

(5) Be original. A lot of cassettes and photos are going to cross the desk of the guy who will review your movie. Even getting him to actually watch it is a challenge. Try to think of a way to make your package stand out. When I sent out *Contact Blow* I wrote a note that said "We suggest watching this movie with a six-pack ... enclosed." I actually enclosed a six pack of beer. This certainly made the size of the package stand out if nothing else. But I imagine it also made it the choice package when a magazine employee had to take something home with him that night. Wouldn't you take the one with the free beer? Of course, this cost ten times the money to send the package but that's what made it so funny. A six pack across state lines. I sent Brooklyn Beer so whoever was getting it could taste a bit of New York. It is after all where the movie was shot.

THOMSON: Everything we got from completion of our project came because someone saw it and liked it ... and that was a result of our efforts to press it into as many hands as we could, however we could, if it was within our financial means to do it.

First thing we did upon completion of our project was to rent a local university theater and show the film for free ... mostly for the benefit of the cast and crew, but we did send out press releases to gain a little attention. Again, on video this is a little harder to do, but museums and universities usually have some sort of video projection means or facilities. If nothing else, we got to say it had shown in a theater. Sending out press releases for an event like this costs nothing and it's a good chance to hype yourself. Send pictures with it. Most publications are starved for cool pictures—it's a great bribe for space.

Then we tried to hit a couple of festivals. Festivals are tough, especially for video, because most want only film prints to show, are expensive, and tend to be highly selective. For videos it's not a real good bet. We got lucky, though, at the Dallas Video Festival, which was geared more to projects like ours.... We showed there to very good reviews, and from there things took off a little.

Reviews are your best selling tools, but they're hard to get and you have to be prepared to take a lot of shit. There is no accounting for taste, and there's no telling how anybody will react to your stuff. You just have to get copies out there and hope for the best. Luckily, there's lots of publications these days that focus on underground-independent stuff. Get out as many copies of your project to these folks as you can find. One good trick if you can afford it is to take out an ad with a mag when you send a copy for review ... but be warned, you usually can't buy praise. And just give out copies to whoever you think might say something nice about it in a public place. Our thought was, we sure can't ever get our money back on this, so what have we got to lose? And in almost every case it was worth it in some small way. You never know where it may go.

ULRICH: I feel publicity is very important. If you can get your area newspaper to do a write-up on you and your movie that's great. But if you can't, check into smaller local papers. We've met a lot of local talent and other filmmakers through local papers. It doesn't matter if it's good publicity or bad publicity, people are hearing about you.

VOLLMANN: Publicity is crucial to a film's success or failure. For instance, if you are shooting a horror film such as we did, getting a magazine like *Fangoria* to cover or review your film can make all the difference in the world. When 250,000 horror fans read about your movie in *Fangoria* you have instant credibility in the horror genre.

Home video artwork for Nathan Thompson's *Contact Blow*.

When your movie is completed, send screeners out to any and all magazines that review films. The more positive reviews you receive, the better your movie is likely to sell. Take many behind-the-scenes photographs while your movie is still in production. These should accompany behind-the-scenes articles and press kits that should also be sent to anyone who reviews or covers movies like your own. Try and get local TV stations or newspapers to cover your movie. Local press never hurts. If you think a nationally known celebrity such as Mel Gibson, Newt Gingrich, or even Siskel and Ebert might like to see your film, send them a copy. A quote from someone famous on your box cover will definitely help sales.

WHITSON & W.A.V.E.: The longer I do this, the more important I see publicity is. It keeps your name in front of the public and lets anyone who might be interested know what you're doing. Unfortunately, it's also very time-consuming. So it's a trade-off.

9. Distribution

If you're making a film that's under $15,000 you're going to have to self-distribute the movie yourself in the United States if it is going to be seen at all. This is both good and bad. First of all, you'll be controlling where the film is going and will be able to keep track of all the sales. But, at the same time, this is all very time-consuming. Expect to put as much effort into distributing as you have into completing your movie.

How does self-distribution work? Being new to this business you are pretty much at the disposal of sub-distributors, companies that buy the tapes from you, the distributor, and resell them to video stores or individuals at an increased price.

You can call the sub-distributors directly to find out if they are interested in viewing your video, but it is cheaper to send them an unsolicited tape with a cover letter and a positive magazine review.

There are three types of distributors you can send your tapes to:

(1) Big distribution companies like Prism or A.I.P. that will buy your film outright and make their own boxes and do their own publicity. If this happens, you don't need to go the route of self-distribution. I have never heard of this happening to any micro-budget feature.
(2) Subdistributors, who will buy your professionally boxed and shrink-wrapped cassettes at 40 to 50 percent of the market or retail price. These companies have already established relationships with video stores and video store chains.
(3) Video catalogs (like Science Fiction Continuum, Scorched Earth, E.I. Independent Film) that will run advertisements in the various genre magazines, which is better than you fronting the money for an ad in a magazine. They will ask your permission to put you in their catalog and then order copies when they get orders. In the course of the year you may sell 10–1,000 copies this way.

With *Vampires & Other Stereotypes* I was certain it was going to be picked up by a national distributor who would publicize it and do all the promotion and, most importantly, get it out into the stores. But, after I pursued this avenue for nearly three years, spending over a thousand dollars in shipping, duplication, and phone calls, no one took it. It wasn't because it was a horrible movie. It was because of three things: (1) It wasn't a Hollywood movie; (2) It had no "name" actors; and (3) It had no nudity. This is what the distributors told me over and over again.

If you wish, go ahead and send it to the bigger distributors who would buy it outright. But only do this for a year. If nothing has happened in one year, do it yourself. If

VAMPIRES

AND OTHER
STEREOTYPES

VAMPIRISM...DON'T BELIEVE THE HYPE!

A BRIMSTONE PRODUCTION Presents
BILL WHITE • WENDY BEDNARZ • VAMPIRES AND OTHER STEREOTYPES
Starring ED HUBBARD • RICK POLI • ANNA DIPACE • SUZANNE SCOTT • MICK McCLEERY
Original Soundtrack THE KRYPT • Special Make-up Effects IMAGEFFECTS STUDIOS
Director of Photography TULLIO TEDESCHI
Written, Produced & Directed by KEVIN LINDENMUTH
Copyright © 1994 Brimstone Productions. All Rights Reserved

Home video artwork for *Vampires & Other Stereotypes*.

your direct-to-video feature was intended for an audience—well, get it out there! It does you no good sitting in limbo. Besides, all the money you spend in postage, duplication and phone calls to "distributors" can be better spent getting boxes made, duplicating and eventually selling the tapes yourself.

This is exactly what I did with *Vampires & Other Stereotypes*. I found someone who did the design and layout for video boxes, gave him an idea of what I wanted, and within two months, going back and forth over details, et cetera, the artwork for the box was done. At that point it was ready to be sent to the printers, where I had to have a minimum of 2,500 boxes printed up. All of this cost under $900.

Sales were nothing spectacular and at this point I'm still selling copies through subdistributors, magazine ads, and horror conventions such as *Fangoria* Weekend of Horrors and *Chiller*. I have not made my money back, but I may one day.

Sales for *Addicted to Murder* went much better. Since I had learned all about distributors and how to sell the tapes with my previous movie, I knew exactly what to do. Immediately after the boxes were made I sent screeners to (1) my various subdistributor connections, small companies that already had ties to video store chains and mom-and-pop video stores, (2) genre magazines that were willing to put their own ads for my movies in their magazines and would then buy tapes off of me at 50 percent when they'd get an order; and (3) video tape catalogs that would also buy tapes from me.

Within two months I made all my money back on this movie, and within the year it was picked up by Blockbuster Video, who purchased nearly 1,900 copies for their rental stores.

Foreign distributors are much more receptive, particularly to shot-on-video features. There are usually two ways they operate: (1) They'll pay between $2,500–$5,000 outright for a 3–5 year period in which to distribute the movie. You must supply them with a submaster from which they can do their own duplicating; or (2) they'll work out a percentage, somewhere between 15–20 percent. Again, they'll want a submaster for duplication. You can also sell copies yourself to distributors, who will buy 20–100 cassettes in one shot, though this means you have to worry about duplication and shipping. I've done deals all three ways, with varying success. It's always much more gratifying getting that money up front.

As with any distributor you should ask them for references, so you can check up on them. If they are legitimate and trustworthy they'll readily comply. Also, they'll probably want you to sign a contract. They usually have no problem with you making up the specifics of the contract. The idea is to be as up-front and specific as possible so there is no possible confusion. Clearness is a big preventive measure.

To date, I've sold movies to England, Germany, Malaysia, Spain, Denmark and Thailand.

For a list of distributors, see Appendix 2.

Video Boxes

Video boxes are a necessary expense to your production if you are selling tapes to subdistributors. *Get them made.* They are probably more important than your movie because that's what people see first. In the world of video rentals and purchases people do judge a video by its cover! A lousy box will not sell a great movie but a great box will sell the worst piece of dreck. Real boxes aren't as costly as you think. Twenty-five hundred boxes (usually the minimum you can order) cost $500. Actually designing the box and making the four-color separation from which the boxes are printed will run you another $300–$400, depending on who does it for you.

When designing the box it is preferable to use publicity photos taken during the shoot rather than lifting images from the video, which is expensive and always a bit fuzzy. Write up a synopsis for the back cover, decide on effective photos that represent the film, and add great quotes from the magazine reviews or articles you obtain.

Then, work out on paper just how you want all the photos laid out, so you can clearly and specifically explain to your graphic designer what you have in mind.

If you do not have the cash flow to make real boxes or if you just plan on selling tapes through magazines and at convention tables, it is cheaper to make boxes yourself. First, buy plastic VHS boxes with clear full window sleeves. Then, design a color one-sheet with the front, spine, and back of the box that you can insert in this sleeve. From this you can simply make more copies at your local copying store and produce boxes as you need them. Both methods of creating boxes will require that you purchase adhesive labels to stock on the faces of the actual video cassettes—stating the title, running time, and copyright information. The labels can be printed on your home computer. Your local stationery store should carry adhesive video labels.

Tape Duplication

Once you have your boxes you are ready to make copies of your videotapes. You should be able to find a tape duplication place that can do them between $2–$3 each. This includes the tape stock, putting the tape into boxes, and shrink-wrapping. There is usually a minimum order of 50.

Shrink-wrapping each cassette is very important. If you are duplicating cassettes yourself, small shrink-wrap machines can be purchased for under $200 from video or office supply catalogs such as Markertek and Staples.

Appendix 2 offers some addresses for tape duplication services and tape stock suppliers.

Prices. Ideally, if you're selling the tape retail at $30, the subdistributor will buy it at half that price (wholesale price). Some people will try to talk you down on the price, depending on desperation, et cetera, but never go below $10 per cassette because you have to make money. Some may even try to make you believe that they're doing you a favor by buying it for $6. They're still selling it for $30. Do not fall into this trap.

Response Time. Distributors are never in a rush to get back to you. It may be as long as half a year before you get an order from any of them. Beware that they often try to get you to go down on prices. Also, they may want "exclusives" on your film so they'll have no competition. This helps them but not you. *Never* sign an exclusive contract with a subdistributor. I say this from past experience. I signed a contract with a wholesaler who promised, in writing, that he'd buy a minimum of 200 tapes per month for a year and would pay C.O.D. with every delivery. In the five months I supplied tapes he ordered only 300 units as opposed to the 1,000 promised in the contract. He also bounced all his checks. After a dozen false promises of ordering more tapes, I tore up the contract and told him he couldn't order any more tapes. This company is not listed on the distributor list.

Since you are a distributor, do not sign an exclusive deal with subdistributors. This does you no good as they will only order 50–200 tapes at most. If the company says they won't do business with you if you will not sign an exclusive, do not do business with them. Do not be desperate. If your film is good and entertaining and technically competent, you'll sell copies. It may take years but if favorable word gets around about it, companies will eventually buy. Only recently have I begun to sell mass orders of *Vampires & Other Stereotypes*.

Remember, if you are selling packaged tapes yourself, you are the distributor and companies can buy as many copies from you as they need when they need them.

Receiving Orders. Upon receiving an order, try to get this in writing. Have the company purchasing the tapes FAX or mail the order to you. Make it clear that they are paying for the method of delivery—mail, UPS, whatever, and that this will be added to the amount. You can ask them to send a check beforehand. If they do not agree to this, send the package certified mail. C.O.D. (cash on delivery) through the United Parcel Service is the best way to do this. The purchaser gives the check to UPS, they receive the package, and then the check is forwarded to you within ten days.

This ensures that they pay you when the goods are received. The only bad thing about this method is that the check may still bounce or get canceled in the interim. The safest way is to request a money order or certified check, though they may only agree to send a regular check.

After a few orders a distributor may want the leeway of paying within 30 days (net 30) after they receive the goods. You can agree to do this or not, but remember, there's always the possibility the check may never arrive.

I have found that the easiest orders come from the people who have catalogs. They will usually send a check with a written order.

THE INTERVIEWEES WERE ASKED, *How have you handled distribution?*

ARSENAULT: I would have loved for *Night Owl* to have been taken out of my hands by a distributor. I got a few offers, but since they didn't offer an advance [cash upfront] I turned them down. I attempted to self-distribute it, but didn't have the time or the money to do it properly. Self-distribution is a full-time job. I felt it was more important to move on with my second feature, so I abandoned my distribution for a year. Some filmmakers can do both, but it takes a lot of discipline!

BALLOT: The route I chose to get distribution didn't work. Why outline a losing tactic? Unless you have *Hoop Dreams* or *The Brothers McMullen* or unless you have a represented, financed project, then you're dealing with E.I or Bookwalter or Michael D. Moore or somebody like that.

Alex Kogan from Films Around the World told me that ten or fifteen years ago there were a bunch of companies that would have paid me a $100,000 advance for *The Bride of Frank*. Now they're all out of business. The studios have such a stronghold on the current film business that the only way guys like me can make money is self-distribution.

He told me to contact Tim Ritter and Tim will explain it.

So, who am I to answer the question "What about distribution?" My fucking movie was plugged on Howard Stern's show and I still managed to lose money!

BERGER: Watch your ass! I defer to Scooter McCrae and Leif Jonker for the horror stories—and they should be heeded! In my experience with *Sins*, I have no real complaints. I have wonderful rapport with all our foreign distributors—friendships, really. And I insist that a constant and honest communication form in that arena. Just realize that the trickiest part of making a movie is letting it go. There are a lot of disreputable corrupt slime out there, but if you take your time, research and discriminate, you may find a tiny pot o'gold at the end of the rainbow. Now, the only other practical advice I can offer is this, and it may not apply to everyone: If your script contains nudity or violence of any kind—research all of your foreign markets before filming! Let me explain why: Japan customs has deemed *Original Sins* pornographic—not for the bountiful amounts of sex and gore—but for the below-the-waist nudity! Pubic hair is a no-no in Japan and even though some distributors may want your film regardless and decide to digitize the offending screen areas—called "cubic hair"—the trick is to get it past customs. Not an easy task! In the UK, *Sins* has spent almost a year with the censors! This is an expensive burden for the distributor who has to spend a thousand or so dollars every time it is submitted! And *Sins* had over eight minutes of footage removed! Most of it dealing with the image of blood on breasts. Other cuts were ridiculously random. Hard to figure out what they were worried about in most cases. And now, after all that, we have just heard that it went back before them for a third time and might well be banned! Great for publicity; bad for income. So plan ahead when filming such scenes. Cover yourself—pun intended—with "soft takes"—alternate clothed takes of your nude scenes or toned-down gore effects sequences. This way you can have another less explicit version of your film instantly prepared for just these problem markets.

BONK: What has worked best for me in terms of sales is reviews. It has led to extra sales, new contacts with subdistributors, et cetera. And the free press through press releases. Most ads I have placed in the genre publications have only broken even—but they have led to new movies being sent my way for distribution. My biggest source for retail is my Internet site—the cost is relatively cheap and the sales relatively big! I love it—what a great concept the Internet is! It's like having a store front that is open 24 hours a day, and you never have to be there! Just update it once in a while.

But the true key to success is to promote yourself—and not to be afraid to do so! I'm working at submitting articles to magazines for printing—many magazines at this level are manned by one person who is so busy he gladly accepts articles written by others—and hoping to increase the familiarity of the titles. No one did this better than Kevin. His movies have been covered in every genre publication, and horror fans seem to know about them as readily as some of the big budget Hollywood horror movies. Kevin is the exception. The average Joe really isn't going to see much of a response for his little backyard camcorder epic—there is so much to compete with—and he has to deal with a certain aversion to shot-on-video movies. So we need to really get out and promote our titles ourselves. Get on the phone and call those magazines, those distributors! We're like the producers of old who travel around from town to town, buying theater space and putting on a big show to lure the public in. We need to do the same—no one is going to treat your movie like a classic if you don't first. You're going to have to be a talker—yes, you actually have to sell your title! Talk to subdistributors every week until they give you a "yes" or "no" answer. Consistently send them reviews, articles, and any sort of press that you might get on the title. Make them think your title is the greatest thing to hit the video market since *Re-Animator*. Next to the website, that route of publicity has worked best for me. Get the audience to start looking for your title, get the movie on their brain, then finally offer it directly to them for sale.

Outside of that, at least potential-wise, the foreign markets seem like the best buys. The domestic market is going through a lot of lulls lately (though it appears it might finally be on an upswing)—more often than not, in fact—and foreign territories that pay lump sums for X number of years are a good alternative. They especially like the gore and sex! A strong movie in a strong territory can pay for your entire budget.

BOOKWALTER: I get asked about distribution all the time. It amazes me to this day how filmmakers can so quickly disregard the selling of their movie like it's not important. Man, the selling of your movie is the thing! You can have the best movie ever made, but if nobody sees it, it doesn't do you any good. I started Tempe Video in 1991 and it's scary how much the home video market has bottomed out since then. Very soon the rental market will be gone entirely. So filmmakers have two choices: join up with companies who will be making movies for 500-channel cable systems, or sell to collectors. Selling to collectors is nice but there's only so many people out there who actually *buy* videocassettes. It's really not enough to make a living from a few titles. I do continue to encourage filmmakers to package and promote their movies by themselves. No one will ever push your movie better than yourself! The problem is that few filmmakers are also good promoters, and the ones that are usually make really rotten movies. I've never gotten a single royalty check from any distributor I've ever dealt with. I think that speaks for itself. The key is having a really great box. Most distributors could care less what's inside the box, although some of them want to play film critics. They just want to be able to turn around and have a telemarketer hype how great the packaging is to a video store so they can entice people to come into their store and rent! That's a pretty sobering thing to discover—that your movie is really the last thing that anyone in this business seems to care about. It's more about politics. I think that the more filmmakers break away from the traditional independent distribution scenario and start handling their movies—and eventually their careers—themselves, the better things will get.

CAMPISI: It's every independent filmmaker's dream to get picked up by a major distributor. You can potentially do this by submitting your film to the many video distributors, and or exhibiting your film at the many festivals scattered across the country.

Major distribution, of course, would be the ideal situation. All too often, however, projects aren't good enough; they lack production value or technical quality, or even creative significance.

Sometimes self-distribution is the only alternate way to go. This can be difficult and costly. First, you've got to commission the

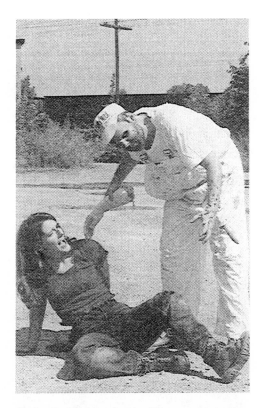

Sasha Graham is terrorized by a zombie in Ron Bonk's *The Vicious Sweet*.

jacket-poster and promotional artwork which tends to be rather expensive. Then you've got to *sell* yourself. You've got to contact the video houses, sales agents, et cetera. A whole book could be written on this subject alone.

A less-costly alternative is to place advertisements in the independent production magazines, including *Independent Video*, *Alternative Cinema*, and *Film Threat Video Guide*. Other genre magazines have comparable advertising rates.

For *The Law*, several advertisements were placed in the above-mentioned magazines and several sales were made. However, we didn't make our film with the intention of selling it, but rather with the intention of promotion. Hence, after a few sales, we shelved the advertisements. A few years later, I still continue getting orders for *The Law*. I guess some older issues of the magazines we advertised in are floating around somewhere.

A GABRIEL CAMPISI FILM

SHADOWDANCE

Empty your mind.

Clear your soul.

Then ask yourself
what you believe.

STARLIGHT PICTURES

Promotional artwork for Gabriel Campisi's *Shadowdance*.

An interesting anecdote: A friend of mine did a small film and submitted it to a handful of video distributors. Little interest was expressed. It was their first film and lacked in every degree. In the end, they gave the film away to a small distributor. They'll probably never see a dime from their film, but their philosophy is "at least we have something on video shelves to prove we're filmmakers." To each his own.

CRAMER: I've worked with dozens of distributors and I must say that only a handful are what I would call honest. For that reason, I try to retain the right to sell copies myself—since only on those transactions can I account for every dollar.

FORD: Distribution is very bad, especially for the little guy. I was luckier than most because my partner, Mark Gordon, is well-connected enough to be able to make a showing at all the film markets. The little guy usually has to be content with catalogs and exchanges and self-distribution. The pickings are pretty slim right now. The home video market is bleak, especially in the U.S. Everybody's losing their shirts. *Alien Force* is pretty new to the market, but it still has not found a U.S. distributor at this point. It has done very well around the world in most territories, but the U.S. still remains elusive. Without this sales force behind me, I don't see how I could possibly have made my money back. The only hope for guys doing it all themselves is to make their movies as cheaply as possible, hit the exchanges and the catalogs. You can probably make your money back that way and keep going, even if you never make much of a profit. It's all about making movies, not about making money, right?

GALLAGHER: When I made *Gorgasm* I was really hyped on getting a distributor. I sent the movie everywhere and everyone seemed interested but I couldn't land any deals. Then *Film Threat Video Guide* wanted it, and I decided to go with a sub-distribution deal with them instead of giving them full rights. I had dreams of mega money, but the sales were pretty pathetic to say the least. At one point I thought I could do better than this and reedited the movie, got it a new box and put a little behind it. It was like a brand new movie and sold like crazy. I realized then that for no-budget videos you are just as well to handle it yourself and find people that you can sell to in wholesale lots. I work with some of those companies and have be-

come one myself with the *Draculina* mail-order business. I do pretty good business with other people's videos, and they are happy because I pay up-front. People can talk big—but unless you actually see the cash, they're usually full of shit. I had one company telling me they could sell thousands of my tapes and wanted to list them. It sounded pretty good and we kept going back and forth but sometimes he'd call me and use a different name than he did the time before—and it became obvious that he was running several scams at the same time and couldn't keep his contacts straight as to what name he used with them. I let it drop, but I know a couple people that got burned by him with rubber checks. You're better off handling things yourself and dealing with people you know you can trust. Most people are full of shit and will slip up if you feel them out.

GINGOLD: Distribution ain't what is used to be. Back in the mid–80s, Mark Pirro sold *A Polish Vampire in Burbank* to a home video company for $40,000; today, an Indie filmmaker will be lucky to reap a fraction of that sum. I haven't gone through the distribution process myself yet, but based on talking to numerous other filmmakers, it seems that there are very few trustworthy distributors out there. From the biggest video labels down to the smallest, there are plenty of sharks waiting for unsuspecting people to jump in the water without a cage. The best advice I can give is to network with other filmmakers to find out who the better distributors are, and to do some research with regards to prospective buyers. And when you do get to the point of signing a deal—and make sure there is something to sign; never get involved with anyone who won't put all the terms on paper—get as much up front as possible. That might be tough, and you may have to settle for a pretty small sum, but it may well prove to be preferable to chasing down a distributor for profits they'll swear to God they haven't made. The alternative is self-distribution, which is best addressed by people with more experience at it than I. The

FBI agent Jack Vincent (Michael Wayne) has his arm shot off in Ron Ford's *Alien Force*.

only thing I can say is that in this case, good box art is all-important. Do your best to make your boxes—from what I'm told, cardboard sleeves are far preferable to plastic clamshell cases—as slick as those put out by the major companies. Not only will they be more appealing to potential individual buyers, but to video store chains as well.

One other point worth mentioning is that many potential distributors will be paying attention to the level of violence and sex in your movie. It can be a bit of a Catch-22: Many buyers, especially for foreign territories, won't touch something that has no nudity in it, while others will be turned off if they think it has too much sex or gore— combining the two is a particular no-no in some areas. While this is not something that should be uppermost in your mind while making your movie, it is worth considering.

HOWE: My experience with distributors is not only limited to *Original Sins*. I know the trouble both Leif Jonker and Scooter McCrae had with the people handling

their films, and I've seen the directors of the films I've shot go through the same shit, although on a larger scale.

I would warn the prospective filmmaker to be very careful in dealing with any and all distributors. Distributors always want you to think they have your best interests at heart. They don't; they have their own. If helping you will help them, then great; if not, look out because you're screwed.

Read every contract carefully, every line of it. If possible, run it past a lawyer. Make sure you have an out, in case you do realize later on that they're fucking you over. When you finally do sign, keep your fingers crossed that they treat you squarely.

If they don't, don't be afraid to make a fuss. If you don't get satisfaction, pull out of the deal any way you can and move on to someone else.

JACOBS: With this it's pretty much been touch and go. I'm always looking for avenues to push my videos down. I've gotten distribution in Canada through a group called Video-Pool. I'm going to be getting distribution through a distributor called Tapeworm, who puts videos in stores. I'm still waiting to hear back from a few others. I've taken the track of an Uzi. I went to the library and got a list of as many distributors as possible. I'm going to write letters to all of these people. I'll send copies to the ones that want to see my video. I'll just take it from there. I'm assuming it's going to get pretty costly, but I'll do as much as I can. The only possible horror story was with this one distributor; I sent them a copy of my movie, and they sent me a contract. It was "exclusive" and they had options on my projects for the next seven years. This was a pretty big company so I called them up to do some modifications. After five minutes of talking with the person I realized that they hadn't even watched my movie. The person told me that everyone is looking for distribution but that nobody can get it. That's the service they provide. When I told him what the film was about—a love story—he said that because it wasn't a "special interest" video, he didn't think they'd be able to help me. That has really been the only low point on this journey so far. With distribution I think it's a matter of getting your stuff out to people and believing in what you've done. Like it or not, you become a salesperson, a publicity agent, an accountant, everything. The goal is to stay on top of all this.

LEGGE: What can I say about distributors that isn't true? They are honest, capable people who are working hard to sell your movie to the best of their ability, with a substantial profit to you. Now, the truth. Most distributors I've dealt with are lazy, shifty, unresponsive, sleazy liars who will steal you blind if you let them. I first dealt with a distributor who wanted to handle *Working Stiffs*. We signed a contract with him—means nothing—and he proceeded to do nothing from that point on. He didn't take calls or return letters. Fortunately for me, the contract was only for a year, so when it expired I was clear of the useless bastard. Then it got worse.

Another distributor wanted to handle both *Working Stiffs* and *Loons*, and boy did he talk and talk and talk. He had the manner of a used-car dealer, which gave me the willies, but I think I'm insulting used-car dealers. Cut to the final reel. Again, this clown turned into Mr. Stonewall, and wouldn't answer calls or letters. And did nothing. My master tapes were tied up in the lab he was using. Since we had signed a contract with this scumbag I finally had to resort to a lawyer, who threatened him with legal action since he was not honoring the terms of the contract, and we managed to break the contract. Of course, I had to pay lawyers fees and shipping costs and storage for my material at the lab. Don't trust them. The road I've taken lately is to sell my stuff direct wholesale to catalog distributors on a pay-up-front or C.O.D. basis. You can't beat it. You're only responsible for defectives, and you're not under exclusive contract with anyone. You have to do the necessary work to track them down and try to sell them on you, but it's ads in mags if you want to. The more films you have to sell, the more people will take you seriously. And you can't give up after the first try. Be persistent. Even if you never make enough money to buy a box of Ring Dings there is a certain satisfaction in being someone who just isn't going to go away.

McCRAE: Distribution, huh? Well, here's the trouble spot, kiddies. One thing to watch out for is getting involved with distributors who are also producing their own material while trying to get yours out there. I have nothing bad to say about this situation, except to point out the simple logic of human nature; there's *your* stuff and there's *his* stuff—who's stuff are you gonna push harder? My first distributor did a very good job of advertising *Shatter Dead* in its own publication but never took out ads in any other magazines. It seems to me a very sound idea to have an order form handy within a few pages of a good review. But advertising costs were being kept down to funnel what profit was being made on the title into more other lucrative areas, i.e. the company's next video project and the continuing publication of their magazine. So, to make a long story short, I got *Shatter Dead* back from my distributor and the monies owed to me are finally starting to come trickling home. It was a sad and desperate period for too long a while as good reviews were published, people who had bought a copy of the project told me how much they enjoyed it, and the Best U.S.A. Independent Film Plaque from the Fantafestival arrived and I was living on a can of cat food while trying to avoid the telephone calls about my double-defaulted student loan.

So remember to be firm about establishing a payment schedule in your first distribution agreement. People who say "trust me" are usually liars. If a person cannot backup in print what they are verbally presenting to you, however simple it might be— it doesn't need to be one of those "party of the first part" affairs—they are to be avoided unless you enjoy being screwed over by a total stranger whose wallet will grow thicker with the sweat of your labors. Beware the distributor who acts like they are doing you a favor; they are not. They need your product more than you need their Rolodex. And if anyone tells you all they want to do is make lots of money for you, politely hang up the phone and unplug it from the jack in the wall for about a week and hope they don't have your home address.

I have currently given *Shatter Dead* to Something Weird Video to distribute. They have a large distribution base, and I'm looking forward to seeing what they can do with the title. I don't expect to see much money from this endeavor; I know they'll keep the title in print and available, which is all I care about right now. When people ask to take a look at something you've completed, it's nice to be able to say, "Go rent it at such-and-such" or "It's available for sale through this-and-that." The biggest, and sometimes scariest, sense of accomplishment sometimes is knowing that your project is out there in the big wide world apart from you and gaining an independent life of its own. Congratulations; you're a professional.

MURPHY: That's a tough one. Everyone seems to get fucked over the first time into it. But that can be okay, too. I learned so much when I finally dove into the distribution world. I was scared. And I got ripped off. And I got ripped off more. But I learned a lot and I gradually took charge and now I am kicking ass in distribution.

First off, you have to remove the filmmaker hat and think like a businessman. You have to present yourself like a businessman. Don't go to meetings with your finger in your nose. Don't be artsy and don't be annoying. Be direct. And don't *ever* sign contracts without a lawyer first reading them over. Be clear about what you want and get it in writing.

Sooner or later, if you're lucky enough to get a company who's interested in your work, you have to decide to take a chance on them. Don't sit on your masterpiece for too many years waiting for that perfect deal. It may never come and in the meanwhile your movie is getting old. Don't be too scared. Take a risk if you can get one. And know that you are swimming with sharks.

Or ... you could distribute it yourself. That's a whole world of work unto itself. But it can be very profitable. Self-distribution is where it's at, in a way. It's power. But it can also eat into all your time when it comes to making the next picture. So you have to just try out everything and anything until you find out what works for you. Distribution can be such a slap-in-the-face stage of your picture. You'll hear all kinds of figures by your distributor of what he can make for you. But the truth is when you sign the only money you will probably see will be the money you got up front. Put a cap on expenses in the contract or you may end up owing them money.

And be real careful of anyone saying they need you to sign over the master to them, the copyright to them, or the right attorney to them. Just be careful. If you're not sure about something *ask*. Ask everyone. Call other filmmakers. Beg a lawyer. And if you get locked into a bad distribution deal remember you *can* sometimes still get out of it. It's a tough one, distribution. But you have to get in there. Get your feet wet. Watch another filmmaker go through it if you can. It's part of filmmaking. Good luck. Be lucky. Don't get too cynical. Use the force, Luke.

POLONIA: Self-distribution is a hard egg to crack. We have had the luxury—or is it misfortune—to experience both sides of the fence. Being picked up by a legitimate distributor is nice because they package your movie and work hard to push it to every store, but most often they do not work hard to make sure you get what you deserve. In plain English you get ripped off! If you do it yourself there is a large amount of work to do and it will cost some, but you stand a better chance of making out better. You have control of everything. You just have to build a good rep with other stores and subdistributors. But be forewarned, you still run the risk of being ripped off!

RITTER: *Day of the Reaper* and *Twisted Illusions* were basically sold out of the trunk of our cars, so that was how we started. *Twisted Illusions* actually still sells—we licensed the rights to Moore Video out of Virginia and that's worked out good. It's weird to have something you made ten years ago or more still selling.

Truth or Dare was financed and released by a distributor. This was in '85 and '86, so that's harder to get done these days on smaller levels, but it's possible. This was a double-edged sword. It was great in the respect that they handled all the advertising, shipping, and sales reports, but I had a falling out with the producer before the movie was released. He tried to steal all of my credits after I had written and directed the movie. I had to sue just to get the writing credit back, and I ran out of money, so he got away with stealing the directorial credit all for himself! This can happen when you have a lot of other people involved in a bigger project. So that's the biggest downside to working with bigger money and distribution. You can lose control over any aspect of your project at any stage. Anybody with any sense would have chosen a different career after going through that nonsense, but what the hey, I was eighteen.

With *Killing Spree*, the offers I was getting were so low that I eventually decided to try self-distribution in 1989–90. I actually spent four years distributing that movie. I call that period a distribution abyss. It's so easy to hang your whole life up on phone calls, mailing, projections, wheels and deals. I learned the business up and down during this period. But when you want to *make* movies, not *sell* them, this can get very frustrating.

Basically, we made our boxes and connected with subdistributors and wholesalers all across the country, shipping directly to them on a C.O.D. basis. We did set up credit with some of the larger distributors. But let me tell you ... the accounting, the lawyers, the aggravation of all this ... it can weigh you down. I sold *Killing Spree* on the basis of the success of *Truth or Dare*, so that's what got me in the door with a lot of distributors.

We also printed up thousands of big 18" × 26" posters to go along with copies of the film. That was hugely expensive and cut into profits. These days, I'd do like a 8" × 10" color flyer to save money.

Truth or Dare sold 30,000 copies in the U.S. alone. I expected *Killing Spree* to do well, but in the end, we only sold about 10,000 units altogether, including a licensing deal we later made with Magnum Entertainment. They released the movie a second time in a new box to the rental market. Both times *Spree* was released, it had a wholesale price of $40, retailing for $59.95.

I also dealt with three or four companies for foreign rights and got ripped off almost every time. It's very difficult to control your movie once you mail a copy of it out to someone.

Let me tell you what I learned in my "distribution abyss." This may help you when trying to sell your film. Never trust anyone. Pretty much all these distributors will take you to the cleaners if you let them. There are some honest ones, but move very cautiously. Never mail anyone a master tape unless you have received an advance. You can pretty much count on the money you get up front for a project is all you're ever going to see. That's the rule of thumb. A foreign distributor may give you a list of what he thinks he'll make off of a movie in the long run and your share, but I have yet to see a dime from any "royalty" situation like this. It's all a scam so *they* can make money! Let me give you some examples.

One distributor had *Killing Spree* for two years. They sold "nothing" on paper. Their contract was up, so I demanded the rights back. They sent me a bill for $50,000 for their "expenses" in representing the film for two years, taking it to festivals, et cetera. Needless to say, lawyers were hired and things were out of control. So insane! I later found out that they sold a Japanese deal and Italian television! And I had received no money up front! They still have a master tape of *Killing Spree* to this day! Again, this was my mistake for not taking any money up front and giving them a master tape to begin with. But I got caught up in their fancy "projections" of sales and my portion.

Another thing that's obvious these days, but wasn't when I started: always send either time-coded or screener copies to *any* distributor. I sent a second-generation one-half inch copy of *Killing Spree* to a Canadian distributor with no time-code number or "screener" burned into the picture. He bumped that lousy copy up to 1" video and went to all the film festivals with that "master tape" he created. The producer of *Killing Spree* actually ran into the guy at a video show. He was trying to sell his 1" master to a company for $15,000. And it almost worked!

You think, well you can sue to stop all this. Wrong. Unless you're independently wealthy, legal fees will break you. And suing

someone in a different country ... you have to extradite them to the U.S.A. first—*at your expense*!

Copyright laws on movies that are not registered with the MPAA are very vague. It's almost as if it doesn't come from a major studio, then it's up for grabs. So protect yourself as much as possible ahead of time. But be warned: I've had people sell "screener" copies of my movies as well! Nothing will stop a pirate if they want to take it.

Keep in mind these foreign horror tales are for movies shot on 16-millimeter. For video movies, the foreign markets are almost nonexistent. Distributors just will not buy movies shot on video, even if they are film-looked. It's just their way of doing business. They don't care how good it is, it's just too cheap for them simply because it was shot on video. Even if it's Betacam SP! If you get a good foreign offer for a filmlooked video production, never tell your distributor the truth, otherwise he'll drop you like a hot potato.

Even foreign deals for 16-millimeter productions have soured lately. In 1986, a movie like *Truth or Dare* with no big stars would command $60,000 for the Japanese alone. Nowadays, the same movie might land you $3,000, if you're lucky. The market has changed drastically.

The best way to sell movies overseas these days that are shot-on-video is one movie at a time. Make your PAL copies and sell the tapes to distributors overseas that will peddle to your types of customers or video stores. And make them pay up front.

Some really well-done SOV movies can make a few thousand here and a few thousand there, but I wouldn't count on grossing anywhere over $6,000–$10,000 on any filmlooked SOV movie for total international sales. Sad but true.

Remember the rule of thumb: Money up front or forget it. Unless you're willing to take a financial loss. And try not to license your movie to anyone for more than three years. This way, if they don't perform, you can get your movie back sooner.

Filmmakers get ripped off all the time. You just don't expect it to happen to small projects, especially your own. But remember the horror stories surrounding the distribution rip-offs of *Night of the Living Dead* and *Texas Chainsaw Massacre*. It's more than a reality, and it's tough to overcome. The business realities of filmmaking make it tough to keep your passion for making movies. You get very bitter.

After the *Killing Spree* nightmare I plugged ahead with self-distribution on *Wicked Games*. Mainly concentrating on the U.S. video market, I sold directly to retailers, wholesalers, and consumers. *Wicked Games* was a better experience, but let me tell you a few things.

First of all, when you ship tapes to a distributor, do it C.O.D.—cash on delivery. If you accept a check, then it could bounce. It takes ten days to get your check back, then another week for it to clear. In twenty days, that distributor could've changed names or even be out of business. Start out getting cash, then if you work up a trustworthy relationship with a distributor and his checks, then go into it cautiously. Watch out for sudden big orders. If this guy orders like fifty tapes a month, then suddenly wants five hundred immediately—on the check system—don't do it. You're being set up for a scam.

With *Creep* I had one distributor that I had dealt with for three years or more very successfully. I shipped them tapes, and I accepted their checks from UPS C.O.D. I was used to this company ordering, like, fifty tapes a day at times. It was a good relationship and we were all making money. Part of the reason I made *Creep* was due to my successful business relations with this operation.

Anyway, in one week they ordered 1,000 *Creep* VHS copies. And the checks came in ten days later. Another week goes by and we find out the account that the checks are written on is closed. We are talking major dough here, and I had a massive duplicating bill due in fifteen days. And no money to back it up.

Again, personal financial devastation almost ensued. I had to get the state attor-

ney's office involved and another filmmaker friend who I had involved with this company had the same thing happen. It was a complete nightmare.

It turned out that some of this company's accounts had screwed them over. In other words, people they sold *Creep* to gave them bad checks. Then they had no positive cash flow in their accounts. Then one of their head officers quit, and allegedly stole funds. The excuses went on and on.

Anyway, I was able to successfully sell enough tapes through honest distributors to pay off that duplicating bill by the skin of my teeth ... and finally get some money back the company owed me for *Creep*. But they still owe, and it's very frustrating to get ripped off.

If you deal with the big chains, be sure to get a purchase order before dubbing off copies. They all work with 30–60 day credit plans—they pay 30–60 days *after* receiving tapes!—and they are usually honest. However, I know of cases where major chains have ordered a couple thousand copies of a movie, and after the filmmaker had them run off, they canceled the order. Since he did not get a purchase order number or anything in writing, he had to eat that cost. So watch it with the big chains.

The big chains seem to only toy with independent movies anyway. They usually aren't very nice to the independent, especially if it's shot on video. I had one chain buyer tell me over the phone, without even seeing the movie, "If you and your friends got together with a camcorder and filmed a little movie, we don't care. We don't even want to see it."

Another chain rejected *Creep* because of lead actor Joel Wynkoop's expression on the front of the box: "The man's rage is too intense for our renters."

So be wary of enthusiastic chains that yank your chain. Things like "it's good, but could you recut this" or "redo your box art and we'll consider buying a few" are really euphemisms for "no" with these pretenders. They're just busting your chops for their own sick purposes.

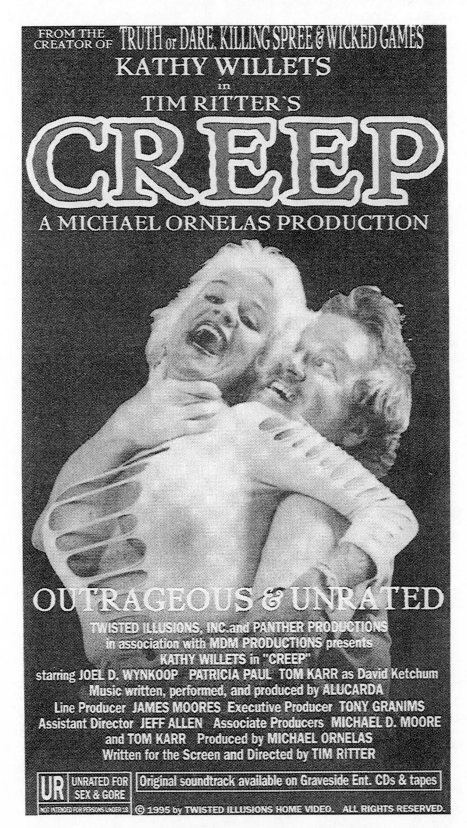

Home video artwork for Tim Ritter's *Creep*.

Blockbuster did carry *Truth or Dare* and *Killing Spree* to a limited extent, but keep in mind they are part of the studio monopoly now, owned by Viacom. They would profit more by buying a "B" picture from a sister company like Republic Pictures rather than anything made by an outsider. There's always a shot, but to get in there, your odds are likened to winning the state lottery.

One company that ordered *Killing Spree* actually wanted to mail me tapes instead of cash after one of their checks was never mailed. They wanted to give me one hundred copies of a Frank Stallone movie in place of hard cash! Always expect the unexpected in this business.

The other issue is price. In the old days, I could get a wholesale price of $30–$40 for *Killing Spree*. Nowadays, you're lucky to get $10 a unit wholesale for your professionally packaged movie. Try to stay at $10 when dealing with these distributors and wholesalers, but it gets tough. It costs you at least $4 a tape with dubbing and packaging, then these people come along and offer you $6 a unit. Sometimes it's better to pass on a deal rather than go further in debt. However, the market is changing so fast that I think in the future, the $6 to $8 a tape is going to be it! Roger Corman is known in the business to sell his direct-to-cable movies to the video market a year later for $6 a unit. And these are 35mm movies with star power. I've had several distributors tell me about his program. He makes all his money off cable and foreign sales, then turns over 10,000 tapes that way, making a few bucks off each tape. But it really crushes out the small guys like us. You can't compete with that very easily.

The horror video market is rapidly becoming like the adult video market. I used to manage an independent video store and was amazed at the cutthroat prices of adult films shot on video. With these huge glossy color boxes, they were selling brand-new for $3.00 or less. A guy in a truck would come around and say, "Take your pick." You rent 'em out one time, you make money. Also, you could sell them to customers for $30

apiece. Well, the same thing has happened in the horror video business. An oversaturation of product has lessened the value of 'em all as a whole.

Another way to get maximum value out of your tapes is to sell them directly to video stores yourself, by phone or car. I've done that quite successfully on all of my movies. It's tough, especially at the retail level, but you will make some money eventually.

Also, direct-mail ads placed in genre magazines get decent responses from the fans. They send you a check up front for $24 or whatever, it clears, then you mail them the tape. I've never had a check bounce yet from a fan. Personal checks are like gold in this business, as far as I'm concerned.

You can also sell tapes at the horror shows and conventions, either taking your product there yourself or have someone represent you there with your tapes. There is honesty among fans and fellow filmmakers, I've found. So that will get you some money back.

If all these distribution war stories are scaring you off from making a movie, don't let them. After all, the passion comes first, the money later—hopefully! My advice in this particular climate is don't spend too much money on the first feature. I'd say it's safe to spend between $6,000–$10,000, including your box and duplication expenses. Ads in magazines will run you more money, but over a period of a year or so you'll probably do okay in the U.S. video market alone. Usually, with a decent box, a filmmaker can self-distribute 500–1,000 units of his tape nationally in a year. That's a realistic number. Plus, the idea is to get your name out there, get your work seen, and hopefully move on to a new project. No investor is going to give you money for a movie unless you can prove you've made one, so this is why you're doing it. You have to make either a short film that's a dynamite showreel or a feature shot-on-video that looks good and does well in the market to get taken seriously on the next level.

So don't let the horror stories deter

you—learn from my mistakes and the mistakes of others. Just be cautious. Don't be taken advantage of if you can help it.

The bottom line is that all of my films have really gotten out into the marketplace, so at least that in itself is satisfying. Lots of people I've worked with have used my early movies as stepping stones and gone on to bigger and better things. So that's the point of the whole thing.

Don't forget about cross-promoting merchandise with your movies. Over the years we've made money off of behind-the-scenes videos, T-shirts, soundtracks, posters, and autographed pictures to help offset other costs or being ripped off. My documentary *Blinded by the Blood: The Making of Killing Spree and Wicked Games* was a two-hour presentation aimed at the how-to market and was a big success due to the low production cost of the presentation. I had tons of behind-the-scenes footage shot from each movie set and used clips from interview shows and the movies themselves. So don't forget to film "behind the scenes" events on each movie you make. You can profit from it later. And fancy boxes aren't necessary in the how-to market. I just designed a laser copied artwork stuffed in a hard shell case for the release of *Blinded*.

To sum up distribution, you have to be prepared for a long journey of unexpected pleasures and pains. Accounting, banking, check writing, massive phone bills and mailing are just the beginning. It's tough. It's not for everyone. So when you arrive at that stage, be ready for anything. And have a good lawyer on standby. And never sign any contracts or paperwork involving your movie unless your attorney has closely analyzed the agreements.

STANZE: Distribution is a tricky game. I suppose that self-distribution would give you greater control over the product. Also, you would not have to worry about a distribution company ripping you off—and they have a tendency to do that. However, I am not interested in spending the time it takes

to effectively distribute my own product. I feel it is worth the risks to get a distribution company to carry your movie and make the sales. Usually, after each project, I have realized the mistakes I made on it and am ready to dive into another movie to use what I learned from those mistakes. I would get frustrated if I could not start another project because I was spending the time and effort to self-distribute my last movie.

If a distributor is interested in your project, ask them for references. Call other producers who have had product distributed by that company. Ask the producers to be honest about their relationship with the company. Did the company maintain acceptable communication with the producer? Did the company work hard enough to promote the product? Did the company provide accurate quarterly statements in a timely manner? Did the producer ever discover or suspect that the distribution company ripped them off in any way? If the distribution company refuses to give out phone numbers of producers they have distributed for, you should probably seek distribution elsewhere.

THOMPSON: The first thing I realized when I finished my first feature-length piece was that I had only done half the work. Selling it—or at least getting it out—was to be the second half. You learn a lot of tough lessons. In the low-budget world there are certain things that will sell your piece and you need to not only have them in the movie but be able to show that they are in the movie fast. A guy with a hundred pieces to look at that night is likely to only look at the first ten minutes. I have friends who are script readers for agents and they claim to know if they are even remotely interested after only a few pages. This explains the ridiculous little phrases on the front page of scripts these days: "*Dirty Harry* Meets *Boyz N the Hood*." They are designed to tell you the story in a moment. What they really do is tell you who they stole their ideas from. But that's Hollywood.

So you want to give a taste of everything

you have to offer in the first ten minutes. If you had Tom Cruise in the movie you could hold out, but you don't. You need to sell them fast. I had a wild phone call with a prospective distributor several years ago. "Nathan," he said. "Do you realize you're selling a horror movie and it's eight minutes before anyone dies?" "I was trying to set up the story," I said. "I don't care," he said. "You need some violent or scary action up front and if you can't get nudity, then at least suggest some." "Look," I said, "If you tell me you have a buyer I'll shoot more, but otherwise I can't afford to." "I'm not asking you to shoot more," he said. "I'm sending you the scene." "What to you mean?" I asked. "I'm sending you a scene that resolves itself and could go in front of almost anything. It was from a movie that got money to reshoot with a budget and this scene was cut out. The actors will be glad it got used. You're an editor; you'll make it work." In the mail arrived three hours of raw footage and a rough cut that showed us what they felt could be done with the scene. I did what I was asked and was surprised how well it did fit into our movie. This trick, however, did not sell the piece. Another part of lesson one—selling is a huge job.

Some people will offer you nothing but distribution. It's not a bad idea to take that if you are starting out. Just having a piece "in the store" is great PR. And it feels good to see it there. Just get some guarantee that they actually have plans to box and distribute your project. I have two friends who took deals only to discover that a company invested in their work with the plan of shelving it in case the next piece by this artist was getting attention. Then they would package and distribute it in order to capitalize on the moment. By buying the rights, they also bought the right to do nothing with it. This would be a good argument for self-distributing. Having never gone that route, I can't give much information on it.

THOMSON: There is a lot of self-marketing going on these days, small low-budget

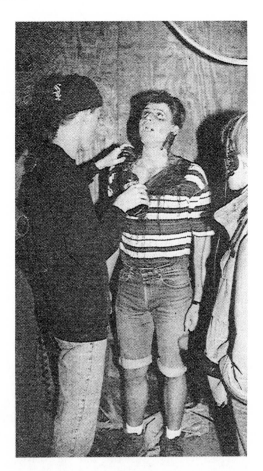

An artist applies fake blood to an actor on the set of Eric Stanze's *Savage Harvest.*

producers selling their own shows through magazines and the like, and many are quite good at it, and have good enough products that it can work that way. When we started *No Resistance* we thought we might shoot for that. But I think we just weren't good enough marketers. It takes a lot of time, energy and money to do that yourself.

We had the ability to sell a few copies of our tape directly to a few local and regional independent video stores ... the key here is to make it cheap and have some good packaging. We also sold a few copies we had on consignment at a local alternative media store. But this was basically just candy. We sold a few through mail orders but never enough to cover our costs of the advertising. Others have been able to do it, but if you ask me, getting a distributor is going to be your best bet every time, if it can be done.

Because the market for video entertainment is so huge, and getting huger all the time, that there has never been a better time for low-budget independent moviemaking. Even if you're working on tape. People are willing now more than ever to forego strict standards of format to find new, interesting and original pieces of expression. Video stores can carry weirder and weirder things, because the costs are relatively low for them, and most anybody has a buck or two to spring on an interesting video to watch that night. *No Resistance* rented over 70 times at the local store ... the store made back 300 percent the cost of the tape ... and that is mostly due to the packaging. Course, you don't make more money the more they rent, but you can always take those numbers and use them to sell to others. Or a distributor. What this means in the end is, there are a lot of distributors out there looking for a product, and almost anything that is technically competent is worthy of their attention.

The technically-competent part is a live or die rule: You *have* to have a decent picture and decent sound. Lose this and you'll never make it. You cannot have dark or out-of-focus scenes. You cannot shoot with a camcorder and leave the autofocus or the autoiris on. Beyond this, and only beyond this, you should have an interesting product ... something you can prove you own ... and you'll at least have the initial attention of any home video distributor in the country. Or the world, for that matter. In the video market the United States is not the only market by a far, far shot. Any good distributor will have copious international contacts.

Get some magazines that review your type of film. Learn who is distributing these types of videos and give them a call. It's their job to try to get product, so of course they'll watch anything you might have to send them. Be prepared for the process to take some time and be prepared to take a little rejection, but really, the market is pretty wide open. It never means you'll see enough money to get

a return, but if you're in this just to make money, you're reading the wrong book.

People get burned by distributors all the time. There's not much you can do as a starting filmmaker except check out who you do business with, see if you can talk to someone who has had dealings with them in the past, and always have a lawyer read a contract. In speaking with a contract lawyer on my first venture into the field, I asked what I could do to protect myself and the lawyer said, "Not much. Like, what if the guy doesn't report to you the $500 he made off you in Denmark? What can you do, go to Denmark and sue him for it? It's worth the $500 just to tell other people you're being distributed. Either you take the plunge or you don't." In the end for us, it was a form of currency just to say we have distribution, regardless of the return. And it will be a huge amount of help when it comes time to raise funds for the next project.

ULRICH: Every independent filmmaker will tell you that getting distribution is hard, especially if you shot your movie on video. But shooting on film isn't all that much easier. The facts of distribution is can your movie make money for the distributor. Try to get as many distributors' addresses that you can and send them a screener copy of your movie and see what happens. If you can't land a distributor then distribute it yourself. Put ads in various film magazines and try to sell your movie to local video stores. I'm still learning about distribution myself.

VOLLMANN: Unfortunately I have learned the hard way about distribution, as have many other first-time filmmakers. My advice, in no particular order:

(1) Technical quality: Distributors watch hundreds of films a year, most of them bad. Make sure your picture quality and sound quality are top notch. After all, if you went on a job interview, would you wear cutoff jeans and a T-shirt?

Home video artwork for Tom Vollmann's *Dead Meat*.

(2) The first ten minutes of a movie has to grab a distributor's attention. If your movie takes too long to get interesting the distributor presses the eject button and moves on to the next tape.

(3) A name actor. This was almost always the first question asked of me. On *Dead Meat*, all my actors were unknown. Except for extra work in big budget films such as *Home Alone*, and *The Untouchables*, no one was known outside of Chicago. If possible, try and find someone who is somewhat nationally known and willing to act in your movie for little or nothing. I met cult movie actor Conrad Brooks at a convention and we struck up a friendship. For those of you who do not know him, Conrad appeared in many of Ed Wood's films, including *Plan 9 from Outer Space*. Recently, he has appeared in Fred Olen Ray's *Bikini Drive-in*, which is being shown on Showtime. There are many actors who would love to be in a feature film, no matter how small.

(4) Another problem concerning distribution could be your movie's running time. A big mistake I made with *Dead Meat* was making it 107 minutes long. That's after I made some cuts. Distributors like their films under 90 minutes. The reason for this is, a movie like mine has to fit on a 120-minute tape. That equates to an extra forty or fifty cents per tape that the distributor has to incur if he wants to handle your movie. Multiply

that by a few thousand units and you get the picture.

(5) There's always self-distribution. If you decide to go this route, like I did, you need to print up professional-looking sleeves for your tape. This is essential. People often judge a book by its cover. My first two cassette covers consisted of color Xeroxes inserted in plastic cassette shells. They really are embarrassing to me now that I have professional sleeves.

(6) Something else I'd like to touch on as far as what distributors are looking for: nudity. I know, I know, porn is the last thing you want to get involved with. When *Dead Meat* was making the rounds, at least half the people I talked to said nudity—my film has none—would have been helpful in getting me some sort of distribution deal, especially overseas. This might be something you would want to think about doing.

WHITSON: Our best success has come from direct mail solicitation. Our latest mailing generated over $12,000 in sales and the orders are still coming in. We also run ads in *Fangoria* for our list and info and that attracts new people each month. Trying distributors hasn't been successful. They don't want things shot on video and when they do, they only want to give you a fraction of what you should get. We have had some of our tapes sold through *Scream Queens Illustrated* and EI Communications is carrying some of our tapes as well.

10. Thoughts on Being a Filmmaker

If all the information in this book discouraged you—good! You probably couldn't complete a feature anyway if you're this easily dissuaded. If it encouraged you to do your own project—great! You're somewhat prepared. Yes, there are easier things than wanting to make a movie.

When I'm asked by someone what I do for a living and I tell them, "I'm a filmmaker," they'll usually reply, "Gee, that sounds like fun." Such a reaction makes me want to smack them in the head. Filmmaking is satisfying—it's what I *want* to do; it's what I do—but fun is not a word I'd use to describe it. Try provoking, nerve-wracking, frustrating, depressing, exasperating—when someone says "It sounds like fun" in those condescending tones it galls me because I know I'm working far harder than them at their 9-to-5 job. Who else will work twelve-, fifteen-, twenty-hour days, not because they have to, but because they want to? A filmmaker, of course.

Try as hard as you can, but don't expect a lot with your first movie. With one under your belt you'll know if you want to make another one, another one that will probably be that much better. If the finished product costs $3000–$10,000 you'll probably make your money back, perhaps even a profit, all depending on publicity and response. But whatever you do, don't expect it to change your life, enable you to quit your job at the T-shirt shop, or make a half-million dollar movie the next time around. In reality, this just doesn't happen. It may simply motivate you to make another—and another—and another—and slowly your skills will grow and the films improve and one day you may make a living. But that's a ways off. Perhaps even a daydream.

So why even make a movie to begin with? Because, for whatever peculiar reason, you want to.

THE INTERVIEWEES WERE ASKED,
Do you have any final thoughts on being a filmmaker?

BALLOT: If independent filmmaking is analogous to Off Broadway plays, then independent moviemaking on videotape is Off Off Broadway. *Pulp Fiction* is considered an independent film yet it cost eight million to make. Mainstream thinking calls films independent despite the fact that they were made with multi-million dollar budgets. There's a huge distinction between the world of "the independents" and the world of "the underground." If Miramax or Fox Searchlight were to finance and distribute my next feature, then I could sit on my fat ass and pontificate about what a brilliant filmmaker I am. But when you try to put together a feature all by yourself by whatever means possible, it's a whole different ball game. I hope that soon, somebody will come along with a shot-on-video feature that'll be bumped up to 35-millimeter film, get theatrical exhibition, blow everybody away and elevate the credibility of the underground. Until then, everybody is basically on their own, with no clear road map to follow.

The odds of making it as an independent filmmaker are overwhelmingly against you. That shouldn't stop anyone from trying. If you have a vision that you want to bring to life, by all means, give it everything you got. Just don't set your expectations too high or you might be disappointed. And try to ignore the voices of negativity around you. If anybody tells you that something can't be done, it's only because they can't do it or it hasn't been done yet. Good luck!

BONK: One thing I have started to exploit, and as far as I can tell, I'm really the first and only to do it with B-movies (at least at this level), is Internet sales. I set up a web site offering not only my titles but those of other filmmakers like myself. I started with my four and now I have over 150 titles—with 150 more to add! Some titles sell extra well—like *Creep, Killing Spree, Ravage, The Vicious Sweet*—other sell maybe one in a year. Overall, it is pretty equal, though. I gave the site a B-movie attitude (*B-movie Theater*, http://www.b-movie.com), and advertised myself as offering fans titles you couldn't readily find anywhere else—and the die-hard fans come out of the woodwork! But one problem I still faced was lack of familiarity. So this led to my popular free Internet B-movie magazine called *Dark Gallery* (http://www.b-movie.com/dghome.html). The entire site itself now gets over 100,000 hits a month, and steadily increases by over 5,000 each month, and the magazine itself accounts for about 20,000–25,000 of those hits. Since I'm offering it for free, fans can't help but take a look. Best of all, it's usually the filmmakers writing the articles themselves—which helps the fans get to know them that much better. The site continually grows in popularity, and now I host *Draculina Online* as well as web sites for Debbie Rochon, Gunnar Hansen, Sasha Graham and Kevin Lindenmuth. With more certain to come! And very soon I am adding free online serials—*Tales of the Living Dead* to be first—which should prove just as popular as everything else.

CAMPISI: The greatest satisfaction I get out of making movies—and my greatest motivating factor—is watching audiences gasp and awe at something they see on the screen, and knowing I was the creative force behind it. Breakneck special effects and visuals get that response, but I give more import to emotional interplay and reaction. If I can get audiences motivated, excited and emotionally involved in rooting for the hero, or angry and vengeful toward the nemesis, I've satisfied my thirst.

Persistence is the key to success. There will be many ups and downs, many successes and many steps back in your pursuit of visualizing your dreams. In the end, no one can stop you but yourself.

CRAMER: All I can add is that my worst film and life experience was losing my best friend Andrew Scott [who starred as "Marcus Templeton" in *Even Hitler Had a Girlfriend*]. We were about half done shooting the sequel [*The Hitler Tapes*] when Andy was murdered. His killer has never been found, and I don't imagine I'll ever get over the loss. Those of us who were lucky enough to work with him all miss him terribly.

FORD: I have decided to try to make my living as a filmmaker, and to accomplish this I am working at putting together packages to raise money on larger film projects. I have decided that the profit margin is too small in the home video market to make a living, and so I must somehow make the switch to larger scale projects. But I admire anybody who can see an idea through to a completed feature film, especially guys who do it and hold down a regular job and family life all at the same time, risking their own money just to satisfy that moviemaking bug. Making the kind of movies they love, their own way, just for the love of it. How could there be a filmmaking more independent than that? Where could you find an artist more dedicated? No matter how large or small a movie is, it's somebody's dream. And it's just as much work to make a little movie as it is to make a big one.

GINGOLD: All I can add is that to me, the key to making a good movie finally lies in making the kind of film you want to make. Don't feel bound to either extreme—the safe, formularized, "commercial" Hollywood style, or the outrageous, break-all-the-rules, taboo-smashing approach. Following the mainstream formulas doesn't guarantee mainstream acceptance or success, while throwing in a lot of over-the-top sex, violence, or other excessive material doesn't mean you're breaking new ground unless you've got the creative convictions to back them up. That's not to say, of course, that you shouldn't go for a mainstream approach or push the limits of taste, but whatever you do, be true to your own instincts, and your love for the work you're doing will shine through. Don't worry about the people who will look down on your project, either because of its budget or its subject matter; frequently they'll be people who want to do something similar, and even talk about it a lot, but don't actually get around to doing it. And finally, be prepared to face a lot of obstacles, but remember that every roadblock you encounter while making your movie will only give you a greater sense of pride when it's finished.

A phone sex employee (Karen Zaczkowski) listens to one of *The Hitler Tapes*, directed by Ronnie Cramer.

HOWE: I'd like to mention one other point. Why make microbudget movies? Is it for money? It better not be, because chances are you won't be making much. Is it for fame? Again, better not be. The best you can hope to get out of a microbudget feature, especially one not shot on 16-millimeter or 35-millimeter, is a little recognition, hopefully enough to scare up the dough for your next, possibly slightly bigger movie. And even this modest gain isn't a sure thing.

Howard and I made *Sins* for two reasons: (1) because no one else seemed to be making the type of movies we really wanted to see; and (2) because we love movies and love making movies. Do it because you love it. If you can make a legitimate career of it, so much the better.

LEGGE: Making a movie is something anyone can do with the right talent and resources. But becoming a moviemaker is different. Lots of people make a movie, the emphasis on *a* movie. One. Uno. That's all, folks. Why? Because your first time out you think it'll be a blast, easy, and one big party. What you find out is that making a movie eats up your time, energy, money, sanity, self-respect and ego. You'll find yourself in a daze wondering what possessed you to start this; you'll keep suppressing the urge to strangle various people; you'll wonder why you're always broke; you'll wonder why that guy you thought was such a great actor is a royal pain in the ass. And when you finish it and screen with a crowd, you have to think, was it worth it? Once, yea. Would you do it again? And again? If the answer is no, you've only made a movie. If yes, you may be a moviemaker. Good luck, and keep the car running for a fast getaway.

MCCLEERY: My last comment. Make sure to take the time to preproduce your film. Preproduce the hell out of it. Use this time working by yourself without bogging down your cast and crew because if you waste time with them they will get very bored and disillusioned with the project. There is nothing worse than going out for a big day of shooting and then it not working out because you were unprepared. Use checklists, graphs, overhead views of your scenes, storyboards, the works to make sure when the day comes to shoot you know what the hell you want and how the hell to get it. The more in control you are, the more in control the project will be.

MURPHY: Don't expect things to happen overnight. And don't go into it thinking the world owes you anything. If you have a crappy attitude, you're not going to get many favors. And favors go a long way in lower budget filmmaking.

Don't commit suicide. If your production gets that bad, remember your commitment to completing it. As Nietzsche said, "Art seducing me to a continuation of life." Find a way. Stay strong. Keep going. If you haven't made a movie yet, the above rambling may not make sense to you … you'll see…

And don't forget to send everyone that helped you a comp copy on tape of your finished movie. They deserve it.

Be grateful. Be original. Be pure energy. It's all you. If you want this ship to move, be prepared to be the wind in its sails. Use your inner light and inspiration and determination and perseverance to excel. And by all means, do try to excel.

And never, never take no for an answer.

POLONIA BROS.: In closing, my brother and I would just like to encourage you to keep pressing on and making films! Success takes time, and time is a filmmaker's most accessible commodity. No matter what, don't give up. We have good days and bad days, hits and misses. If you don't finish the race, you don't know what the winning prize may be. Good luck!

RITTER: Be creative. If you don't have a lot of money, concentrate on characters and plot twists. That's why I make mainly psycho-thrillers. It's economical and it tends to be where my mind wanders anyway, so I'm in luck.

It's a tough business. Be prepared for a lot of rejection from sources you may not expect. But trudge on.

If you write your own scripts, read a lot. This is inspirational and you can get a lot of ideas from horror novels. I'm also inspired by soundtracks and heavy metal music. But novels will help you structure your own writing—especially screenplays. We need better writing in the industry as a whole. If you concentrate on a good story, half the battle is won before you film your flick.

Also, watch a lot of movies, even bad ones. You learn from them all as a filmmaker.

And when you finish your first film, you'll feel so accomplished. There's nothing like finishing a movie—every time I do one, when the final edit is done and all the music and sound effects are laid down, it's such an exhilarating time! A natural high that most people probably get from playing sports or whatever, but for me, that end cap when it's done, when the war is won … you can't beat that. And all the people that have ripped you off in the past can never take that feeling of completion away. That's what makes it worth it … completing what you started on just paper, sending it out to entertain the fans. That's what it's all about, even more than the making money part, for me anyway. It's always for passion first. You keep that attitude and you will progress forward.

So what are you waiting for? Write your script, grab some gear, and get started!

THOMPSON: In closing I would only say that if I had a dollar for every guy I know that planned to, or still plans to "make a movie," I'd be rich. There are a million reasons why you haven't made one yet. If you don't have the ability to do it as you want to, do something else in the meantime. Just do it. Start shooting something tomorrow on whatever format you have. Getting a piece done is one thing no one will criticize you for.

THOMSON: I know more people who talk about making movies and never do a damn thing about it than I ever thought would be possible. And remember, I work in the video biz, so I definitely know a lot of people with the knowledge and the means. I also know a lot of people who tell me it's not worth it, so don't bother. The fact is, if you want to do it, *just do it*. It's one of the toughest things in the world to pull off, but that's why not everybody can do it. The worst thing you can do is spend a little money, screw up, learn some stuff, and have some fun. The odds are definitely stacked against you … but if you go into it with only a mind to have some fun in the process, you can't lose. Everything else is gravy.

ULRICH: The only comment I have is to stay true to your visions, don't let anybody tell you that you can't do something, and when you make a mistake make sure you learn from it.

VOLLMANN: Filmmakers are a lonely breed. They live and breathe movies. They spend all their time and money to see their projects come to fruition. Sacrifice personal relationships for their craft. No one believes in a filmmaker more than himself. If you can dream it, you can do it. Sooner or later all the hard work will pay off.

WHITSON: I would tell each person to make the movie they want to make. Stay true to your vision and create a unique product that is easily recognizable as your own. Listen to criticisms, but stay true to what you want to do. Develop your own signature so that there is no mistaking that the movie is yours. Our movies are unique because they combine mainstream concepts along with some adult elements not usually found in your typical movie. I believe that's why we've been as successful as we have.

Epilogue

If your video makes it to the video stores you have succeeded in self-distribution, not to mention succeeding as a filmmaker. How many other films are completed each year that never see the light of day, never get distribution, never get a chance? If your movie is out there and finds audience, you have accomplished your goal.

But keep in mind that it is in competition with other tapes on the shelf, movies that cost millions more than your production. Although your project was probably completed for what one day of lunch costs on one of these features, you do not want your renters to feel like they were ripped off after they watch it. On the other hand, how many videos have you rented that were truly terrible? How much better is your movie?

It seems that low-budget filmmaking has received a bad reputation during the past decade, reviewers and such equating low-budget with "bad," "schlocky" or "kitschy," not to be taken seriously solely because they do not have a budget. Yet the reason we don't have a budget is because there's no one supporting us. We're doing it ourselves.

With what I think is a new wave of independent filmmakers that has recently emerged, this view will hopefully change. Ultimately, it's up to us independent filmmakers to improve the market and make a living at making films. Good luck!

Appendix 1.
The Interviewees Collaborate:
The *Alien Agenda* Movies

During the year I was working on this manuscript, dealing with some two dozen independent filmmakers who had similar stories about making movies and distribution and how hard it was to go about doing all of this, it occurred to me that this would be a prime time to collaborate on a project. I already had the idea of an alien invasion series in mind, and as I scripted the first movie I asked some of these people if they were interested in helping and many of them were. Some had access to sophisticated graphics equipment; others even had stories of their own that they wanted to do, which I incorporated into the basic premise. What ended up happening, within a year, was the creation of three distinct movies under the banner of *The Alien Agenda*.

The first one, *Out of the Darkness*, deals with the subtlety of the invasion, how the "Gray" aliens are experimenting with humans and planting hybrids into the general populace, hybrids that prey on humans. Although this first movie contains three separate stories—two by me, one by longtime associate Mick McCleery—they all add upon each other and connect, so I can't really call it an anthology. It stars McCleery, Sasha Graham, Scooter McCrae (director of

Shatter Dead), Rick Poli (*Twisted Tales*), and John Collins. Visual saucer effects were done by Mark Polonia (director of *Feeders*) and the rest of the extensive digital effects by Tim Thomson (director of *No Resistance*). There's also cameos by Jeffrey Arsenault (director of *Night Owl*), Mike Gingold (*Mindstalker*) and Candice Meade (a victim in *Addicted to Murder*). The second *Alien Agenda* movie, *Endangered Species*, deals with a future world where it is revealed that a second type of alien, referred to as "Morphs," are at war with the "Grays" and that mankind is caught in the middle of the conflict. This feature has a segment by Tim Ritter called *Ransom*, a segment by Gabriel Campisi—incorporating his short, *The Law*—and the wraparound or final story written and directed by me. Ron Ford (*Alien Force*) directed the opening interviews of "alien abductees." Computer visual effects were also done by Tim Thomson and Polonia did the saucer effects. Among the actors are Debbie Rochon (*Tromeo & Juliet*, *Hellblock 13*), Candice Meade, and Joel D. Wynkoop (*Creep*, *Wicked Games*), with cameos by Nathan Thompson (*Contact Blow*) and Sasha Graham

The third movie, *The Alien Agenda: Under the Skin*, has a distinct dark comic

Home video artwork for *The Alien Agenda: Endangered Species*.

undertone, with segments directed by Tom Vollmann (*Dead Meat*), Mike Legge (*Potential Sins*), and myself, and deals with what's been going on with the "Morph" aliens and how they "recruit" humans to help them.

Although these three features were a large undertaking and phone, FAX, and mail bills were high, this collaboration went quite smoothly which makes me think that this is probably *the* way to successfully complete and market such low-budget productions. We only had to worry about a section of each movie and the work was divided up among everyone involved. Plus, the cost of production was way down because each director paid for his own segment and a good portion of it was done for barter. For example, in return for "filmlooking" someone's feature they did a great deal of the special effects for me. Props were borrowed from half a dozen others. The signed agreements were very straightforward so there could be no confusion. It works when you deal with kindred spirits.

The best part of all is that people are continuing to work together beyond this initial collaboration—Ron Ford was so impressed with Tim Thomson's (*No Resistance*) effects on *Out of the Darkness* that he had him do the effects on *Alien Force*, in which Evan Jacobs (*Safety in Numbers*) also has a cameo. Thomson may be working on Gabe Campisi's new feature, *Shadowdance*, as well. Tim Ritter's third *Truth or Dare* movie, *Screaming for Sanity*, is scripted by Ritter, Ron Bonk (*The Vicious Sweet*) and myself and I'm currently working on a script with Jeffrey Arsenault (*Night Owl*) that will hopefully see production next year. There's a dozen other collaboration permutations pending.

Appendix 2.
Resource Directory

Film Sources

Anhedenia Films
17860 Newhope St
Ste A-171
Fountain Valley, CA 92708
Send for ordering information.
FILMS: Walking Between the Raindrops;
Safety in Numbers; The Toll Collector

Brimstone Productions
3 W 102 #4B
NYC, NY 10025
Phone/fax 212-662-1084
Add $4.00 P & H for first tape, $1.50 for
each additional tape.
FILMS: Addicted to Murder ($20); Vam-
pires & Other Stereotypes ($20); Twisted
Tales: Special Edition ($30); The Alien
Agenda: Out of the Darkness; The Alien
Agenda: Endangered Species; The Alien
Agenda: Under the Skin ($30 each)

Cool Movies
PO Box 31347
Chicago, IL 60631
$20 plus $3 P & H.
FILMS: Dead Meat

E.I. Independent Cinema
68 Forest St
Montclaire, NJ 07042
Send for catalog.
FILMS: Polymorph; Sandman; Ozone;
Dead Next Door

Empyre Films
1801 Lincoln Blvd #266
Venice, CA 90291
$20 plus $3 P & H.
FILMS: Jugular Wine

Lunatic Fringe Productions
12456 Memorial Dr.
Box 464
Houston, TX 77024
Send for ordering information.
FILMS: No Resistance

Jeffrey Arsenault
PO Box 1398
New York, NY 10156
FILMS: Night Owl

One by One Film & Video
301 American Way
Vorhees, NJ 08043

Send for information.
FILMS: The Killing of Bobby Greene; Don't Watch This Show

Polonia Brothers Entertainment
86 Pearl St
Wellsboro, PA 16901
$20 each plus $3 P & H.
FILMS: Feeders; Saurians; Terror House; Bad Magic; Night Crawlers

Salt City Home Video
PO Box 5515
Syracuse, NY 13220
Send for catalog.
FILMS: City of the Vampires; Darkest Soul; Killing Spree; Savage Harvest; Ravage; Gorotica; Gore Whore; The Scare Game; Wicked Games; The Vicious Sweet; Dark Descent; Final Exam; Dark Descent: Beyond Sanity

Scorched Earth Productions
PO Box 101083
Denver, CO 80250
Send for catalog.

FILMS: Even Hitler Had a Girlfriend; The Hitler Tapes; Back Street Jane

SideShow Cinema
26 Emerson St
Mendon, MA 01756
$15 each, plus $3 P & H.
FILMS: Potential Sins; Cut Throats; Working Stiffs; Sick Time; Loons; Brain Drainer

Something Weird Video
PO Box 33664
Seattle, WA 98133
Send for catalog.
FILMS: Original Sins; Shatter Dead

Starlight Pictures
1725 S. Rainbow Blvd
Suite 2-186
Las Vegas, NV 89102
FILMS: The Law; Shadowdance

W.A.V.E. Productions
PO Box 83
Deerfield, NJ 08313
Send for catalog.

"Filmlook" Services

The following companies provide "filmlook" services.

Filmlook
Wood Holly Productions/Filmlook Inc.
1118 W. Magnolia Blvd.
Burbank, CA 91510-7818
Contact: Robert Faber
    213 462-5330

This is the direct number and address of the official "Filmlook." There are other people across the country selling the same service for a slightly increased price; they are simply go-betweens—they send the stuff you send them to Filmlook. Be warned, though, they are busy and it may take two weeks to a month before they can do it. Also, they will not accept anything shot in VHS or Hi-8, pretty much just D2, 1", and Betacam SP. The cost of tape stock is not included. There is a ten-minute minimum of $600, about $75 a minute after that.

I also suggest you call local postproduction facilities, as they may have their own version of such a process.

Brimstone Productions
3 W 102 #4B
NYC, NY 10025
Phone/fax 212 662-1084

This may be a shameless plug but I've "filmlooked" both *Twisted Tales* and *Addicted to Murder* myself, through an amalgamation of equipment, and the results are quite good. I can do an entire 90-minute movie for $750, which includes the 90-minute Betacam SP stock.

List of Magazines and Fanzines

Sometimes the life span of a magazine is only a year or two so some of these may no longer be in print.

Alternative Cinema
E.I. Communications
68 Forest St.
Montclaire, NJ 07042

Annabel Lee (PAL)
P.O. Box 2191
Sabadell 08200 Spain

Bubblegum (PAL)
31 North End House
Fitzjames Avenue
London, W14 ORS England

Chainsaw Video & Magazine
Han Weevers
Twijnstraat 7, 3511 ZG
Utrecht, Netherlands

Cult Movies
Mike Copner
6201 Sunset Blvd., Suite 152
Hollywood, CA 90028

The Dark Side (PAL)
Allan Bryce
P.O. Box 146
Plymouth, PL1 1AX England

Defect
Pidde Andersson
Repslagargatan 25
261 40 Landskrona Sweden

Draculina Publishing
Hugh Gallagher

P.O. Box 587
Glen Carbon, IL 62034

Dreadful Pleasures
650 Prospect Avenue
Fairview, NJ 07022

Exploitation Journal
Keith Crocker
40 S. Bush Dr
Valley Stream, NY 11581

Factsheet Five
P.O. Box 170099
San Francisco, CA 94117-0099

Fangoria
475 Park Avenue South
NYC, NY 10016

Film Extremes (PAL)
P.O. Box 409
London, SE183 DW, UK

Horror Attraction
932 Brook St
Piqua, OH 45356-3628

Horror Pictures (SECAM)
90 Rue Gandi
46000 Cahors France

Poopsheet
Rick Bradford
P.O. Box 161095
Ft. Worth, TX 76161-1095

Propaganda Magazine
P.O. Box 296
New Hyde Park, NY 11040

Psychotronic
Michael J. Weldon
3309 Rt 97
Narrowsburg, NY 12754-6126

Reel Wild Cinema
2 Glenbrae Court
Berwick, Victoria Australia 3806

Samhain (PAL)
John Gullidge
77 Exeter Road, Topsham
Exeter, Devon EX3 OLX
England

Schlock
John Chilson
3841 Fourth Ave #192
San Diego, CA 92103

Screem Magazine
Darryl Mayeski
490 S. Franklin St.
Wilkes-Barre, PA 18702

Shivers (PAL)
9 Blades Court
Deodar Road
London SW15 2NU
England

Shocking Images
Mark Jason Murray
P.O. Box 601972
Sacramento, CA 95860

Sub-Genre
Marcus Koch
3440 Enterprise Road, E
Safety Harbor, FL 34695

Sub-Terrene (PAL)
Anthony Cawood
6 Daleside Ave
Pudsey, Leeds
UK LS28 8HD

They Won't Stay Dead
11 Werner Road
Greensville, PA 16125

Trauma (PAL)
Kristian Molgaard
Karpedam, 4b.1.th.
DK-6200, Abenraa Denmark

UNREEL
Lionel Laratte
119 E. Mt. Airy Ave #5
Philadelphia, PA 19119

Vex
P.O. Box 319
Roselle, NJ 07203-0319

Video Confidential
8822 Second Avenue
N. Bergen, NJ 07047

Videocrypt
Lamey, Charles
8715 2nd Avenue
Stone Harbor, NJ 08247
(Entertainment columnist, writes for NJ
   papers)

Videooze
P.O. Box 9911
Alexandria, VA 22304

Video Plus
Flohmarkt Milchstrasse i
2000 Hamburg 113
Germany

Videoscope
P.O. Box 31
Keyport, NJ 07735-0031

World of Fandom
Al Shevy
2525 W. Knollwood St
Tampa, FL 33614

Zine Shock (PAL)
Jaume Balaguero
AP, 16056 Barcelona
Spain O8080

Distributors

As of mid–1997 this list is accurate and up to date. It does not list every distributor I've ever dealt with, as many have disappeared and others I wouldn't recommend. So here's a list of companies that are buying already packaged tapes.

Blockbuster
1201 Elm St
Dallas, TX 75270

Broadway Video
Paul Dwoskin
813 E. Republican
Seattle, WA 98102
(Video store in Seattle looking for under-
    ground/cult movies.)

E.I. Independent Cinema
Mike Raso
68 Forest St
Montclaire, NJ 07042
(Buys already packaged films, has catalog,
    puts adds in major genre magazines. Re-
    quests 10–15 tapes beforehand and will
    send checks as he sells them.)

Manic Entertainment (PAL)
Elmar Berger
P.O. Box 1207
73278 Schlierdack
Germany (Buys foreign rights for home
    video distribution in Germany, usually
    for three years.)

Movie Video Trader
Ron Gavito
6870 N. Broadway, Unit A
Denver, CO 80221
303 426-8567

Movies Unlimited (Catalog)
Irv Slifkin, Charlotte
6736 Castor Ave
Philadelphia, PA 19149
215 722-8398
(Buys already packaged tapes wholesale—
    they pay within two weeks, though they
    may only order one movie at a time.)

Paul's Hobby Zone
Paul Piantedosi
229 River Street
West Newton, MA 02165
617 332-8687

Rentrak Inc.
David Watts
7227 N.E. 55th Avenue
P.O. Box 18888
Portland, OR 97218
503 284-7581

Salt City Home Video
P.O. Box 5515
Syracuse, NY 13220
315 488-1399

Science Fiction Continuum (Catalog)
Sue Braviak
1163 Inman Avenue
Edison, NJ 08820
908 755-2331

Scorched Earth (Catalog)
Ronnie Cramer
P.O. Box 1001083
Denver, CO 80250

Screen Edge (PAL)
Attn: Richard King
28/30 The Square
St. Annes on the Sea
FY8 1RF England
Tel: 44 1253 712453
Fax: 44 1253 712453

Video Wasteland
Attn: Ken Kish
214 Fair Street
Berea, OH 44017
Tel: 1 800 532-1533
(Catalog, rents through the mail.)

West Coast Entertainment
Attn: David Vallaire
709 Hwy 90

Waveland, MS 38576
800 476-1026
(Buys already packaged films wholesale.)

Miscellaneous Suppliers and Services

The following is a list of mail order suppliers for adhesive labels and plastic video boxes. Write or call for catalogs:

United Ad Label Company
P.O. Box 2345
Brea, CA 92622-2345
800 998-7700

Polyline
1233 Rand Rd
Des Plains, IL 60016
708 390-6464

Markertek
4 High St Box 397
Saugerties, NY 12477
800 522-2025

Here are the addresses of some companies that perform tape duplication services:

Video Images
Attn: Joe Abinanti
15805 1/2 Stagg St
Van Nuys, CA 91406
Tel: 818 988-8123

Corporate Duplication Solutions
375 N. Street
Teterboro, NJ 07608
Phone: 201 342-3060

Vaughn Communications
7951 Computer Avenue
Minneapolis, MN 55435
Phone: 612 832-3100

If you have access to a tape duplicating facility and have to supply your own stock, the following two companies sell VHS tapes at reasonable prices:

VU Videos
1420 Blake St
Denver, CO
303 534-5503

Steadisystems
212 947-7666

Index

189